The Mountain War

The Mountain War

A Doctor's Diary of the Italian Campaign 1914–1918

Isaak A. Barasch

Edited by
Shulamit Kopf

Translated by
Michael Wooff

Introduction by
Sir Hew Strachan

Pen & Sword
MILITARY

First published in Great Britain in 2021 by
Pen & Sword Military
An imprint of
Pen & Sword Books Ltd
Yorkshire – Philadelphia

Copyright © English text of diary Shulamit Kopf 2021
Copyright © Introduction and chapter introductions Hew Strachan 2021

ISBN 978 1 39909 310 1

The right of Isaak A. Barasch to be identified as Author of this work has been asserted by him in accordance with the Copyright, Designs and Patents Act 1988.

A CIP catalogue record for this book is available from the British Library.

All rights reserved. No part of this book may be reproduced or transmitted in any form or by any means, electronic or mechanical including photocopying, recording or by any information storage and retrieval system, without permission from the Publisher in writing.

Typeset by Mac Style
Printed and bound in the UK by CPI Group (UK) Ltd, Croydon, CR0 4YY.

Pen & Sword Books Limited incorporates the imprints of Atlas, Archaeology, Aviation, Discovery, Family History, Fiction, History, Maritime, Military, Military Classics, Politics, Select, Transport, True Crime, Air World, Frontline Publishing, Leo Cooper, Remember When, Seaforth Publishing, The Praetorian Press, Wharncliffe Local History, Wharncliffe Transport, Wharncliffe True Crime and White Owl.

For a complete list of Pen & Sword titles please contact

PEN & SWORD BOOKS LIMITED
47 Church Street, Barnsley, South Yorkshire, S70 2AS, England
E-mail: enquiries@pen-and-sword.co.uk
Website: www.pen-and-sword.co.uk

Or

PEN AND SWORD BOOKS
1950 Lawrence Rd, Havertown, PA 19083, USA
E-mail: Uspen-and-sword@casematepublishers.com
Website: www.penandswordbooks.com

Contents

Preface vi
List of Plates viii
Maps ix
Introduction 1
Letter to My Great-Uncle 39

The Diary 57

Chapter 1   The Isonzo 59

Chapter 2   Tyrol 105

Chapter 3   Gorizia 137

Chapter 4   From the Isonzo to the Piave 177

Afterword 213
Index 215

Preface

by Shulamit Kopf

So many historical documents crumble to dust, vanish, get tossed or lost by people not cognisant of their value. Thousands languish in attics, shoeboxes, drawers, buried underground or forgotten in archives. That could have easily been the fate of the six diaries handwritten during the First World War by my great-uncle, Dr Isaak A. Barasch, who served in the Austro-Hungarian army on the Italian front. He didn't survive the war having succumbed to the Spanish flu epidemic on 12 September 1918. Had the diaries remained with our family in Poland, the diaries would have vanished in the next world war. It was lucky that his sister, Helen Mehlman, took them with her when she immigrated in 1922 with her family to New York City. There, in her antique-filled apartment on Riverside Drive, they stayed in a drawer for almost 100 years.

There are several people who have helped me rescue Dr Barasch's words from oblivion.

I want to thank Helen's daughter, the late Irene Fingerhut, for entrusting the diaries to my care.

My son, Jonathan Waldmann, got the project going by finding an excellent and dedicated German-to-English translator, which brings me to my big heartfelt thanks to Michael Wooff who took the project as a job until it became a mission. He fell under the spell of Dr Barasch's prose. 'Your great-uncle is such good company. He seems to have a knack for befriending people and of appreciating the finer things of life ... Good for him,' he wrote. 'Your great-uncle deserves to be bequeathed to posterity.'

British military historian, Hew Strachan, professor at the University of St Andrews, is accustomed to receiving letters from people in possession of historical documents relevant to the First World War that they would like him to examine. He was kind enough to read Dr Barasch's diaries and immediately recognised their importance. He has my heartfelt gratitude for deciding to take on their publication as a project. I couldn't have accomplished this mission without him. It is thanks to him that this book exists.

My gratitude also goes to Erwin Schmidl, a military historian in Vienna, who was kind enough to send me his book *Jews in the Habsburg Armed Forces*, and to patiently answer my numerous questions. We were both shocked when I discovered a family connection to General Alexander Ritter von Eiss, one of the generals he mentions in his book.

Sonja Lessacher at the University of Vienna Medical School archives sent me Dr Barasch's academic records.

Thank you to my son, David Beyer, and Dana Beyer who made some excellent editorial suggestions for the chapter I wrote.

A big thanks to Rupert Harding at Pen & Sword for accepting the diaries for publication with such great enthusiasm.

And you, dear reader, if you stumble across yellowing letters, journals or old documents when you clean out the homes of your grandparents, don't throw them out.

List of Plates

Portrait photograph of Dr Isaak Barasch

Lea Barasch Mehlsak, Dr Barasch's mother

Pages from Dr Isaak Barasch's diary, written in German

A formal studio portrait of Dr Isaak Barasch and members of his family, 1914

Moses Mehlsak, Dr Barasch's father

Dr Isaak Barasch with his cousin, Dr Schilem Jung, on his father's estate, c. 1910

Dr Barasch at a clinical lecture, 15 January 1912

A photograph taken in a studio in Vienna, 24 December 1914

Dr Isaak Barasch standing in front of the army field hospital in Grassaga, November 1917

Dr Isaak Barasch at 'Makuči' medical help centre with Medical Orderly Sadek and an ensign, December 1916

Dr Isaak Barasch with a group of officers

A group photograph, 17 December 1917

Dr Barasch with fellow soldiers in front of a coffee house

Dr Isaak Barasch with a group of medical officers in Grassaga, 1917

Dr Barasch on a well-deserved break from his military duties

Dr Isaak Barasch on a sea trip in the Kvarner Gulf of Fiume (now Rijeka), April 1917

Dr Barasch's younger brother, Leon (standing), on the Italian front, 1918

Dr Yoel Chaim Mehlman, Dr Barasch's brother-in-law

Dr Isaak Barasch's gravestone in the Jewish section of Vienna's Wiener Zentralfriedhof cemetery

Maps

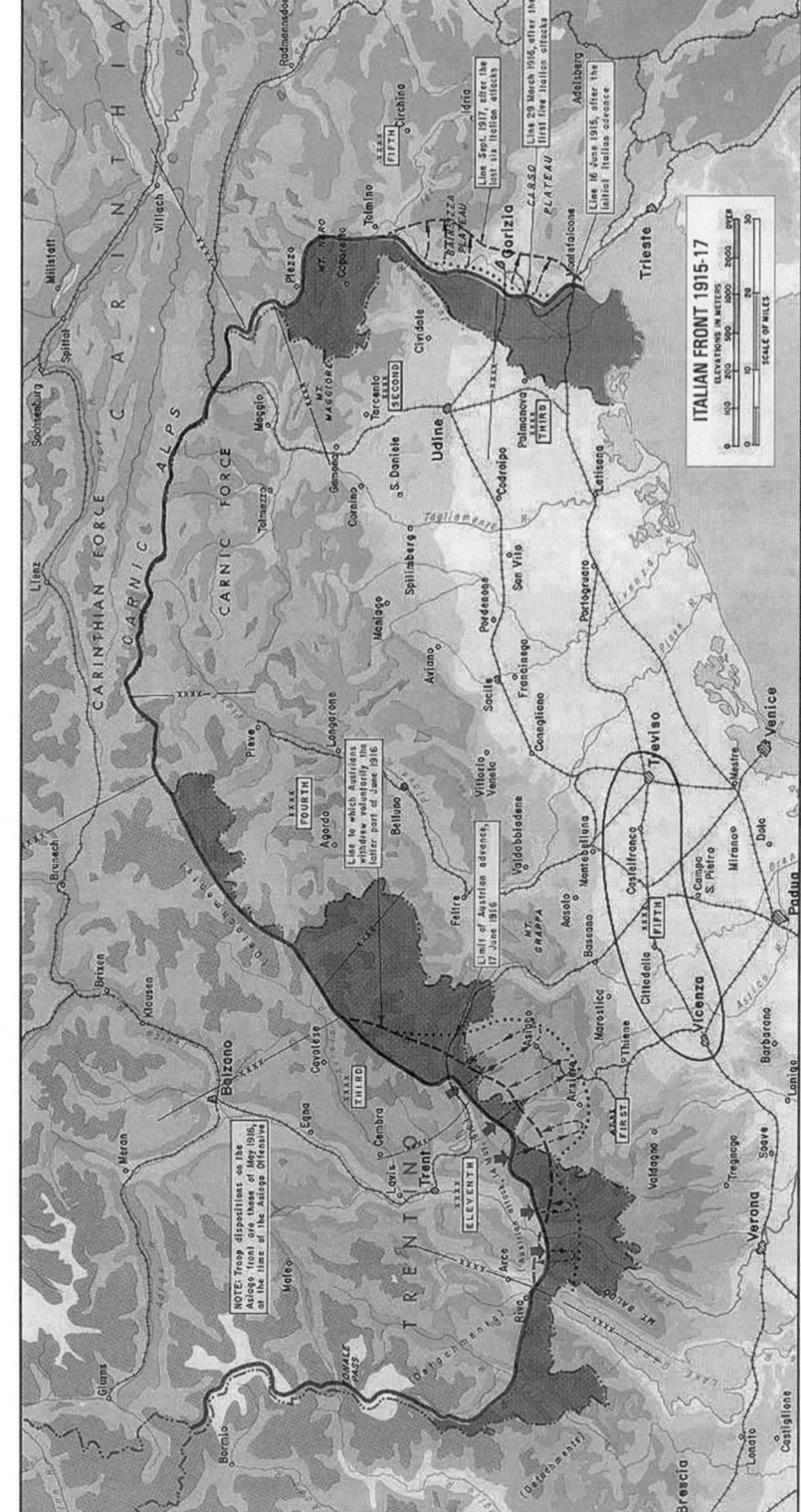

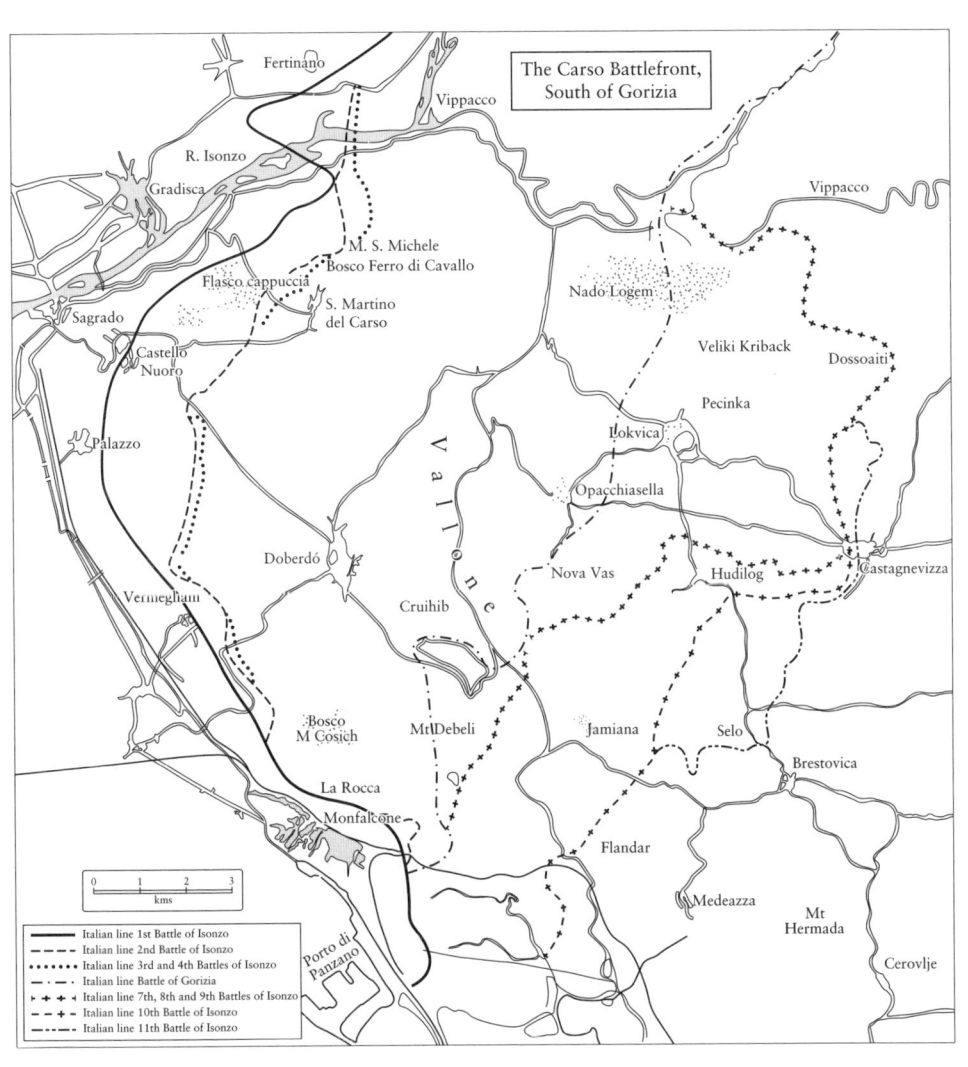

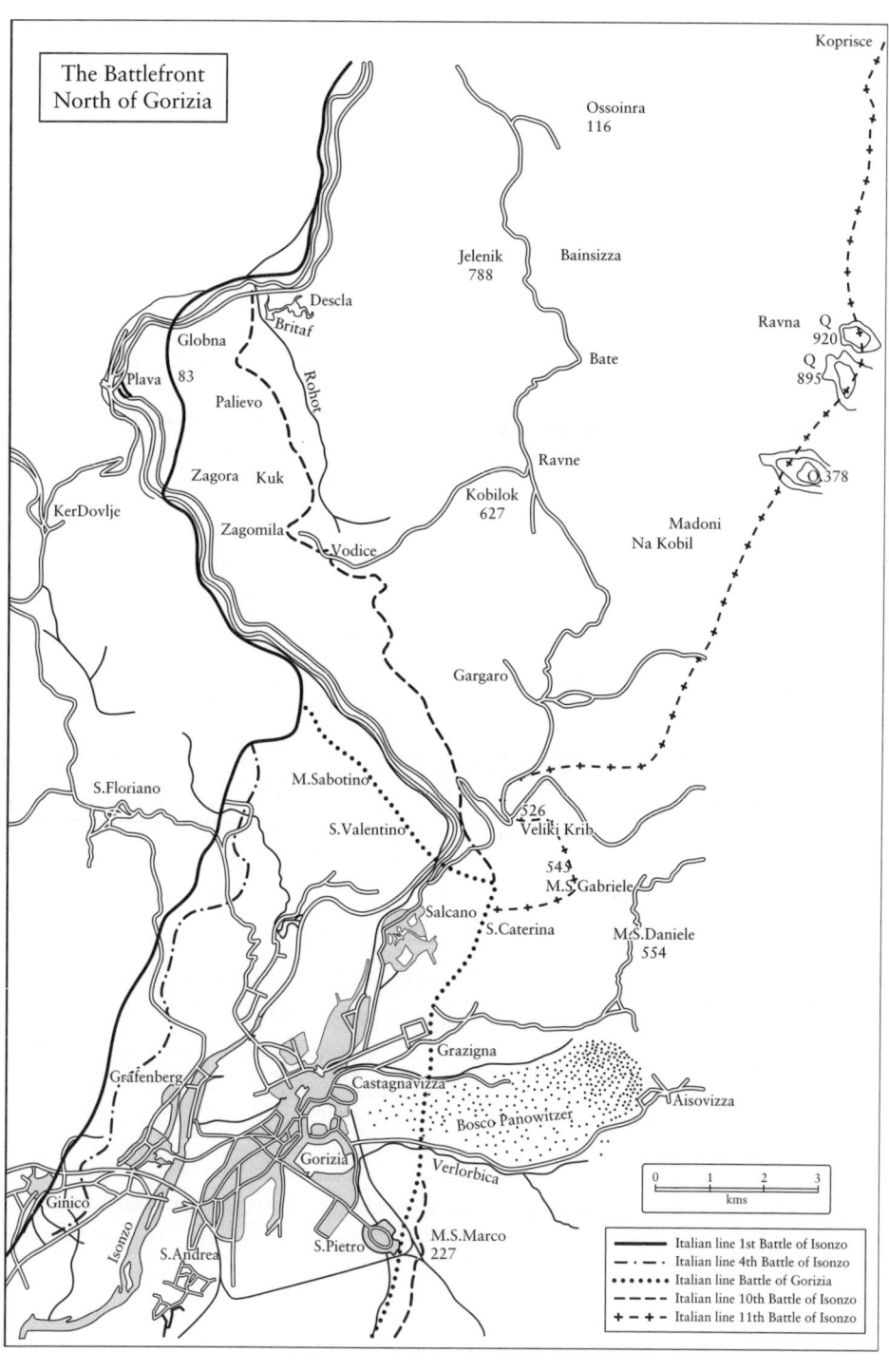

Introduction

by Hew Strachan

Austria-Hungary and the Outbreak of the First World War

On 28 June 1914 Archduke Franz Ferdinand was killed in Sarajevo in what was then Bosnia-Herzegovina. The conspiracy theories which followed his death and the counter-factual accounts of what would have happened if he had lived testify to the confused status of the Habsburg empire at the beginning of the twentieth century. Some saw the heir apparent as the victim of an internal plot, deliberately exposed to a terrorist's bullet by the decision that he should visit the newly annexed province without adequate security. Others speculated as to the course he would have followed if he had succeeded his aged uncle, Franz Josef, as emperor.

According to one side he would have saved the empire by re-centralising control. In 1867, after Austria's defeat at the hands of Prussia, the empire had been reconstructed as a dual monarchy, one part Austrian with its capital in Vienna and the other Hungarian and based in Budapest. An alternative view countered that he planned to take the 'compromise' of 1867 further, creating a separate South Slav entity (which would have included Bosnia-Herzegovina). In Viennese eyes, a tripartite solution to the governance of the Habsburg lands would have put the bumptious and often fractious Magyars from Budapest in their place, so allowing Austrian common sense to divide and rule. The Magyars were outnumbered by Slavs even within Hungary; they would be definitively weakened if the Slavs formed an independent political identity.

While alive, Franz Ferdinand had toyed with both options, initially favouring federalism or a three-way split and then veering towards renewed centralisation. Both were means, indirect or direct, for asserting his authority, and both confirmed that the current structure was confronting imminent and dramatic change. Franz Josef had ascended the throne at the age of 18 on the abdication of his uncle in 1848. Few could remember a time when he had not been emperor, but he was now 84 and his subjects had to ready themselves for the end of an era. Many did so with trepidation. Franz Ferdinand himself was not a particularly attractive personality or a natural reformer. He seemed to be more radical than he was thanks to his decision to marry a comparatively humble Czech countess in a genuine love match. He had also countered the more bellicose instincts of the chief of the army's general staff, Franz Conrad von Hötzendorf, and would probably have blocked the rush to war which followed his assassination. But he was also a bully with a short fuse, an anti-Semite, and as convinced of his royal and imperial authority as any of his predecessors.

The divided opinions which surrounded Franz Ferdinand were a metaphor for the Habsburg empire as a whole. For some its decline, evident since the end of the Holy Roman Empire in 1806, was terminal. In 1815 the adroit statesmanship of Metternich had slowed its onset by masterminding the creation of a European international order which contained both war and revolution, and so in turn held in check the twin forces of liberalism and nationalism. These were the long shadows cast by the French Revolution of 1789 and the two decades of European war which had followed – 'the last great war'. In 1861 Austria lost its lands in Lombardy as Italy united under the leadership of Piedmont. The creation of the Italian state confirmed that nationalism was not a liberal prerogative; it could also be effectively harnessed by conservatives. Otto von Bismarck, the minister president of Prussia, took the point: the way for the old order to keep power was to ride the tiger of nationalism and so catch the liberals in a cleft stick.

In 1866 Austria suffered a second defeat, this time at the hands of a Prussian-led alliance, and so forfeited its leadership of Germany as it had done that of Italy (although its armed forces fared much better against the Italians this time round). The Habsburg empire was now confined to south-eastern Europe, where the writ of the 1815 settlement was weaker, and where nationalism flourished. In 1878 Bulgaria and

Greece extended their frontiers at the expense of the Ottoman empire and three new states were formed – Serbia, Montenegro and Romania, all of them with borders which marched with the Habsburg lands. As a multi-national empire, Austria-Hungary ruled over subjects whose languages were the same as those of these now-independent states, just as it still ruled over Italians and Germans. Habsburg foreign policy, therefore, carried domestic implications, with the rise of adjacent nation states seeming to put Austria-Hungary on permanent notice as to its future.

In the event the Habsburgs played a difficult hand with some skill. Franz Josef knew when to bend with the wind, enabling the monarchy to weather the 1848 revolutions, keeping out of the Crimean War in 1854 and recognising the wisdom of the 1867 Austro-Hungarian solution. The advent of the railway enabled his empire to attain an economic unity which its geographical configuration – landlocked except for its access to the Adriatic and girded to west, south and east by the mountain ranges of the Alps, Balkans and Carpathians – had hitherto blocked. Nor could the smaller independent states which implicitly threatened its unity to the south match the culture of its cosmopolitan elite. Like Franz Ferdinand, Franz Josef was no radical but, as he aged, he presided over an empire which provided a home for at least fourteen different languages and their cultural traditions and enabled freedom of worship for multiple faiths, including Judaism and Islam. German may have been the language of army command and central government and Catholicism was the dominant faith, but for those of different persuasions life in Austria-Hungary was more congenial than life under Ottoman or Russian rule. For the affluent and educated classes in Vienna, a city rejuvenated by the building schemes of its mayor, the anti-Semitic Karl Lueger, and by the decorative designs of the Jugendstil, it was even better than that. Here the arts and sciences flourished, the musical modernism of Gustav Mahler or Richard Strauss, the painting of Gustav Klimt or Egon Schiele, the philosophy of Ludwig Wittgenstein or psychology of Sigmund Freud, the poetry of Rainer Maria Rilke or the prose of Robert Musil, all suggesting a vibrancy which faced forwards, not backwards.

Externally *fin-de-siècle* Vienna prompted some of the Habsburg empire's critics to rethink their assumptions. Its successful annexation of Bosnia-Herzegovina in 1908–9, formally still part of the Ottoman empire but under de facto Austro-Hungarian control since 1878, was achieved initially with Russia's connivance but then in the teeth of its opposition. It convinced Robert Seton-Watson, the British historian who during the First World War would argue for the creation of a Yugoslav state, that Austria-Hungary was 'likely to become stronger, not weaker, in the immediate future'.[1]

Seton-Watson accepted and even embraced the pre-war Habsburg empire as readily as did most of its inhabitants. After 1918, Czechs in Bohemia, who supported the creation of an independent Czechoslovakia, or Poles, whose country had been partitioned for the third time between Austria, Prussia and Russia in 1795, would make the collapse of the dual monarchy seem inevitable. That was not how things looked to most Czechs and Poles in 1914. On the war's outbreak they duly rallied to its defence – as did the empire's other nationalities. The story of disintegration grew with the telling and became stronger with hindsight. Those who remained loyal to the Habsburgs until the end would come to blame the empire's collapse on the treason of Czechs, Italians, Poles and Slavs and trace its antecedents to 1914 and earlier.

The empire's defeat had many other causes, and nationalism was as often an after-thought as much as a prime mover. The diary to which these words are an introduction was written by Isaak Barasch (or Barasz in its Polish form), the son of Jewish farmers who were tenants on a largish estate owned by a Polish nobleman and located in the empire's north-east, near Złoczów, now Zolochive in Ukraine but then in Galicia. More than half of Galicia's population in what was the empire's most under-developed province were illiterate but Barasch was multi-lingual: he wrote in Polish to his family and in German to himself – or at least in this diary. In addition to Hebrew, Greek and Latin, he spoke Yiddish and taught himself Italian. He might most obviously have identified as a Jew and a Pole. In the pages

---

1. Harry Hanak, *Great Britain and Austria-Hungary in the First World War: a Study of the Formation of Public Opinion* (London, 1962), pp. 12, 25.

that follow he does the first just once (on 2 November 1917 and then only in passing) and the second never. On the evidence presented here, he was neither a Zionist nor a Polish nationalist, but – like other Jews – a Habsburg supra-nationalist. His entries frequently criticise the fat cats in the rear, and particularly the higher administration of the army, but never is there a whiff of disloyalty or sedition.

The failure of Austro-Hungarian multi-nationalism would not become fully evident until 1917, and it gained traction as much from its external exploitation as a weapon of war as from internal pressures. In Britain Seton-Watson was an early convert to the idea of undermining the empire from within but until late in the war the Foreign Office wanted Austria-Hungary to survive in order to balance the power of Germany to its north. This allied consensus fragmented on 8 January 1918, when the President of the United States, Woodrow Wilson, in part deferring to the views of émigrés who had settled in America, laid down the principle of national self-determination as one of his war aims or 'Fourteen Points'. Over the course of the last year of the war allied propaganda used this promise to promote the dissolution of the Austro-Hungarian army on its southern front.[2]

Despite its wartime support for the maintenance of the empire, the British Foreign Office before 1914 was less persuaded of Austria-Hungary's resilience than was Seton-Watson. Sir Edward Grey, the Foreign Secretary, under-estimated Vienna's appetite for independent action and regarded it as the pawn of Germany. In two Balkan wars fought in 1912 and 1913 Austria-Hungary saw south Slav nationalism grow as Serbia doubled its territory at Ottoman expense. Austria-Hungary kept out of both conflicts but was not rewarded for its restraint. In 1913, under the terms of the Treaty of London, brokered by Grey in conjunction with Germany, the Balkan states gained from their belligerence and the dual monarchy lost. The Austro-Hungarian foreign ministry realised that the Metternichian concert of Europe was no longer serving its interests and concluded that it needed a new way forward.

---

2. Mark Cornwall, *The Undermining of Austria-Hungary: The Battle for Hearts and Minds* (Basingstoke, 2000).

Its preferred solution to its Balkan problem was to secure an alliance with Bulgaria. Lying to the east of Serbia, Bulgaria had no common border with the Habsburg empire and, after the first Balkan war in 1912, had fallen out with Serbia over the spoils. Germany did not like the idea: it wanted to formalise an existing secret deal with Romania. However, the Austro-Hungarians recognised that Romania would demand territorial compensation in Transylvania in return for any deal. The idea was a non-starter, first because Transylvania was part of Hungary and the latter would never agree to its loss, and secondly on a point of principle. Once the empire accepted that it would have to hand over territory to appease its neighbours, it would be on a slippery slope that would end with its dismemberment.

The murder of Franz Ferdinand – who was personally close to the German emperor, Wilhelm II – resolved this impasse. Serb complicity was as much a given in Berlin as in Vienna and Germany might now be open to the idea of a Bulgarian alliance. On 30 June, Leopold Berchtold, the Austro-Hungarian foreign minister, proposed a full and final reckoning with Serbia and, with Franz Ferdinand out of the way, Conrad von Hötzendorf had free rein to call for a Balkan war, something he had urged on a reluctant monarchy recurrently since 1909. However, if Austria-Hungary was to fight Serbia, it would run the risk of Russian intervention. Its neighbour to the north-east was still smarting from the humiliation inflicted on it by Austria-Hungary over the annexation of Bosnia-Herzegovina. Vienna needed a guarantee of support from Germany to deter Russia from supporting Serbia. On 6 July 1914 Germany gave that guarantee. In doing so, it confirmed the view in London that, rather than taking its own decisions, Austria-Hungary was the instrument of German foreign policy.

Both Austria-Hungary and Germany were playing a high-stakes game. Franz Josef himself recognised that it could end in a world war and – extraordinarily given Austria-Hungary's lack of preparation for such an outcome – was prepared to condone the risk. But the running in both Vienna and Berlin was made by those who in a fit of wishful thinking convinced themselves that the most likely outcome was a limited war between the dual monarchy and Serbia, which would end quickly and be geographically confined. Neither Berchtold nor Conrad paid sufficient attention to the possibility that Russia might come to Serbia's aid, and the German chancellor, Theobald von Bethmann Hollweg, convinced himself that the danger of a major European war was precisely what would keep the lid on one.

Russia was not deterred. On 24 July 1914, the day after Austria-Hungary delivered its ultimatum to Serbia, the Russian council of ministers took a strong line. It asked Austria-Hungary to postpone its deadline for a Serb reply by 48 hours and at the same time supported partial military mobilisation. Mobilisation itself did not mean war: Austria-Hungary had mobilised its army during the Balkan wars but had not committed it to action. Rather, it signalled serious intent. The Tsar approved these steps on 25 July. They did not work. Austria-Hungary did not give in to Russia's pressure. Instead, Russia's actions gave Serbia a freer hand as it now knew it did not stand alone. Its adroit but robust response to Vienna rejected the Austro-Hungarian ultimatum. On 28 July Austria-Hungary declared war on Serbia and committed to the Balkan front not just its 5th and 6th Armies, intended solely to defend its southern border, but also its reserve, the 2nd Army. In doing so Conrad von Hötzendorf gave vent to his belief that the best – possibly the only – form of war was offence. As a result, he left the 1st, 3rd and 4th armies, tasked with the defence of Galicia in the event of a Russian offensive from the north-east, without support. On 30 July, the Tsar ordered the general mobilisation of the Russian army and the chief of the German general staff, Helmuth von Moltke the younger, pleaded with his Austro-Hungarian counterpart to prioritise Galicia and so act in concert with its German ally to the north, concerned to protect East Prussia from Russian attack while it focused on France in the west. Conrad responded as though he thought that either the war could still be limited or at least Serbia could be defeated before Russia could bring its full weight to bear. Although he mobilised the armies on the Galician front on 31 July, troops going to the Balkans maintained their priority on the Austro-Hungarian railway network. The 2nd Army continued its concentration in the Balkans. It did not begin to arrive on the Galician front until 28 August and its transfer was only completed on 4 September.

It was too late. By then the Austro-Hungarian advance into Russia had been checked and its forces were falling back. Isaak Barasch's family was in the eye of a storm and they were not alone. The largest concentration of Jews in the Austro-Hungarian empire lived here, making up 10 per cent of the population of Galicia and 16 per cent in adjacent Bukovina. The Russian 3rd Army pushed past Złoczów on 26 August as it advanced on Lemberg (today Lviv). Russia had actively discriminated against its own Jewish population, denying them political rights, forbidding them to own property, barring their entry to the army or civil service, and limiting their educational opportunities. The Tsar himself had condoned anti-Semitic pogroms as a form of patriotism. Accompanying his advancing army in the autumn of 1914 was a programme of Russification promoted by the Orthodox church. For Austro-Hungarian Jews, the Russians were a terrifying enemy. Those of the civilian population who could fled to other parts of the empire, to Bohemia, Moravia and Hungary, which collectively housed over 105,000 Jews by 1 October 1915. By then too 137,000 refugees from Galicia had ended up in Vienna, more than half of whom – 77,090 – were Jews. Among them was Isaak Barasch's family. The Russian gains would be reversed in 1915. Some then returned but regretted doing so when Russia's so-called Brusilov offensive tore into Galicia once more in June 1916. It was checked with German help. By 1917 Barasch's family were back home, but there were still 21,105 Jewish refugees from Galicia receiving state aid in Vienna on 1 January 1918.[3]

Italy's War with Austria-Hungary

In 1914 Isaak Barasch was not fighting in Galicia in defence of his home and hearth. When the war broke out, he was in Vienna, having just completed his studies to become a doctor. His war would be spent facing not the Russians, the obvious enemies of an Austro-

---

3. Helmut Rumpler and Anatol Schmied-Kowarzik (eds), *Die Habsburgermonarchie 1848–1918*, Band XI, *Die Habsburgermonarchie und der Erste Weltkrieg*, 2. Teilband, *Weltkriegstatistik Österreich-Ungarn 1914–1918: Bevölkerungbewegung, Kriegstote, Kriegswirtschaft* (Vienna, 2014), p. 138.

Hungarian Jew, but the Italians, who – at least ostensibly – were the empire's allies. Although the Austro-Hungarian army had fought Italians three times in Franz Josef's reign – in suppressing the 1848 revolutions, in countering Piedmont in 1859 and in protecting its rear when confronting the Prussian and Saxon armies in Bohemia in 1866 – in 1882 they had become allies.

'Italy provides an upside-down example of the primacy of foreign affairs', as Richard Bosworth has memorably put it.[4] Having become a united kingdom in 1861, it was anxious to assert its right to be considered a great power and sought a foreign policy to enable it to do so. By 1878 two opportunities presented themselves: the decline of the Ottoman empire, especially in the Balkans, and the rise of colonialism, especially in Africa. Both converged to give Italy its chance. In 1878 Russia overplayed its hand in the Balkans, with the result that the so-called League of the Three Emperors – those of Austria-Hungary, Germany and Russia – fractured. Set up in 1873, the league had been designed to manage eastern Europe while keeping it separate from the imponderables of the Balkans. Bismarck's first step towards the reconstruction of the imperial triad was to form a Dual Alliance between Germany and Austria-Hungary in 1879. In 1881 the three emperors went on to form a fresh alliance, but it looked fragile from the outset. Meanwhile Italy was eying up possible gains across the Mediterranean at the expense of the Ottoman empire, whose hold on north Africa was increasingly nominal. Here its obvious rival was France. Its gratitude for France's support in 1859 in the achievement of Italian unification was offset by the payment which France had demanded in return, the cession of Savoy and Nice. In 1881 the French, already masters of Algeria, trumped Italy by occupying Tunis. Italian hostility to France and French engagement in north Africa – rather than in continental Europe – suited Germany; for Austria-Hungary a treaty with Italy would neutralise the persistent threat it presented on its south-western frontier; and for Italy a deal with both the others provided the international recognition it sought. In 1882 the three powers formed the Triple Alliance. Its terms pledged mutual

---

4. Richard Bosworth, *Italy and the Approach of the First World War* (London, 1983), p. 34.

support if either Germany or Italy were attacked by France and if any of the signatories was attacked by two or more great powers.

Italy's colonial efforts moved on to the Horn of Africa but met with humiliation at Adowa in 1896, when it was defeated by the Ethiopians. It turned its attentions back to the Mediterranean and in 1911 invaded Libya, still formally part of the Ottoman empire. Some historians now interpret the Italian conquest of Libya as the initiation of the First World War. That may be a leap too far, but it brought colonial warfare to Europe's doorstep and in the short term, by diverting Ottoman attention back to north Africa, enabled the Balkan war of 1912. Bulgaria, Greece and Serbia seized the opportunity to drive the Turks further out of Europe, almost to Istanbul itself, and in turn undermined the indirect Austro-Hungarian suzerainty of the region which had been established largely at Ottoman expense.

The southerly direction of its foreign policy left Italy with a conundrum. Both its colonial ambitions and their maritime dimensions made it dependent on British support or – at the very least – forbearance. In 1904 Britain had resolved its own Mediterranean problems by reaching an understanding with France which left the latter free at its western end, in Tunisia, Algeria and increasingly Morocco, while allowing Britain to focus on Egypt, Sudan and the route via the Suez Canal to India. Germany engineered two crises over the French occupation of Morocco, in 1905 and 1911, intended in large part to rupture Anglo-French relations. They had the opposite effect. The Anglo-French naval agreement of 1912, which specifically addressed their security concerns in the Mediterranean and the North Sea, became central to France's pressure on Britain in the July crisis of 1914, and after the outbreak of the First World War became pivotal to the strategies of both powers. Italy, with its boot dividing the Mediterranean in two and with its long coastline dependent on overseas trade, could not afford to incur the wrath of either of them.

Nor did it do so in the run-up to 1914. Despite its membership of the Triple Alliance, it kept its distance from Germany in the two Moroccan crises. By 1912 Raymond Poincaré, the French president, was conscious that Italy, which deemed itself a liberal state, might not require much persuasion to abandon the Triple Alliance, but he feared that such a move would undermine the balance between the Triple Alliance and what was now – after the British understanding with Russia in 1907 – a Triple Entente. For France, the peace of Europe was being kept by the mutual deterrence of two seemingly equal blocs and so could be destabilised if a member was subtracted from one alliance and added to the other. As Austria-Hungary was also to realise, it was no longer Metternich's concert of Europe that was maintaining international order – even if that did not become fully evident until July 1914 itself, when Grey's attempt to convene a great power conference on the lines of London in 1913 was rejected by Germany.

Moreover, just as the Triple Entente tightened, with an Anglo-Russian naval agreement under discussion in 1914, so did the Triple Alliance – in some respects. In 1887, Austria-Hungary and Italy agreed an additional clause, which stated that changes in the Balkans could only occur if there had been an earlier agreement for 'reciprocal compensation for every advantage, territorial or other' which one of the two might gain from such an alteration. The last of the regular renewals of the Triple Alliance came in the wake of the first Balkan War, in December 1912. The war's outcome alarmed Italy as much as it did Austria-Hungary, because both feared that Serbia would acquire a port on the Adriatic.

During the July crisis in 1914, Austria-Hungary acted unilaterally. Italy was not told of Austria-Hungary's intentions to change the status quo in the Balkans until 23 July and by then they were already being put in train. Anxious to keep its deliberations in advance of its ultimatum to Serbia secret, Vienna had little faith in the confidentiality of diplomatic communications routed to and through Rome. Its fears were justified, but they did not mean that Italy did not realise what was afoot. On 20 July the Italian military attaché in Vienna reported that Austria-Hungary had passed the draft of the demands it would make of Serbia to Franz Josef for his approval, although he did not know their content. The Italian army was so distanced from the formation of Italy's foreign policy that it would not necessarily have passed on the intelligence it received from its military attachés. By the same token, the general staff was not privy to the terms of the Triple Alliance.

Nonetheless, the Italian army's planning assumptions were framed in conformity with its government's treaty obligations. In the 1890s its general staff focused on a possible war with France and considered breaching Switzerland's neutrality to get there. In December 1912 its thinking had shifted in that it now respected the principle of neutrality, but in becoming politically more circumspect it also grew geographically more ambitious. It aimed to get three corps to the Rhine in order to cooperate with the Germans in the west. The German chief of the general staff, Moltke, protested that Germany's mobilisation plans were too advanced to incorporate the Italians and preferred the idea of deploying them to the east, to fight Russia. Whichever the direction in which Italy sent its army, Moltke's Italian counterpart, Albert Pollio, saw a war waged by the Triple Alliance as an opportunity for the army to reap gains for Italy. By early 1914 he was even ready to begin fighting pre-emptively.[5]

Pollio got on well with both Conrad and Moltke, and earned their trust at a personal level, but Moltke did not expect the Italians to turn up on the Rhine and Conrad had inherited the Austro-Hungarian army's visceral animosity towards its Italian neighbour. Franz Ferdinand had briefly dismissed Conrad from his job because of his repeated calls for war against Italy. Similarly, for most Italians, the pursuit of colonies in east or north Africa were displacement activities when put alongside the completion of the Risorgimento, the unification of all Italians within the Italian state. In 1914 Italy's frontier with Austria-Hungary ran from Lake Garda in the west, through the Venetian and Julian Alps, before executing a right turn and following a course across the plain of Veneto, west of the Isonzo River, to the Adriatic. Italy wanted control of the Italians who lived beyond this line, from Tyrol to Trieste. Its ambitions also extended further east and south. They followed the Dalmatian coastline to include Croatia and Albania. Much of this area was populated and cultivated by Slav peasants but the cities, including Trieste, Pola and Fiume, were largely inhabited by Italians. The Italians were richer but their birth rate was falling in relation to that of the Slavs: time was not on their side.

---

5. John Gooch, *The Italian Army in the First World War* (Cambridge, 2014), pp. 36–8.

The outbreak of war in the Balkans was therefore an opportunity for territorial compensation in line with the 1887 provisions of the Triple Alliance. Italian ministers responded to the Austro-Hungarian ultimatum to Serbia by concluding that the circumstances of the war's outbreak cancelled their treaty obligations and requested an indication as to what they would get if, nonetheless, Italy decided to fight. It did not get an answer. On 2 August Italy opted to remain neutral but did not withdraw from the Triple Alliance. In the frenetic atmosphere of the last week of July Italy was the only great power to take a conscious decision not to fight. Its ministers did so without fully concerting their intentions with the army, which for much of July continued to assume that it would join its alliance partners. Pollio himself died suddenly on 1 July 1914, but his successor, Luigi Cadorna, did not immediately change the direction of his thinking. He too saw the opportunities for Italy if it hitched itself to a successful Triple Alliance war effort; his worry was that the army was not ready for conflict on such a scale. It lacked both guns and men. Pollio had wanted 30,000 more conscripts a year and the national rail network was not adequate for the scale of mobilisation required.

Once Cadorna became aware of what his government would do, his caution increased. First, he was well aware of the torrent of anti-Italian rhetoric emanating from Vienna as a result of Italy's neutrality. Conrad was in the van, but Moltke also vented his spleen. The war which Italy now confronted, if it were to fight, was less likely to be fought against France and more likely to be waged on Italy's north-eastern frontier either with or – more probably – against Austria-Hungary. Although the dual monarchy was already committed to war on two fronts, in Serbia and Galicia, it seemed to be better prepared for a major European conflict than Italy, whose resources had been poured into Libya. Moreover, the army had to re-orientate itself intellectually, and in terms of intelligence collection and operational planning. Cadorna's advice was that it would not be ready until the spring.

A bidding war began between the Central Powers and the Entente. Italy's military potential, which both sides had denigrated before the war, whether on land or sea, now became a desirable asset. However, although the negotiating position of the 'least of the great powers' was considerably enhanced, it was not the only potential ally to have withheld its hand in July 1914. Romania, whose support Conrad still wanted while recognising the obstacles in his path, had secretly committed itself to the Triple Alliance but also remained neutral. On 23 September 1914 it agreed with Italy that neither power would forfeit its neutrality without informing the other. Both Bulgaria and Greece were also weighing their options. All three, like Italy, knew that the redistribution of territory and influence in the Balkans would be dependent on their success in choosing the ultimate winner and in their timing as to when to jump. The opening weeks of the war complicated, more than they eased, their decision-making. The attractions of Germany as a land power were blunted by its defeat on the Marne in early September. For those on the Mediterranean littoral, the enhanced probability of a long war increased the weight of Anglo-French sea power, but it too did not deliver in line with its reputation. At the beginning of August two German warships had escaped the clutches of the French and British navies for the safety of Ottoman territorial waters. The fact that Turkey was now allied to Germany and Austria-Hungary, and became an active belligerent at the end of October, only complicated neutral calculations, especially for Italy. It thought it had settled Libya; the widening war, especially if the Italian army were fully committed in Europe, might loosen its hold in north Africa.

In 1902 Bernhard von Bülow, Germany's chancellor and foreign minister, and the architect of its pre-war 'world policy', remarked of Italy's membership of the Triple Alliance that 'in a happy marriage the husband must not get violent if his wife ventures to dance an innocent *extratour* with another. The main thing is that she doesn't run away from him, and she won't do that as long as she is better off with him than with anyone else.'[6] As his wife was Italian, Bülow presumably knew what he was talking about. In December 1914 he was appointed German ambassador to Rome in order to prove that his judgement was correct. After all, Italy was still 'married' to the Central Powers and their task was therefore to reward their spouse for that implicit

---

6. Bosworth, *Italy and the Approach of the First World War*, p. 4.

loyalty rather than to punish her for a presumed breach of faith. The way to do that was to honour the commitments of the alliance's 1887 clause. If Austria-Hungary's war against Serbia had gone with the speed and decisiveness that Conrad and others had anticipated in July, that might have been achieved at Serbia's expense. But Hungarian fears of having yet more Slavs than Magyars inside the empire meant that the dual monarchy had committed itself to keeping Serbia intact. In any case by the end of 1914 the Serbs were still successfully holding the Austro-Hungarian army at bay and the latter could not afford to prioritise its Balkan front while Russians were advancing on Budapest through Galicia. If Austria-Hungary was going to reward Italy for its loyalty to the alliance, it would have to hand over its own territory, not lands it hoped it might acquire at some point in the future. Germany proposed that Austria-Hungary give Italy the Trentino. Franz Josef responded that he would abdicate before doing so. The price which Germany was asking the Habsburg empire to pay for getting Italy into this war on their side might help to win the war in the short term but could also initiate Austria-Hungary's eventual disintegration. It had rejected that option when wooing Romania in peacetime; it could not countenance it now its existence was on the line in wartime. It seemed to some in Vienna that, in becoming the advocate of Italy's aspirations, its German ally was becoming the mouthpiece of its enemies.

Austria-Hungary did not reject the German suggestion outright. Instead, the idea grew that whatever it lost in the south-western empire should be offset by gains in the north-east. The war had re-opened the manner of Poland's partition and even its possible reconstitution. Russia had suggested enhanced self-government, albeit within Russia; the Central Powers promised potential liberation from Russia. But – however they calculated it – none of Germany, Austria-Hungary or Russia was ready to preside over the resurrection of a fully independent Polish state. The dual monarchy's demands in Poland set it at odds with the expectations of interest groups in Germany, not least the army, which saw a German-dominated Poland as a necessary future buffer against Russia. Moreover, the Austro-German military position in the winter of 1914–15 was not yet strong enough on its eastern front for either of the two allies to be the arbiter of Poland's future. That was so particularly for Austria-Hungary, which had lost ground in Poland, not gained it, since the war's outbreak. On 8 March 1915, the Russians took the Austro-Hungarian fortress of Przemysl and Italy responded by increasing its demands for concessions in the south-east. Bülow could not get Germany to give enough in Poland to keep the Austro-Hungarians happy and the Austro-Hungarians were consistently unwilling to match Italian demands, which escalated in step with the empire's worsening military situation.

The Entente powers were not so constrained. They could offer the Dalmatian coastline as well as the Trentino, since neither required any sacrifice on their part. Austria-Hungary was not in the same position: Trieste was the empire's principal port and Cattaro and Pola were the bases of the Austro-Hungarian navy. If it forfeited them, it would be landlocked. Vienna's best hope lay with the Italians themselves, many of whom opposed entry to the war. Italy's former prime minister, Giovanni Giolitti, spoke for many liberals in Italy who favoured continued neutrality. He reckoned Italy might get most of what it wanted from the war without fighting. However, Italy's liberalism, given its low level of industrialisation and high levels of illiteracy, was not as firmly rooted as its rhetoric suggested, and in any case Giolitti was not in office. On 16 October 1914 Italy's foreign minister, Antonino San Giuliano, died and Antonio Salandra, the prime minister, selected as his successor Sidney Sonnino, an opponent of Giolitti. Two days after San Giulano's death Salandra himself declared that his aim was to gain 'frontiers on land and sea no longer open to annexation, and [to raise] Italy, in reality, to the status of a great power'.

Sonnino set about putting what Salandra called *sacro egoismo* into practice. On 2 April Austria-Hungary finally offered Italy the Trentino, but six days later Sonnino responded by also demanding the islands off the Dalmatian coast, Gorizia (or Görz to the Austro-Hungarians), Gardisca and primacy in Albania – and this just to keep Italy neutral. Austria-Hungary realised how this negotiation was likely to end and Conrad began to prepare its defences along the Italian frontier, reinforcing them with troops from Serbia. On 26 April the Entente signed the Treaty of London, under whose terms Italy would renounce the Triple Alliance and enter the war on the Entente side.

In return Italy was promised the Trentino, Trieste, the Dalmatian coast and its islands, and recognition of the gains in the Dodecanese ceded by the Ottomans after their defeat in Libya. There were also ill-defined promises of compensation in Anatolia and the Horn of Africa. None of this was published until 1917, but on 3 May Sonnino followed up on the terms of the Treaty of London by withdrawing Italy from the Triple Alliance.

In early May it looked as though the Italians had backed the wrong horse. The Entente's attack on the Dardanelles on 25 April 1915 miscarried and Britain's hopes that victory here would bring the Balkan neutrals into the war on the Entente's side were put on hold. On 2 May the success of the Austro-German offensive at Gorlice-Tarnow reversed the situation in Galicia; the Russians retreated, abandoning Poland and the Baltic states. The eastern front would not stabilise until September, and when it did Bulgaria joined the Central Powers to overrun Serbia. Italy did not, however, renege on its undertaking. Although Salandra resigned on 13 May 1915, Giolitti hesitated, calculating that by the Treaty of London Italy had now vested its aspirations to great power status in the Entente. He opted not to take office and make the case for continued neutrality. Pro-war demonstrations buoyed Salandra's return to power. On 24 May Italy declared war.

It did so only against Austria-Hungary; it would not do so against Germany until 28 August 1916 and it refused to take an active part in the war against the Ottomans, despite the fact that it was still fighting a covert war against them in Libya. The lopsidedness of Italy's relationship with the Entente was striking but not wholly without parallel. Britain was the principal agent in recruiting Italy to the Entente despite the fact that its forces were not at that stage of the war engaged in direct hostilities against Austria-Hungary. Italy was therefore effectively fighting its own independent and local war, within the framework of the First World War, for the completion of the Risorgimento.

Although the mobilised strength of the Italian army was 1.2 million men, it could only equip 732,000 of them. It was short of officers and of heavy and mountain artillery. The conditions of trench warfare elsewhere had created a demand for the former but those of the Italian front also required the latter. The frontier with Austria-Hungary was 600km long and four-fifths of it was made up of mountains, some of them rising to over 3,000m. Given rock, snow and ice, these were not the conditions for the construction of deep entrenchments, but they did favour the defence. Cadorna, however, was going to have to attack. He had banked on simultaneous offensives from Russia and Serbia: neither was on offer. He concentrated 400,000 men on the frontier and put 14 of his 35 divisions into the sector closest to the sea, on the Isonzo, south of Gorizia. They were still going to have to advance uphill. Cadorna told the war minister he would need another 50 regiments, 14 battalions of *Bersaglieri* and 40 companies of *Alpini*, trained for mountain warfare, as well as all the artillery he could get, before the army was likely to make much progress.[7]

On the Austro-Hungarian side, the mood was quietly confident – in some ways extraordinarily so given the empire's experience in the war so far and the fact that it was already fighting on two other fronts. In this case, its lack of panic proved justified, and it did so in large part because Italy's treachery rallied Austria-Hungary in a united response which overcame any suggestion of ethnic differences. The response to such perfidy was revenge. 'We can expect anything from plausible, sly people', Isaak Barasch wrote in his diary on 9 February 1916. Despite his lack of sympathy for the church, which he saw as complicit with the state in the maintenance of the war, he pitied the Pope, marooned in Rome 'in that country of criminals and scoundrels' (26 July 1916). So duplicitous were the Italians that he thought it not impossible that even now Italy might turn against the Entente and especially against France, so that it could regain Savoy and Nice. However, such outbursts were unusual: he had enough friends who were Italian – whether they were so by citizenship or whether they were Austro-Hungarian – to resist national stereotypes. When he blamed the war and its horrors on Salandra, as he did on 9 February 1916, he bracketed him with other Entente leaders, Grey, Kitchener and Poincaré. After all, this was a coalition conflict and Austria-Hungary had tensions with its own allies, especially the dominant partner, Germany.

---

7. Gooch, *The Italian Army*, p. 95.

The Austro-Hungarian Army

The Austro-Hungarian army was an institution 'common' to both parts of the empire. This made it exceptional in the era after 1867 and yet also central to ideas of patriotism and Habsburg identity. The Heeresgeschichtliches Museum – the army museum – is the oldest museum in Vienna. Built after the 1848 revolutions to house the imperial armoury, by 1891 it had become the 'hall of glory' to the Habsburg army as Franz Josef had wanted. Both Franz Ferdinand and Conrad von Hötzendorf believed that, if the dual monarchy was to coalesce, its army would play the key role in its achievement. Its domestic functions therefore in some ways weighed more heavily than did its responsibility for external defence. Symbols – uniforms and military bands, the status of its officers and the link to the Crown – seemed at times to make its outward form as important as its military professionalism. From October 1915 until November 1916, while Isaak Barasch and countless others were fighting on three fronts (and a fourth after Romania joined the Entente at the end of August 1916), three soldiers were kept at the army's supreme command (Armee Oberkommndo or AOK) to model new uniforms for the post-war army. The work was supervised by an able staff officer, Edmund Glaise von Horstenau, and the emperor himself inspected the results of his efforts on 30 March 1916.[8] The white parade uniforms proposed for an imperial army which would never come into existence are still preserved in the Heeresgeschichtliches Museum. The museum itself resumed collecting in 1915, accumulating objects associated with the current war in order to project its influence into the future. Conscious of its past, this was an army deeply alive also to posteriority. Glaise von Horstenau himself, who became a Nazi and a general in the Wehrmacht in the Second World War, devoted the inter-war years to working on the seven volumes of Austria-Hungary's official history, *Österreich-Ungarns letzter Krieg* (or Austria-Hungary's last war). In some ways the title's retrospective note said it all.

The long peace which the army enjoyed between the war of 1866 and the First World War consolidated these trends. Its officers took

---

8. Peter Broucek (ed.), *Ein General im Zwielicht. Die Erinnerungen Edmund Glaises von Horstenau*, 2 vols (Vienna, 1980–8), Vol. 1, pp. 360–4.

seriously the study of war, but some of their thinking became divorced from reality. Despite his prolific contributions to military theory, Conrad himself never saw action before 1914, beyond the occupation of Bosnia-Herzegovina in 1878. In 1868 all men aged between 19 and 42 became liable for military service. Austria was to provide 50,000 recruits and Hungary 45,600. They were allocated by lot: those who drew a low number completed twelve years' service in all, three in the 'common' army (denoted by the prefix *k.und k.*, an abbreviation of *kaiserlich und königlich* or imperial and royal), seven in the reserve and two in the Landwehr (prefix *k.k.* for imperial-royal) or the Honved (prefix *k.u.* for *königlich und ungarisch* or royal and Hungarian), the former being the home army of Austria and the latter of Hungary. Those who drew middle-ranking numbers, about 20,000, served for 2 years in either the Landwehr or the Honved and then transferred to the reserve for 10 years. Finally, those who drew high numbers were exempt from any form of immediate service and placed in the Landsturm, which was only activated in time of war. Isaak Barasch was in the Landsturm.[9]

Although the annual recruit contingent was raised to 103,000 in 1889, its size by 1903 no longer reflected the growth in the empire's population base (which reached 52 million in 1910) or kept step with comparable European armies. The Hungarian Diet refused to approve an increase unless Hungary had an army that was fully its own. The method chosen to avoid such a concession was to widen the Hungarian franchise, which was the most restrictive in Europe, so undermining the Magyar dominance of the Diet with an influx of Slav votes. It was a shrewd gambit: Magyar intransigence would prove counter-productive if it resulted in the loss either of their control of Hungary or of Hungary's status within the dual monarchy. Nonetheless, the impasse lasted until 1912, when the Diet passed an army bill, and 42,000 recruits were added each year. As a result, an entire decade had been lost, in which too few men had been trained and passed into

---

9. The discussions of the army in English include: Laurence Coles, *Military Culture and Popular Patriotism in Late Imperial Austria* (Oxford, 2014); Istvan Deák, *Beyond Nationalism: A Social and Political History of the Habsburg Officer Corps 1848–1918* (New York, 1990); Gunther E. Rothenberg, *The Army of Francis Joseph* (West Lafayette, Indiana, 1976). Graydon E. Tunstall, *The Austro-Hungarian Army and the First World War* is forthcoming with Cambridge University Press.

the reserve. Moreover, the reorganisation which followed the army's increase both disrupted its running in the short term and was not due to be completed until 1918, when the annual recruit contingent would reach 236,000. In 1914, the common army had a peacetime strength of only 450,000, about half the size of the German army. It was swamped on mobilisation, when the reservists, Landwehr and Honved added 2.9 million, to give a total force of 3.3 million. Its paper strength was now comparable with its peers in Germany and France, although only 2 million of that total went to the front.

The army's quality was further diluted by the addition of almost a million men from the Landsturm before the end of 1914. Their units lacked not only training but also officers and non-commissioned officers. In another concession to Magyar conservatism, commissioning officers from the ranks was banned. Officer numbers remained comparatively low throughout the war and declined in proportion to the army's growth. As losses mounted the relationship between rank and responsibility was lost. Battalions were meant to be commanded by majors but, as Barasch's diary makes clear, they could often be led by captains and even lieutenants. Given the ban on promoting non-commissioned officers, the Landsturm was one way to expand officer numbers, but a gulf opened up between the pre-war officer corps, with its devotion to the emperor and the army, and the newer entrants, who were often university-educated professionals, more conscious of their ethnic origins and anxious to return to their pre-war careers. Isaak Barasch came in the latter category, and his diary frequently expresses his frustration with the surviving pre-war officers and their set ways of doing things. He regularly identifies his fellow officers with their jobs in civilian life. A sort of reverse take-over was occurring. By 1918 the Landsturm had contributed 4.6 million men and, given the heavy losses suffered by the common army in the opening months of the war, had converted the professional ethos of the pre-1914 supra-national Austro-Hungarian army into that of a multi-national citizen force.[10]

---

10. Helmut Rumpler and Anatol Schmied-Kowarzik (eds), *Die Habsburgermonarchie 1848–1918*, Band XI, *Die Habsburgermonarchie und der Erste Weltkrieg*, 2. Teilband, *Weltkriegsstatistik Österreich-Ungarn 1914–1918: Bevölkerungbewegung, Kriegstote, Kriegswirtschaft* (Vienna, 2014), pp. 141, 146.

The key building block of the army at the tactical level was the regiment. Until 1912, an infantry regiment consisted of 4 battalions, each of 4 companies of 4 platoons, with an establishment of 4,200 or more of all ranks. This four-by-four structure was reproduced at higher command level too. A brigade contained two such regiments and there were two brigades (or four regiments) to an infantry division. The 1912 reorganisation reduced the regiment to three battalions. It also disrupted their ethnic identities. Regiments were locally recruited, and officers were expected to master the language or languages of those they commanded. Two, three and even four or five languages might be required. Although German was the language of command, and although Germans were the dominant ethnic group among the officers, German was the recognised language of only 31 of the 142 units which were monoglot in 1914. After 1912 conscripts were no longer necessarily assigned to their local regiments and so the linguistic challenges increased just before the war and spiralled out of control after its outbreak. The turnover in both men and officers deepened the problems of communication and comprehension for both sides, an issue exacerbated by the uncertainties surrounding national loyalties. An incident on mobilisation in Prague created early if exaggerated doubts about the dependability of Czech units which never disappeared. On the Russian front, Romanians, Ruthenes and other Slavs were thought to be likely to desert. Barasch was less preoccupied with these issues, because on the Italian front the loyalty of all ethnic groups except the Italians themselves could be assured.

As in other European armies in 1914, the corps – a self-contained formation made up of all arms and typically composed of two to three divisions – was the key higher command on mobilisation, although its importance declined in operational terms as manoeuvre was replaced by positional warfare and the division acquired assets of its own. The empire was divided up into sixteen military districts, each allocated a corps with its headquarters in a major city or town. VII Corps, in which Barasch was serving when his diary opens in January 1916, was based before the war in central and southern Hungary, with its headquarters in Temesvar. It had fought on the Galician front until July 1915, when it was moved to the Isonzo and stayed there for the rest of the war. On mobilisation, the whole force was divided into six Armies of two to three corps, whose commanders and staffs were appointed from scratch. More followed and from March 1916 two to three armies were formed into Army Groups.[11]

Many of these senior commands were held by members of the royal family. As in the other absolute monarchies the emperor was the supreme warlord but Franz Josef's age ruled him out from active command in the field – and he had in fact wisely kept such responsibilities at a distance when younger. In 1914, although Conrad had de facto command as the chief of the general staff, the army's overall command was in the hands of Archduke Friedrich. In 1915, another archduke, Eugen, was given command of the south-western (i.e. Italian) front, albeit with the able Alfred Krauss as his chief of staff. The commander between November 1914 and November 1916 of VII Corps, in which Barasch served, was Archduke Josef. His wife moved to Trieste so that both could enjoy the pleasures of the city. Barasch reported on a social occasion with them at corps headquarters without his customary censure for those in the rear. When Franz Josef died on 21 November 1916, his youthful successor, Karl (who was born in 1887), removed both Archduke Friedrich and Conrad from their posts. He appointed Arthur Arz zu Straussenburg in Conrad's stead and took over the supreme command himself. Much of his motivation was sensible: Friedrich was accused of corruption and Karl wished to break the increasing control of the Austro-Hungarian army which the German high command was putting in place. He also wanted to take the empire out of the war, recognising that its scale and length were now breaking his inheritance. His attempts to negotiate a separate peace in 1917 failed, with the result that his attempt to undermine the Austro-German alliance rebounded. The charge of betrayal tied the dual monarchy yet tighter to Germany. His efforts to intervene more

---

11. The most recent overall study of the empire in the war is available in English in its revised edition: Manfried Rauchensteiner, *The First World War and the End of the Habsburg Monarchy* (Vienna, 2014), here p. 51; *Österreich-Ungarns letzter Krieg*, ed. Bundesministerium fur Heerwesen und Kriegsarchiv (7 vols and 7 vols of maps [*Beilagen*], index vol. [*Register*], 1929–38) provides detail on the army's order of battle and the distribution of its units during the war.

directly in the operational direction of the war were equally flawed, partly because it was not something in which he was particularly expert (he had commanded a corps on the Italian front for four months in 1916), and partly because Arz zu Straussenburg, unlike Conrad, was insufficiently robust in his exercise of authority. Just as the decision of Tsar Nicholas II of Russia to take over Stavka, the Russian high command, in the autumn of 1915 backfired when the generals asked him to abdicate in March 1917, so did Karl mire himself too deeply in military affairs to evade the political responsibility of defeat.

The military collapse, when it came, was suffered most directly on the front on which the army had proved most successful. The Central Powers overran Serbia and Romania in 1915 and 1916 respectively. The Balkan problem, for which war in 1914 had seemed to be a solution, was apparently resolved. Then the two revolutions of 1917 took Russia out of the war that winter. Although the Austro-Hungarian army was also committed in Macedonia, Italy was now its major front. In October 1917, having checked the Italians on the Isonzo in fighting to which Barasch bears witness, it combined with the German 14th Army to break through at Caporetto (to the Italians but Karfreit to the Germans, and today Kobarid in Slovenia). The Italian army suffered a major defeat and fell back across the plain of Veneto to the line of the River Piave. The Austro-Hungarian army stood at a high-water mark, but what looked like victory, at least on the map, did not feel like it. It had been achieved at the price of self-inflicted wounds from which the empire could not recover.

At the end of 1917 Barasch took part in the advance to the Piave, following the Adriatic coast from the line on the Isonzo. His description of the abundance he found once into Italy bears comparison with the responses of the German units that broke through on the western front on 21 March 1918. Seeing the enemy rear made both armies aware of the economic imbalance between the two blocs. At the heart of their responses was food. Although theoretically self-sufficient in agricultural terms, Austria-Hungary drew both manpower and animals from the land when it mobilised its army in 1914. Like Germany, it was subject to the Entente's blockade, but unlike Germany it had no access to maritime trade through neighbouring neutrals after

Italy entered the war in 1915. Austria depended on the granaries of Hungary for its survival, and Hungary looked after itself first. Hunger gave wings to political discontent, ethnic difference and ultimately revolution. The problem was as much distribution as production. Internal communications were inadequately maintained but overworked, not least by continuous troop movements. After its failure to cross the Piave in June 1918, the army broke and was defeated by the Italians at Vittorio Veneto on 24 October. It had already sought an armistice on 4 October, the day after Germany did so. As the army collapsed, so did the empire it served. The demands of the First World War aligned the two, ensuring that the strengths of the first could no longer compensate for the tensions within the second, but that each reflected the other.

Jews in Austria-Hungary during the First World War

Food and its lack became the trigger for anti-Semitism, which waxed with increasing strength in 1917–18. Although many of the Jewish refugees had returned home as the Russians retreated, not all did so. Moreover, as the empire faced dissolution, especially after Woodrow Wilson's support for the principle of national self-determination in January 1918, many Jews were uncertain where they belonged. The dual monarchy had given them protection and a home. Jews were emancipated in both parts of the empire in the 1860s and returned the trust which the Habsburgs showed in them with loyalty to the dynasty. They had greeted the war's outbreak as an opportunity to demonstrate their gratitude. Those from Galicia in particular saw the fighting against Russia as 'a holy war'. However, in 1918 it became clear that Galicia was likely to be partitioned between Poland and Ukraine, the former overwhelmingly Catholic and the latter Orthodox, and neither offering the security to Jews which they had enjoyed before 1914. They wanted to remain loyal Habsburg subjects at best or neutral at worst. Neither was an option.

Those who had fled to Vienna, Prague or Budapest and those who had eked out a living as refugees in Bohemia and Moravia were about to become foreigners. Even assimilated Jews who had been pre-war

Austrian residents, although assured of their citizenship in the new state, grew nervous as the rhetoric of German nationalism flourished. They were better off than Jews in Hungary. In 1914 the Magyar government had refused to provide support for refugees, passing the responsibility on to Austria, and the populist politics of Admiral Horthy at the war's end traded on anti-Semitism.

By 1917 the populations of cities like Budapest and Vienna saw refugees no longer as objects of compassion worthy of humanitarian support, as many had in 1914, but as additional mouths to feed from a diminishing supply. In February 1918 there were 496,018 refugees in Austria without the means to live, of whom 143,349 were Jews. In September, despite the peace treaty signed with the Russians at Brest-Litovsk in March, there were still 326,281, of whom 68,286 were Jews.[12] They became the scapegoats for the sufferings of the wider community. Unlike their co-religionists who were assimilated and middle-class, they wore strange clothes, spoke Yiddish and were conservative in their religious observance. Although middle-class Jews supported them through charitable activity, they did not necessarily empathise with them. Moreover, popular assumptions about these richer Jews were then also attributed to those who were clearly poor. All Jews were blamed for the black market and were castigated as war profiteers.

The army was comparatively exempt from these pressures, although it was not free from hunger. Nor were citizen soldiers unaffected by the prejudices and beliefs of their families at home. The pre-war Habsburg army had been remarkably unconcerned by the confessional proclivities of its members. Nonetheless, Jews were both under-represented in its ranks and their numbers were falling. In 1911, Jews constituted 4.4 per cent of the empire's population, but made up only 0.6 per cent of the career officer corps, down from 1.2 per cent in 1897, and 3 per cent of the rank and file, down from 3.9 per cent

---

12. Marsha Rozenblit, 'Der Habsburg-Patriotismus der Juden', in Helmut Rumpler (ed.), *Der Habsburgermonarchie 1848–1918: Band XI. Die Habsburgermonarchie und der erste Weltkrieg: 1 Teilband*, 2 vols (Vienna, 2016), pp. 887–917; here p. 902. See also Maureen Healy, *Vienna and the Fall of the Habsburg Empire: Total War and Everyday life in World War I* (Cambridge, 2004).

in 1902. Neither trend was a product of discrimination, although it undoubtedly existed. Rather, they reflected the changing career aspirations of young Jewish males as their educational attainments rose. Between 1848 and 1910 987 Jewish career officers had passed through the army and 19 had been promoted to general, some admittedly on their retirement. These figures compare very favourably with other nineteenth-century European armies. Jews still served but they did so while pursuing another career: in 1911 17 per cent – an extraordinarily high proportion – of reserve officers were Jews.[13]

Furthermore, any suggestion that Isaak Barasch might have found the army uncongenial on the grounds of race or religion is not borne out either by his diary or by that of Bernhard Bardach, another Jewish military doctor, albeit a pre-war career officer who served on the Russian front.[14] Relevant in this latter case is the fact that, while the opportunities in civilian medicine were multiplying before 1914, those for military doctors were not to be ignored. Of the 19 Jews who reached the rank of general between 1848 and 1910 11 were in the medical department, as were 469 – or roughly half – of all Jewish career officers. In 1911 1.9 per cent of career medical officers were Jews, twice the percentage who served in the infantry. As a result, the Jewish medical officer was an established feature of the pre-war army. Siegfried Plaschke, like Barasch a Landsturm doctor who was Jewish but not a pre-war regular, was twice decorated for gallantry in the field, so giving the lie to anti-Semitic jibes that Jews were 'cowards' or corrupt.[15] Isaak Barasch was also decorated.

When Barasch was called up, he was in Vienna, not at his family home. Galician Jews with ambition and seeking assimilation left the land, in his case first for Lemberg (today Lviv) and then Vienna, to pursue his studies in medicine. Just as he would have felt comfortable in a city nearly 9 per cent of whose inhabitants were Jews, so he would have had good cause to be confident that both the army and

---

13. Deák, *Beyond Nationalism*, pp. 171–8.
14. *Carnage and Care on the Eastern Front: The War Diaries of Bernhard Bardach 1914–1918*, trans. and ed. Peter Appelbaum (New York, 2018), pp. xv–xvi.
15. Birgitte Biwald, *Von Helden und Krüppeln. Das Österreichisch-ungarische Militärsanitätswesen im Ersten Weltkrieg*, 2 vols (Vienna, 2002), Vol. 1, pp. 100, 109.

its medical department would not discriminate against him on the grounds of his faith. It could not afford to do so: over 300,000 soldiers who served the empire in the war were Jews, about 25,000 of them as reserve officers like him. There is no evidence in the diary that he was religiously observant, but the army was solicitous of those who were, where possible giving leave for major festivals and providing field kitchens for kosher food. Unlike Jews on the north-eastern front, Barasch was not fighting a holy war against the Russians, but he was defending an empire which had protected the rights of his people.[16] He did so by fulfilling his vocation – to be a doctor.

The Medical Services of the Austro-Hungarian Army

Given the long peace which the Austro-Hungarian army enjoyed between 1866 and 1914, its medical services might have been expected to atrophy. The armed forces of the other great powers of Europe were engaged in colonial campaigns which not only gave their doctors experience in the treatment of battle wounds but more significantly hammered home the importance of basic hygiene and preventive medicine. Before the First World War, disease was a bigger killer of soldiers than combat. In 1895 the French army incurred twenty-five combat deaths in conquering Madagascar but lost one-third of the force to disease, 72 per cent of them to malaria. Between 1899 and 1902 the British army in the South African War suffered heavily from enteric fever and disease caused twice as many deaths as combat. Both armies learnt that prevention was better than cure and that basic sanitation was central to military effectiveness.

Within Europe, it had been the experience of the Austrians and their enemies that had led to the establishment of the Red Cross. Henri Dunant, its prime mover, had been behind the battle front at Solferino in 1859 and was so disturbed by what he saw that in 1863 he convened a meeting in his home city of Geneva to set up an international organisation to help the wounded and to organise

---

16. Rozenblit, 'Der Habsburg-Patriotismus der Juden', pp. 892–6; see also Erwin Schmidl, *Habsurgs judische Soldaten 1788–1918* (Vienna, 2014).

casualty evacuation. Its result was the Geneva Convention of 1864, which established the International Red Cross for 'the amelioration of the condition of the wounded in armies in the field'. Patriotic and charitable groups dedicated to helping those injured in Austria-Hungary's wars affiliated themselves with the Austrian branch of the Red Cross in 1879. The fact that the umbrella organisation had royal patronage gave it official standing but Johann Steiner, who became the head of the medical department at AOK in the First World War, was worried by the Geneva Convention's presumption that the wounded and those who came to their aid were to be treated as neutrals in international law. That could not be the case for the medical services of the army of a belligerent state, and nor could it apply to soldiers who, once recovered from their injuries, might return to the front line. In 1906, the powers which met to draw up the Hague Convention took the opportunity to revise the Geneva Convention, recognising these points and adding that wounded enemy soldiers and the military doctors who were treating them, who were then captured, were to be accorded belligerent rights as prisoners of war. The Austrian Red Cross (which was deployed to Bulgaria in the Balkan wars), as well as its Hungarian counterpart and the voluntary bodies with which they were both associated, were therefore free to contribute to the empire's war effort in 1914. They provided about half the disposable capacity for medical care and casualty evacuation at the outbreak of the conflict.[17]

The employment of the Austrian Red Cross in others' wars gave the army's medical officers some knowledge of modern combat conditions. They learned from the Russo-Japanese War as well as the Balkan wars, and they produced a raft of publications to analyse the results. The medical school in Vienna became well known for its excellence in military medicine. The first field regulations for the Austro-Hungarian medical services were published in 1879, and they were updated and revised in 1904. From 1885 war games and military exercises tested medical arrangements. An inspection report

---

17. Biwald, *Von Helden und Krüppeln*, Vol. 1, pp. 37–44, 57; see also Geoffrey Best, *Humanity in Warfare: The Modern History of the International Law of Armed Conflicts* (London, 1980), pp. 141–54.

of 1908 criticised the tendency for such events to become parades and public spectacles, and in 1909 an officer was appointed specifically to counteract any such trend. In 1913 an exercise at corps level, with each corps deploying thirty doctors, reckoned that in a battle lasting up to two days losses would run at between 10 and 15 per cent and that each corps would require 24,000 beds for those too sick to be moved to the rear.[18]

In peacetime Austria-Hungary had a network of garrison hospitals across the empire and each designated fortress had its own provision. On mobilisation the army deployed 160 field hospitals, 104 mobile reserve hospitals and 47 convalescent hospitals (literally 'field rest houses') for up to 500 lightly wounded. In 1917 the last two were amalgamated to form more field hospitals, and by then there were 291 in all. Each field hospital was designed to care for 200 patients, or 300 in times of need, and was allocated to a corps or division. Its staff comprised 6 to 8 doctors, as well as 78 medical assistants and a team of 29 responsible for medical transport. Much of the work of the field hospital commander (who ranked as a major with the title of *Stabsarzt*) was concerned with procuring the buildings needed for operating theatres and wards, and with bringing up equipment and medical supplies. The divisional field hospital was the collecting point for the seriously wounded, who came in from subordinate formations forward of the division. Under the 1904 regulations, which governed the medical services' organisation and establishments in the First World War, mobile field units were allocated to each infantry brigade and to every infantry and cavalry division.[19]

The army had about 1,500 doctors in all in 1914, about 200 below establishment. The most senior were appointed as *Generalstabsarzten* at army level, or sometimes *Oberstabsarzten I Klasse*, and at corps level as either *Oberstabsarzten I Klasse* (i.e. as medical colonels) or *Oberstabsarzten II Klasse* (lieutenant colonels), but in the war were known more regularly as *Korpschefarzten*. Each regiment was meant to have five doctors, a *Regimentsartz* (ranking as a captain), with

---

18. Biwald, *Von Helden und Krüppeln*, Vol. 1, pp. 37, 42, 44–53.
19. Biwald, *Von Helden und Krüppeln*, Vol. 1, pp. 54–6, 58–9.

beneath him an *Oberarzt* (a full lieutenant or *Oberleutnant*) and three *Assistentartzen* or lieutenants for each battalion. Barasch began his career as an *Assistentartz*, with responsibility for the health of one of the regiment's battalions but was promoted to *Oberarzt*. The latter rank was the one conferred on civilian doctors who were brought into the army but this source slowed and dried up completely in 1918. Medical students were enlisted as medical assistants, serving as non-commissioned officers. A medical *Unteroffizier* and four stretcher bearers were allocated to each infantry company. However, taking potential doctors before they had completed their studies made little long-term sense. Barasch was already qualified when the war began and so in 1915 he entered via the Landsturm, which provided a continuous influx of newly minted doctors. As of 1 February 1917 the army's doctors totalled 7,392 or 2 for every 1,000 men. Within a year the number had fallen to 5,399. By then many regiments had 3 doctors, not 5, and by April 1918 the army had only 4,872 doctors.[20]

As Barasch's diary repeatedly makes clear, a profound division opened up between the pre-war career medical officers and those who joined after 1914. Many of his complaints reflect the hostility felt by those at the front for those in the rear in all armies, regardless of nationality or branch of service. The combination of their creature comforts with the form-filling and bureaucracy of a mass army fighting an industrialised war did not make for a comfortable relationship between the set procedures of those in higher positions and the harassed and exhausted junior officers having to improvise in adverse circumstances. However, the Austro-Hungarian army's medical services had specific drivers for discontent and internal division. Although each of their appointments from *Assistentartz* to *Generalstabsarzt* had an army rank equivalent, the doctors did not have command authority over troops and so could be treated as second-class citizens by officers in combat arms. For the junior doctors exposed to all the dangers of the front line that was self-evidently insulting but it was also felt by their seniors, concerned to advance the professional

---

20. Biwald, *Von Helden und Krüppeln*, Vol. 1, pp. 87–95; *Österreich-Ungarns letzter Krieg*, Vol. VII, pp. 88–9.

status of their calling. They reacted with fury in May 1917, when the war ministry imposed censorship on the publication of scientific papers on military medicine on the grounds that they could damage the army's reputation by discussing the incidence of infectious diseases or of cases of self-harm by soldiers.

The career medical officers had learnt to live with these slights before the war and acquired the airs and behaviours of officers 'with troops' as they did so, but the more they met the army half-way, the more they angered the junior doctors drawn from civilian life. Senior medical officers wearing spurs and carrying swords – quite apart from breaching the Geneva Convention if they had been caught in the front line – were mocked for such affectations. They in turn thought that the junior doctors should learn to adapt better to military life and its requirements – as Barasch himself was advised to do. In September 1916 the 14th section of the war ministry, which was responsible for military medicine, wanted those studying medicine destined for the army to receive specifically military training. The professors of medicine at the universities of Vienna and Budapest charged with their education responded in 1917 that the army should do more to raise the social standing of its doctors and argued that their salaries should be more closely aligned with those they might earn in civilian practice.[21]

The job of an *Assistentartz* was less to deploy the medical knowledge he might have acquired at the university of Vienna and more to process those who were sick and injured along the conveyor belt that took them to the rear, and then out of the line or back to front-line duty. The system of garrison hospitals in peacetime and the concentration of assets at divisional level in wartime put a premium on speedy casualty evacuation from the front line. In Galicia in 1914 getting the wounded back took priority over immediate treatment, with the result that they clogged the lines of communication, a problem compounded by the fact that the army was itself in full retreat. It proved counter-productive in other ways too. First it gave time for shock and then sepsis to kick in, resulting in disproportionately high death rates, and

---

21. Biwald, *Von Helden und Krüppeln*, Vol. 1, pp. 96–7, 103–5.

secondly those who made it back to the security of the interior tended to stay there and so be lost to further front-line service. In 1907 the medical staff had proposed three classifications for those who were sick or wounded – able to walk, fit enough to sit or lie on a transport and unable to be transported. By October 1914 soldiers were simply divided into lightly or severely wounded. Only the latter were to be taken out of the rear area of operations. The remainder were to be treated within it and returned to their units as soon as possible. By 1917 manpower shortages had intensified the presumption against the evacuation of casualties to the rear. Those expected to recover in eight days were to be treated at a battalion or regimental aid station and those who would take a fortnight at a brigade or divisional field hospital. Army hospitals were reserved for wounds which would take a month to heal. By the end of January 1918, of 4,718,000 who had been wounded or fallen sick since the outbreak of the war, 2,964,000 had been returned to the front.[22]

At one level this was no more than a reiteration of the principles set out in the 1904 regulations. They had tended to assume that the army would be on the offensive. The wounded were to be evacuated as soon as possible and therefore a doctor and medical team should accompany the advance. An aid post should be established just behind each forward unit, which would send out stretcher bearers to search the ground for the wounded. During the war dogs were also trained for this role. Every soldier carried his own field dressing – and in 1915 there was a call for him to have two, but later in the war the effects of the blockade meant bandages – as well as medicines – were in short supply. The regulations ruled that the doctors in the aid stations were to focus on saving the lives of those in a critical condition, primarily by compression and dressing the wounds (a process Barasch describes). The lightly wounded should return to the front or make their own

---

22. Biwald, *Von Helden und Krüppeln*, Vol. 1, pp. 65–6, 70–1; see also Wilhelm Kaschofsy, 'Militarärztliche Organisation und Leistungen der Feldspitäler der österreichish-ungarischen Armee im Kriege 1914–1918', in Clemens Pirquet (ed.), *Volksundheit im Krieg (Wirtschafts-und sozials-geschichte des Weltkrieges. Österreichische und ungarische Serie)*, 2 vols (Vienna, 1926), Vol. 1, pp. 108–21; and for brief summaries, Christian Ortner, *Die k.u.k. Armee und ihr letzter Krieg* (Berndorf, 2020), pp. 238–43; *Österreich-Ungarns letzter Krieg*, Vol. VII, pp. 88–9.

way back to the brigade or divisional field hospital rather than divert the attention of the regimental doctors or take places on medical transport. The *Regimentsartz* would establish a second aid post and, with an *Oberartz* to support him, could guarantee that it would have 24-hour continuous medical cover.[23]

This is the pattern that Barasch describes in his diary, but obviously it did not always go according to plan. It assumed that a regiment had a full complement of doctors, which by the later stages of the war it did not. Major action and heavy losses could swamp the system, just as persistent but desultory contact with the enemy would not over-tax it. Complicated wounds could not be fully treated at regimental level, as the aid stations did not have operating theatres and because x-ray machines (the army had over 600) were held at higher command levels. Most of the injuries Barasch was treating on the Isonzo front in February 1916 were caused by shells and so their treatment was often beyond the resources available to him. His view, as he put it on 10 February, was that there were too many doctors at regimental level, and not enough further back in the field hospitals. At this early stage of his service he also itemised the medicines he needed but were not supplied. Thereafter he stopped doing so, perhaps recognising that he was not going to get them and that there were other tasks on which he might more profitably focus.

Even if he had no command authority, the battalion or regimental doctor played a key role in the unit's discipline and morale. Barasch's job was less to cure than to discriminate between those that were really ill and those who were malingering. As all armies in both world wars realised, doctors could not afford to allow men bed rest in the rear just because they had a slightly elevated temperature, but they also had to recognise when a condition might worsen if the soldier had no respite or when it might be the harbinger of an infectious disease which could take even more men out of the line. As a newly qualified doctor, Barasch bridled at having to suspend his care for the individual in favour of ensuring that the collective needs of the unit were pioritised.

---

23. Biwald, *Von Helden und Krüppeln*, Vol. 1, pp. 57–8, 81–5; Karl Kassowitz, 'Der österreichish-ungarische Truppenarzt an der Front', in Pirquet (ed.), *Volksundheit im Krieg*, Vol. 1, pp. 133–42.

'I am playing the role here of a watchman', he wrote on 10 March 1916, 'and even that of a ... detective'.

He also became a clerk of works. Whenever his battalion went into the front line, he needed to find the materials to build a shelter for his aid post. The Austro-Hungarian positions to the east of the Isonzo River were sited on a limestone plateau, the Karst in German or Carso in Italian, where shell holes or caves bored out of the rock provided the only cover, unless timber could be acquired from elsewhere. Out of the line, his tasks were not dissimilar, but here also included the construction of bath houses. The absence of opportunities to wash or to change clothes made front-line conditions ideal breeding grounds for lice. In 1915 typhus cases soared in all the belligerent armies: that of Austria-Hungary suffered 114,280 cases in the year as whole, as opposed to 11,777 in the 4 months between August and December 1915. Vaccination brought the problem under control the following year, although the link between the louse and a second disease, relapsing fever (which was frequently mistaken for influenza), was not fully understood until later in the war. Typhus cases in the Habsburg field army fell to 24,740 in 1916, 9,740 in 1917 and 4,560 in 1918.[24] Barasch's obsession with cleanliness demonstrated the contribution of the unit doctor to the practice of preventive medicine through the enforcement of standards of hygiene and sanitation.

Positional warfare created more opportunities both negatively for the spread of infection and positively for the imposition of medical routines for its control. The army created thirteen *Salubritätskommissionen*, known as *Sakos*, to fight infection, with one allocated to each army's line of communications, and the target was to have hygiene stations at every corps headquarters by the end of 1915. Mobile bacteriological laboratories were formed at the end of 1914; there were 96 by the war's end. They had fumigation units for delousing and battled cholera and smallpox as well as typhus. The *Sakos* insisted on regular washing, on the need to establish latrines away from fresh water sources and to

---

24. Albert Müller-Deham, 'Der Bauchtyphus als Kriegsseuche nach Erfahrungen in der österreichish-ungarischen Armee', in Pirquet (ed.), *Volksundheit im Krieg*, Vol. 2, p. 115.

rotate soldiers out of the line regularly so that they and their kit could be thoroughly cleaned.

On the Karst, water was in short supply in the summer and soldiers died of thirst. They would risk cholera by filling their water bottles from stagnant pools, which were also breeding grounds for mosquitoes and here – as in Macedonia – malaria was prevalent. By March 1918 quinine to treat it was unobtainable across the empire, another effect of the blockade. In September 1918, the Austro-Hungarian army in Italy had between 5,000 and 6,000 malaria cases a week. In the winter frostbite replaced the diseases of the summer, especially further north in the Alps, and was also statistically more obvious because it struck at a time when fighting was less frequent and so battle casualties fell. On 27–8 December 1917 one division reported that it had 87 wounded but 423 sick, of whom 99 had frostbite. In March 1918, with the army on the Piave, the same division had 73 wounded but 811 sick and 86 suffering from frostbite.[25]

Disease remained a major influence on military effectiveness in the First World War, although not as big a killer as it had been in previous wars. Austria-Hungary put 8 million men into the field.[26] Estimates of its war dead range from 1.1 million to just under 1.5 million, with the higher figure seeming more likely, given the collapse of the empire in 1918 and its impact on the collection of accurate statistics.[27] By the end of 1917 war dead when aggregated by locality were already put at just under 1.2 million.[28] Although deaths on the Russian and Romanian fronts slumped in 1918, that was the year in which they peaked on the Italian front at 43,367 (as opposed to 38,519 in 1916 and 42,309 in 1917), with in addition a staggering total of 488,152 captured or missing (as opposed to 85,520 and 84,152 in each of the

---

25. Biwald, *Von Helden und Krüppeln*, Vol. 1, pp. 73–812; Vol. 2, pp. 386, 398.
26. *Österreich-Ungarns letzter Krieg*, Vol. VII, Beilage 37.
27. See Antoine Prost, 'The dead', in Jay Winter (ed.), *The Cambridge History of the First World War*, 3 vols (Cambridge, 2014), Vol. 3, pp. 588–9.
28. Helmut Rumpler and Anatol Schmied-Kowarzik (eds), *Die Habsburgermonarchie 1848–1918, Band XI, Die Habsburgermonarchie und der Erste Weltkrieg, 2. Teilband, Weltkriegstatistik Österreich-Ungarn 1914–1918: Bevölkerungbewegung, Kriegstote, Kriegswirtschaft* (Vienna, 2014), p. 180.

previous years).[29] An unknown number would have been dead. Given that the ratio of dead to wounded was of the order of 1:4, a figure of 1.5 million deaths suggests a total of 6 million wounded. Total cases of sickness were put at 3.46 million, although allowance must be made for double counting between wounded and sick. Rounded numbers of those who were afflicted by war-related diseases totalled just under 3.2 million, of whom over a third had contracted syphilis. All forms of typhus added 448,000, tuberculosis 430,000, dysentery 400,00, malaria 330,000, eye infections 190,000 and cholera 80,000. Of these, cholera was the most lethal, killing over a third of those afflicted by it.[30]

Neither shell-shock, to use the title most frequently employed in Britain for mental problems precipitated by front-line service in the First World War, nor influenza, the biggest killer of late 1918, is included in these statistics for war-related disease. Doctors in the Austro-Hungarian army undoubtedly suffered from the first, especially in the war's latter stages as their falling numbers added physical exhaustion to psychological strain. Barasch's diary provides abundant testimony to the pressures he was under, although it is not always easy to disaggregate his dislike of the war in general from his personal mental health, or the role of the demands which the war put on him from depression for other reasons. The inability to provide for his patients as he would have liked as manpower diminished and medical supplies became increasingly hard to procure must have increased his sense that he was struggling to continue. He secured leave in January 1918 and then his absence from the line was extended. When he was recalled in June he quickly found himself in the psychiatric ward of Laibach (today Ljubljana) hospital and then was sent to the Vienna garrison hospital.

By this time the first wave of the 1918 influenza epidemic had hit, its impact in early April being much like 'normal' flu. It was the second wave, which began to break in August and peaked between

---

29. Ibid., pp. 162–3.
30. Ibid., pp. 164–5, 190; see also S. Kirchenberger, 'Beiträge zur Sanitätsstatistik der österrichisch-ungarischen Armee im Kriege 1914–18', in Pirquet (ed.), *Volksgesundheit im Krieg*, Vol. 1, pp. 47–77.

September and December 1918, which accounted for 90 per cent of the deaths attributed to the so-called Spanish flu outbreak of 1918–19. In the pandemic's immediate aftermath these were put at 21 million, but today's estimates can reach 100 million, or 5 per cent of the global population. Influenza cases spread into Austria-Hungary from the west and did not reach epidemic proportions in Vienna until October.[31] Isaak Barasch was one of the early victims, dying in Vienna on 12 September 1918.

Barasch's diary is a war diary in the most literal sense. He begins his story in January 1916, when he was already at the front, and he breaks off whenever he left it. He never mentions his family or his life beyond the war. Nor does he give any indication that this diary was part of a sequence, which addressed the rest of his life. Instead, it is a deeply personal response to the war itself. It is an introspective document, whose emotional and reflective power derives precisely from its author's own sense of isolation. He struggles to establish friendships with his fellow officers, finding their jollifications and drinking more trying than bonding. This is no paean to comradeship or to a sense of meaning to be found within war. His disillusionment with European culture and its values, as revealed by the war, is almost complete, as is his frustration at the loss of personal control over his own life which the war has imposed. And therein lies its power: this is a book about one man's engagement with overwhelming events and his struggle to maintain his agency within them.

---

31. Elias Herbert, 'Grippe', in Pirquet (ed.), *Volksgesundheit im Krieg*, Vol. 2, pp. 54–66.

Letter to My Great-Uncle

by Shulamit Kopf

Dear Great-Uncle Isaak,
I am writing you an imaginary letter 102 years after your death.

I hope you don't mind, but I have been reading the six diaries you wrote while serving as a doctor in the Austro-Hungarian army during the First World War. More than that, I'm having them published. Your extraordinary words must be preserved in the human archive.

With access to your private thoughts – uncensored, raw – I feel that I have come to know you quite well, more intimately than many of the people in my life.

I like you. I am even beginning to love you and feel close to you. Throughout the war you never lost your humanity, your empathy for the suffering of the soldiers and the beleaguered civilian population, your wry sense of humor, your scathing gaze set on officers who care for more for medals than the lives under their command.

You were acutely aware of the lunacy of it all:

> Yesterday marked the second anniversary of our waging of this war. How much longer must this inconclusive struggle between nations go on? There have already been enough victims for mankind to bear, going on for seven million dead just in Europe these last two years. And then there are the imponderable phalanxes of the crippled and sick. Immeasurable treasures have gone up in smoke. Poor humanity for putting up with this! How cowardly you are! Where are your high ideals? Where is your love of liberty? Where are all your freedom fighters? … You allow yourselves to be enslaved and led astray so easily.

I am sorry to tell you, Uncle Isaak, but humanity has not grown wiser and mobs are still led astray.

Describing 'the disgusting devil's music', as you called the bombardments, you wrote:

> There are ghostly wails and cracks. One could almost believe that all the evil spirits in the underworld have sworn to do away with suffering humanity. It's an inferno that not even Dante could find sufficient words to describe.

But even in that hellscape you never lost your ability to steal a moment to appreciate the wonders of nature.

> The place we're in is a beauty spot. The only thing missing is a society in harmony with it.

Or:

> How beautifully the little birds are singing in the wood today. As if they didn't have a care in the world. They are twittering and trilling all around and do not allow themselves to be disturbed by the ugliness that has been enacted in this vicinity for months now.

Or:

> I only got halfway and contented myself with the splendid view which I had from here over St Vigil ... the little groups of houses and the mountains. Here I lie down in the grass. Various flowers (the purple gentian especially and the yellow first flower of spring) adorn in beautiful samples too numerous to mention the meadows where goats and sheep are grazing.

I imagine you dressed in your uniform taking a few happy moments of peace to lie on the grass, feel it stroke your face, gazing at clouds floating by, reluctant to return to the maw.

You describe events so vividly that I can see them unfold like a movie scene.

Ext. MOUNTAIN SCENERY-DAY
To appear on time for the medical inspection Dr Barasch tries to find a shortcut. He checks his wristwatch, a World War I innovation. The camera follows him as he stumbles over heaps of stones, steps in puddles after yesterday's heavy rain. He is lost, bathed in sweat. A deep silence interrupted from time to time by the far away thunder of guns and shells. Finally, he spots a distant footpath.

The camera follows as he briskly walks towards it. He is on the path and quite unexpectedly:

> There opens up to me a splendid but really quite chilling panorama. The far-off flat mirror of Lake Doberdò, beyond that a part of the township of Monfalcone, and further on, the whole course of the lower Isonzo with its mouth and the hard-fought-for and drenched in human blood chain of hills with their summits … All this lay at my feet, quite near to me. A piece of ground over which crueller events than ever had already been played out … A terrible human tragedy. Hundreds of thousands of people have been torn to pieces here, crushed, blown up and mutilated. It is a great cemetery with its innumerable heroes' graves swarming everywhere with shamelessly exposed corpses.
>
> And all these things on this fair piece of ground were revealed before my very eyes in an instant.
>
> I was like someone intoxicated. I almost lost consciousness. I was as if rooted to the spot and could not stir from there. I stared and I stared.

An explosion nearby.

> I woke up. And only now did I notice in what a life-threatening situation I found myself. This was in the chimney of one of the highest summits here. I was visible to the enemy on all sides as if I had been on a plate. Everywhere in all these high places enemy observers are positioned. The distance as the crow flies from the enemy's lines amounted to four kilometres at most.

> I was frightened and uneasy. I wanted to run away. But it was difficult. I only had one way out. To run away as fast as possible.

Cut.

You show self-awareness:

> I am by and by an unusual person, who cannot easily adapt to new situations.

I sense you were an introvert preferring to read a good book or write in your journal rather than carouse and play cards all night with the other officers.

> I feel a limitless emptiness. I am in an enormously depressed state. This whole current frame of mind is in large part attributable to the circumstances I find myself in. Indeed, I find myself living in a wholly new and unfamiliar world.

You longed for a kindred soul:

> If I only had a warm, sympathetic, pure soul next to me – I long for one so much – I should like so much to tell it things. I should like to pour out all my sorrow to it, to keep it sheltered from all the dirt there is in life and love it so deeply, so profoundly with every fibre of my being and my soul. And where are you now, the one I'm looking for, the one I long for so much, the one I await so impatiently? A single, warm, loving glance from you could confer on me a great deal of spiritual strength to hold out at this difficult time, could bring to me hope and faith for the future. Perhaps this uncanny, dreadful war is responsible for us not being able to find each other?!

Sadly, you never got an opportunity to find her.

On another occasion you wrote:

> A nightmare is burdening my breast and constricting my breathing. My heart beats uneasily. I should almost like to cry out and weep in my despair. No trace anywhere of zest for life or hope. Gloomy thoughts dominate my mind and my ego. I should

like to chase them away, but I am not equal to the task. They torture me endlessly ... I only have one great wish. For all this to be over once and for all. By whatever means it takes. It doesn't matter how, as long as the suffering stops. Because it can't keep going on like this.

... Happy the man who has been spared it. He doesn't even know the actual meaning of that one word: War. He cannot even begin to imagine the terrors it contains. Neither does he know the tragedies being played out here a thousandfold on a daily basis. Nor can he understand the great shame, the immeasurable disgrace this war is for the whole of Europe, for so-called European culture. (How can one still speak of culture? It's just an empty, meaningless word now.)

Such a man has never had the opportunity to look into the real essence of human life, to see man before him naked and unadorned, without the superfluous pretty phrases and the conventional claptrap about culture, as only here such things can be seen.

You never expressed jingoistic hatred of the enemy. You took time from your military duties to visit a bedridden elderly Italian civilian, sad to leave him when you got your marching orders:

It was a farewell sick visit. The sick gentleman was terribly upset when he learnt that I would no longer be able to visit him again soon. He asked me for my address and promised to write to me often. His wife and daughter are in Milan and he is lying here all by himself in a small, cold room and cannot leave his bed because of his paralysis. He is a most sympathetic, intelligent, and sensible gentleman. I shall miss him a lot.

You looked with a jaundiced eye at the politicians, bureaucrats, the shirkers, the profiteers, 'the great horde of rogues and swindlers'. In your fantasy you transported the generals of the fighting nations to the front to get a taste of reality:

They know nothing of the terror of war. If they had to share in it just once, they would certainly make sure that the war was over as quickly as possible ... If they were willing to risk their own skins to feel for just a few hours, they would act differently. It is a misfortune for humanity that these murderers escape scot-free.

You didn't spare the chaplain, 'mean, dirty parasite, this boring, grovelling, self-serving representative of a profession that cares for souls' who comes to say Mass in the field to encourage people to persevere in the war effort only when the regiment is out of danger:

> These 'noble' and devout Christians have now completely forgotten about Christ's teaching of love thy neighbour, since they can now no longer maintain it, and instead preach, for high wages, hate, vengeance, murder and the annihilation of that neighbour who does not pay them.

An officer quarrelled with you bitterly for being too sensitive and not hardened by two-and-a-half years on the front. He ordered you to acquire military callousness at once:

> ... without suspecting that my biggest worry all the time was how to stay untouched by it, and the latter objective I have attained to my utmost satisfaction.

How can I not love you for that?

I admire your initiative and tenacity in building field hospitals, scrapping for equipment, picking up a saw yourself when the army, that 'clumsy war machine', as you described it, did not provide materials or workers.

You got into trouble over and over again for caring too much for your wounded soldiers instead of patching them up and sending them back to the front:

> On the 12th of August 1917, I had to report to Lieutenant General Istvanovic. [Nikolaus Istvanovic von Ivanska] Major Hoch, who commands a battalion in the 79th Infantry Regiment, took me to see him. And why? Because I am too assiduous with my morning visits, send too many people to hospital in Zagreb and diagnose too many illnesses. I am too much of a doctor and not enough of an army doctor. These are the reproaches constantly being levelled

at me by lay people, by men who are not the least bit qualified to diagnose a person's state of health. But yesterday I had to listen to the same thing from a doctor, Colonel Richard Pfeffers, who even went so far as to threaten me with the possibility of losing my position here for this very reason. And today I was placed on report and the same thing was relayed to me again.

I am in awe of you. My admiration grows with every page.
I appreciate your sense of humour:

I have just learned that Senior Doctor Jung was wounded a short while ago. A piece of shrapnel hit his left forearm and broke the bone. How much I envy him. If only something like that could happen to me.

You were a gifted writer. I have discovered that if I choose sentences at random, divide them into short fragments, by magic what emerges is poetry:

Shrapnel and shell.
Echo in the mountains.
These dumb, proud giants
Indignant
That people
Dare
Disturb
Their holy and eternal rest.

Or:

Death has taken up residence
Unmolested.
His blood lust is merciless,
Insatiable.
Daily, he rips out hearts to accompany him to the realm of everlasting
Darkness
Down in Hades.
Hundreds and thousands of them.

I have a photo taken in a studio in Vienna on 24 December 1914, the date of the famous Christmas Truce when soldiers on both sides came out of their trenches to celebrate the holiday together. Apparently, you hadn't enlisted yet because you are attired in civilian clothes, dark wool coat, fashionable Edwardian hat, arm resting on the chair, hand clenched, legs crossed. There is an alert, intelligent look in your brown eyes. You are at ease. Standing next to you is a man in uniform, a close friend or a relative because in the dedication you wrote on the back of the photo which you sent to your cousin, you take it as given that he knows this man's identity. In a lighthearted tone you write: 'If you follow our example you will be Austria's best son.'

In photos taken two years later on the front you look like you had aged a decade. The war had traced its own lines on your face.

It is heartbreaking to read the last few entries in your diary in 1918 from a psychiatric hospital where you were a patient with what today would be recognised as post-traumatic stress disorder. There were about 120,000 such patients in Vienna by the end of the war. The final of the six diaries speaks to this period, the cover having detached along with a few pages, a totem to your own unravelling.

I shudder to think of you in that 'narrow, dirty single cell on the psychiatric ward'. You asked to be allowed to wear your clothes and to go out to the enclosed garden for some fresh air. Your request was denied.

> A truly unpleasant, painful existence here too as I am under constant strict supervision and am treated almost like a criminal. And the only crime that I have committed was to have stayed too long under fire on the front line and to have everywhere done my duty in a spirit of the greatest self-sacrifice and selflessness and not to have looked around, like many others I could mention, for connections and protection in order to get out of doing certain things. I am curious to know when they will take their dirty paws off me. I have already delivered enough victims to the god of war. My whole nervous system has been undermined and shaken to the core.

Yet even in this dire situation in one of the final entries you manage to show empathy for a prisoner of war:

> For the first and second day I was together with an Italian prisoner of war, Senior Doctor Pietro di Laura from Piacenza, a most likeable, sympathetic man who would soon be sent off to the Steinhof Institution. A state of depression had manifested itself following his monastic existence in captivity and the strong yearning to be reunited with his wife and children. Certainly, no doctor could ever hope to cure him. Only going back to his family would heal his innermost soul.

What would have healed your innermost soul?

What you wrote in six diaries spanning two-and-a-half years, the military authorities compressed into a few brief sentences for Dr Isaak Arthur Barasch, second lieutenant in the Landstrum, promoted to first lieutenant on 7 June 1916. They awarded you two Military Merit (*Signum Laudis*) medals.

> His Majesty's commendable recognition for brave and self-sacrificing behaviour in the face of the enemy.
>
> His Majesty's commendable recognition with award of the swords for brave and self-sacrificing behaviour in the face of the enemy.

Viennese military historian Erwin Schmidl says your two medals are extraordinary. 'Given the comparatively low standing of the Landsturm in the military hierarchy, as opposed to the regular army, I feel that these two medals are quite remarkable for a young doctor.' From what I have learned about you, the shiny medals with red ribbon on your uniform didn't intoxicate you. It barely formed an afterthought.

You wrote nothing about the family, which makes me wonder for whom did you write the diaries? To record events for posterity? To remember details in your dotage? An outlet to vent your feelings?

In a rare instance you wrote:

> Today I am unable to get to sleep. I have been especially on edge for a few days now. I have various family problems to think about.

What family problems? Now my curiosity will never be satisfied. I can catch faint glimpses on the back of the cover page where you noted payment of 200 krona each month to your sister, Yanka, perhaps to help her with private high-school tuition in Lemberg (Lwów)?

You write on 25 December 1917 that you will have a week's furlough but make no mention of where you are going. But I know, because that very same day you sent a postcard to your parents to a small village in what is today Ukraine. The postcard, written in Polish, has survived 103 years.

> Dearest beloved parents,
>
> I can't express to you in words the scope of my gratitude and love to you for taking such care of Donia [your younger sister, my grandmother]. It makes me very happy that in a few days I will fall into your arms and your kisses.
>
> What dear ones how are you doing? What's new?
>
> I kiss you warmly and kisses for baby Cecilia,
>
>   Your son,
>
>   Isaak

So, what do I know about your personal life given that I was born thirty-six years after you died of the Spanish flu in September 1918, the start of the epidemic in Vienna?

Your birth certificate says you were born on 3 May 1885 in a small town called Zloczow, now Zolochiv in Ukraine, in what was then Galicia, a region acquired by the Austro-Hungarian empire during the first partition of Poland in 1772. It was the largest, most economically backward province of the Austro-Hungarian empire. An 1887 study compared the standard of living in Galicia with the standard of living in England at the time. The average Galician produced only one-quarter of the quantity of food, ate less than half of the standard English diet, possessed only one-ninth of the Englishman's wealth yet paid twice as high a proportion of his income in taxes. At the time of your birth the peasantry made up 82 per cent of the Galician population, most of whom were illiterate, which makes your academic achievements even more extraordinary.

It states on your birth certificate that you are illegitimate which is why you bore your mother Lea's maiden name, Barasch. Your father, Moses Mehlsak, is mentioned in your birth certificate in the 'comments' column. There is an explanation for that.

Until 1830, the law allowed only one son in each Jewish family to marry. That law was abolished after 1830 but still the Austro-Hungarian authorities levied a special marriage tax just on Jews and so the vast majority of Galician Jews were married by a rabbi in a religious ceremony like they had had for thousands of years, indifferent to the civil authorities. Although this law was abolished seventeen years before your birth, Jews were reluctant to register their marriages with the civil authorities.

You signed the name 'Barasch' in clear, beautifully formed letters that stand upright in military formation. On the rare occasion that you signed Mehlsak, for example on the back of a photograph you sent back home, the letters become spineless and lurch a bit downwards to the right. Do I discern a certain ambivalence towards that name, a sense of discomfort with your official status as illegitimate?

Your given name was Isak Aron, which you later changed to a more European, less Jewish sounding Arthur, to smooth your way in your career as a doctor in Vienna. Your siblings did the same, part of a broader trend of Jewish integration into society. Your sister Hinda became Helen, my grandmother, Kaila (known in the family as Donia), became Klara, Yenta became Yanka, Leib became Leon, Tzilla became Cecilia. In the family you were called Iszui, the diminutive for Isak. The rabbi who officiated at your circumcision ceremony eight days after your birth, Rabbi Feivel Rohatin, went on to become a well-known scholar.

I mention this because I learned that he had received his rabbinical ordination from Rabbi Aron Izhak Ettinger of Lemberg. Just so you know, fifty-four years later, your baby sister, Cecilia, on the run from the Germans, will meet and marry that rabbi's grandson.

Your father, Moses Mehlsak, leased an 800-hectare piece of land from a Polish nobleman in Lisk, a village about 46km from Lemberg. He grew beets, oats for horse feed, corn and potatoes, had a herd of cows, a distillery for vodka, ducks and geese, a dovecot and a stable of about thirty horses. He had a permit from the Austrian authorities for a coach with four horses. Peasants who worked on the farm lived with their families in barracks on the estate, bolstered at harvest time by seasonal workers who came down from the mountains each summer. The Austro-Hungarian government from the reign of Holy Roman Emperor Joseph II onward encouraged Jews to go into farming.

In the 1891 Business Directory your father is listed as a grain and produce dealer in Gliniany, the closest town to the farm. Moses raised his children with the motto that the only thing of value they possess is their word of honour. Your younger brother, Leon, told me that with great passion many years later when I was a child, waving his index finger and invoking the same authoritarian tone your father must have used.

Moses woke before dawn every morning, washed, and put on the *tefillin* to say his morning prayers. On the Jewish Sabbath there was no work on the farm. My mother, Irena, born three years after you died (named after you with the first letter of her name corresponding to yours), remembers a story she heard. You came home from your studies in Vienna to visit the family taking the train from Vienna to Krasne, the closest stop, and then by horse-drawn cart to the house. A few days later it was the Sabbath, and everyone was seated around the table after having eaten a heavy meal of *cholent*, a traditional meat stew simmered overnight to conform with Jewish law which prohibits cooking on the Sabbath. They plied you with questions about Vienna, about medical school, especially your younger sister, Yanka, whose dream it was to become a doctor. They wanted to know about the elegant streets, the theatre, the Opera House, the newest fashions. You were living in the cultural and intellectual capital of the Western world, perhaps sitting in the same cafe as Sigmund Freud, Arnold Schoenberg, Joseph Roth, Arthur Schnitzler or Stefan Zweig.

You were so absorbed in the amiable conversation that you forgot yourself, opened your cigarette case, silver with a cobalt-blue enamel inlay of an atlas, took out a cigarette and lit it.

At that, your father got up from the head of the table, walked over, raised his arm and slapped you in the face. Silence around the table.

You put out the cigarette, bent down to kiss the hand that hit you and apologised for having disrespected the laws of the Sabbath.

As a small boy you studied in the *heder*, the traditional school where one learned to read Hebrew. You later attended a gymnasium in Zloczow, where your maternal grandfather, Judah Barasch, was a wood dealer. Perhaps when the weather was inclement you stayed in town with your grandparents, or else with your maternal aunt, Chaya Jung. You and your cousin, Schilem, born eight days apart, were good friends. He ended up marrying your sister, Klara. Their daughter, Irena, was my mother.

For some reason, my mother thought you began your medical studies in Padua, Italy which is where you acquired fluency in Italian, adding to your already wide-ranging knowledge of Polish, German, Yiddish, ancient Greek, Latin and Hebrew. But records from the University of Vienna indicate you first studied in Lemberg before transferring to the prestigious medical school in Vienna. You enrolled at their faculty of medicine in the winter term of 1909. On the registration form you indicated that your mother tongue was Hebrew, a strange choice since Hebrew would not become a spoken language for a few decades hence in Israel. You studied eight terms until the spring term of 1913 and were finally promoted to Doctor of Medicine on 2 March 1914. You were 29 years old. It is unlikely that you encountered anti-Semitism in medical school since about 40 per cent of the students were fellow Jews.

I have a photo of you in a large lecture hall at Vienna University dated 15 January 1912. You wrote on the back: 'Photo taken during a clinical lecture in the new 1st medical clinic of Professor Carl von Noorden. It was the day of my practical.' I was told you specialised in gynaecology, which would not have been of much use at the front. Four months after you obtained your degree, Archduke Franz Ferdinand was assassinated in Sarajevo.

Your parents, farmers with little formal education, but literate in Hebrew, had great ambitions for their children, expressed mostly as a passion for higher education and academic titles. Your mother's brother, Naftali Barasch, had studied law in Lemberg, the first in the family to attain a higher education. Your parents funded your medical school education and also the education of your sister Helen's fiancé, who broke off the engagement upon gaining his medical degree. Your heartbroken sister, two years younger, came to Vienna to study medicine whereupon you introduced her to a fellow student, Yoel Chaim Mehlman, who went on to become a dermatologist. He was from Gliniany. Their whole lives they had lived a few kilometres from one another yet met and fell in love in Vienna. She quit her studies to marry. It is thanks to Helen that your diaries survived. As the oldest sister, she claimed them upon your death and took them with her when she emigrated to New York City in 1922 to join her husband.

You lived in Vienna on Lerchenfelderstrasse 24. At the beginning of the war, Zloczow was captured by the Russian army, prompting the entire family to flee to Vienna. You arranged an apartment for them on the same street.

In the diaries you mentioned important historical events such as the death on 21 November 1916 of the old emperor, Franz Josef. Our family, like other Galician Jews, venerated Emperor Franz Josef for granting equal rights to Jews. Prayers for his health were recited in Galician synagogues throughout his reign from 1848 onwards. Growing up in Tel Aviv in the 1950s, I often heard your siblings, steeped in German *kultur*, recite poetry by Heine and Goethe. They spoke with great nostalgia and love about some person called Franz Josef, whom they held in great esteem. They brought him up so often and with such adoration that I was sure he must be an uncle.

My mother, Irena, said you liked poetry, books, antiques. Her cousin in New York, Helen's daughter, named Irene, heard that you liked concerts, hiking in the mountains, that you had an open mind, a sense of humour. You read Ibsen and Shakespeare in German. She heard you were also something of a ladies' man, a female friend with whom to go to concerts, another for hiking expeditions in the mountains and another for, well … My mother, in fact, insisted you had been engaged to a Baroness von Larisch. This seems far-fetched as the only von Larisch I was able to find was Countess Marie Larisch von Moennich, twenty-seven years older than you and the niece of Empress Elisabeth of Austria. Most probably you told the family that you spotted her carriage as it passed by, doffed your hat, and the story took off.

Neither of the two Irenes knew about your stay in a psychiatric hospital, probably due to the stigma attached.

You died on 12 September 1918 and were buried in the Jewish section of Wiener Zentralfriedhof, Europe's largest cemetery. About twenty-five years ago my mother visited your grave and had it cleaned and restored.

What happened to your family after you died?

Helen, as you already know, emigrated to New York City with her family. Yanka, ten years younger than you, followed in your footsteps and finished her medical studies in Lemberg in 1923, just nine years after the first female graduated from that institution. Yanka must have had spunk because, according to a story, she found a penis severed from a cadaver in her satchel placed there as a prank by the male students. At the start of class, she stood, held it high and asked if anyone present was missing his male member. In 1936 she went to Palestine, but her arrival coincided with an influx of doctors escaping the Nazi regime in Germany. They got all the good positions, so she went back to Lemberg (at this time called Lwow). In hindsight this was a tragic mistake. In 1942, she accompanied a transport of children from the ghetto to the German death camp in Belzec.

Your sister Klara married your cousin, Schilem, who became a successful lawyer in Krakow where they lived in an antique-filled apartment on Krakow's famous main square. They had two children, Irena and Leonard. When the Germans invaded Poland, they escaped to Lwow and from there, were transported by the Soviets to a labour camp deep in Russia. It was on this journey that your silver cigarette case with the cobalt blue enamel inlay was stolen. It was Klara's only keepsake of you and she was inconsolable.

Your cousin, the lawyer, laboured cutting down trees. In the spring of 1943 Irena joined the newly formed Polish army under the auspices of the Soviets and marched all the way to Berlin, arriving when there was still fighting house to house. It was interesting to note that in letters home her descriptions, her use of musical metaphors for German bombardments, read like pages from your diary.

Your younger brother, Leon, studied agronomy in high school. He enlisted in the army and served during the First World War as a private, also on the Italian front. The two of you didn't meet. Later, he stayed to run the farm. When the Germans invaded Poland on 1 September 1939, he and Cecilia hitched horses to a wagon and escaped south to the Romanian border. On the way they picked up a hitchhiker, the grandson of the former rabbi of Lemberg. They survived in Romania and later made their way to Israel.

Other than Helen in New York, and Yanka, who was murdered in Belzec, your other siblings survived and emigrated to Israel. They lived in Tel Aviv, which is where I was born. That generation is all gone now. They are buried next to each other in a cemetery in Tel Aviv.

And so, Great-Uncle Isaak, I have brought you up to date.

The thought has occurred to me that had you not died of the Spanish flu and had remained in Vienna, they would have knocked on your door in 1942, if not sooner, arrested you and loaded you on a freight train to Poland. There, they would have gassed you and burned your body just like they did your younger sister and other members of our family. 'But I fought for the Fatherland, for Austria', you might have protested when they came to take you. 'Look, this is my medal from the battle of Doberdò.'

So much for your sacrifice.

A tourist website for the Dolomites region boasts of many First World War museums and cemeteries. You were present when the graves, row upon row, were freshly dug, writing:

> The cemetery is getting bigger and bigger. New graves are appearing daily … Everything all over this region speaks eloquently of the bloody, violent, countless struggles, battles, attacks and counterattacks, all the killing, anger and destruction that have been going on here

You must have known some of the dead; comrades, patients.

And then you wrote something that should be inscribed on all the grandiose marble and bronze war memorials, not only in the Dolomites, but the world over:

> The guns should be silent for once. Mankind needs a rest.

Another thought, a happier one, has occurred to me. On 5 June 1916 when you reluctantly left your post at St Vigil in the Dolomites after a month's stay, you wrote poetically:

> Adieu, you fair St Vigil! With your good Monte Sella. Adieu, you broad green meadows with your enchanting splendour of bloom. Adieu, all you little villages up there that gaze trustfully down into the valley. Adieu, all you proud hills, you rushing streams and fragrant pine forests, adieu!! I am taking my leave of you. Farewell, you pious Latin populace with your language that is incomprehensible to me and may you diligently cultivate your fertile open fields. And you, old rattling watermill, whose sound is everywhere audible here. Today I must separate from all of you. I must go on to the mountains, obedient to the call of the hour. I'll see you again in the course of the war. And when the war is over and fate in the meantime has not snuffed me out. If the bloodletting stops and I am still among the living, you'll see me again, fair St Vigil, and then I want to enjoy all your splendour unmolested.

You were unable to keep your promise.

I have decided that when the Covid-19 pandemic is finally over (yes, another respiratory plague like the one that took your life 102 years ago) and it is safe to go, I will travel to fair St Vigil and stay in the same hotel you mentioned, the Monte Sella. I checked, it's still there and the original 1903 Jugendstil structure is intact.

I'll take with me a copy of the book and give it to them. I will time my visit for 5 June, the day you left, and I'll do some hiking in the hills. I will lie down on the grass among the flowers that dot the meadows and think of you.

With much love and great respect,
Your great-niece,
Shulamit Kopf

The Diary

Chapter 1

The Isonzo

Introduction by Hew Strachan

In late May the River Soča, which rises in the Julian Alps to the east of Mount Rombon, flows fast with the irridescent blue of snow melt. At times its pace slows but the narrowness of its steep-sided valleys causes it to gather momentum once more until it reaches Gorizia. Here it leaves Slovenia and, on entering Italy, becomes the Isonzo. The river passes to the west of the town, and then describes an arc as it curves round the Carso, a limestone plateau to its east. The valley broadens and flattens as it gets nearer the Adriatic Sea. Viewed southwards from the principal vantage point on the Carso, Monte San Michele, its wide, calm and shallow waters reflect the light before flowing into the Mediterranean to the west of Monfalcone.

By the standards of Mount Rombon, which is 2,208m, Monte San Michele – at 275m – is a hillock, but its steep-sided slopes command the Isonzo to its north and south. Today in summer the Carso is covered in trees whose foliage obscures the field of vision of those on level ground and so such vantage points have disproportionate significance. In May 1915 the Carso was described as devoid of vegetation, except where erosion had created deep depressions in which water could gather and growth occur. Before 1914 Austrian foresters had planted trees to soften the winter wind but so far they had had little impact. In 1915 and 1916 the Carso – or the Karst in German – would become the principal battle zone on the Austro-Hungarian front.

The Italian army had had plenty of time to mobilise before it entered the war and its first formations arrived on the Isonzo on 24 May 1915. The Austro-Hungarians had blown the bridges and flooded the low-lying areas between the river and the Carso. The Italians did not cross the Isonzo until 4 June and took Monfalcone unopposed on 9 June. Cadorna, the Italian commander, had set up his headquarters in Udine. His 3rd Army was to take the Carso and push on to Trieste, while his 2nd Army was to secure the 3rd Army's flank to the north by taking Gorizia, so exposing Monte San Michele and opening the route to Laibach (today Ljubljana).

By 15 June both Italian armies were across the Isonzo but remained short of heavy artillery, already established as the dominant weapon of the war in its capacity to unlock strong defensive positions. On 23 June they opened their attack. Between then and the end of the year, the Italians fought four battles on the Isonzo. It was their enemy who counted the number. They did so for propaganda effect, to highlight the robustness of their defence and the futility of the Italian attacks. However, Austro-Hungarian losses were proportionately as heavy as Italian, not least because the commander of the 5th Austro-Hungarian Army, Boroević, insisted on counter-attacks to regain lost ground. The fighting was ferocious, with minimal cover and shellfire causing rock splinters to fly off and cause further wounds. Italian losses in the four battles have been put at 230,000 dead and wounded, while Austria-Hungary's – from a smaller force on the defensive – still reached 165,000.[1]

This was the situation when Isaak Barasch picks up the story in January 1916. He fought on the Carso between then and April. For the first two months there was no major Italian offensive, principally because of the weather but also because both armies were pausing to recover their strength. However, one of the characteristics of the First World War was the persistence of low-level conflict even when no big battles were happening. Shorter days and worse light made targets of opportunity less frequent but, as Barasch records, men were still being killed and wounded. Fighting was continuous, with patrols, mining and counter-mining, and exchanges of artillery fire. Boroević focused on restoring his line by recovering Oslavija, on the west bank of

---

1. These figures are calculated from John R. Schindler, *Isonzo: The Forgotten Sacrifice of the Great War* (Westport Conn., 2001), pp. 59, 80, 123–5. This is one of two excellent but contrasting accounts in English. The other is Mark Thompson, *The White War: Life and Death on the Italian Front 1915–1919* (London, 2008).

Isonzo, just north of Gorizia. By 19 January, he controlled its heights, so securing the town for the time being.

Barasch was an *Assistenzarzt* (Assistant Doctor) in a battalion of the 32nd Landsturm Infantry Regiment, which together with the 31st Landsturm Infantry Regiment formed the 110th Landsturm Brigade, whose commander from the middle of January was Eduard Maag. Two brigades, the 110th and the 111th, were combined in the 106th Austrian Landsturm Infantry Division, commanded since November 1914 by Ernst Kletter. They had all begun their war on the Galician front, but had moved south-west in time for the third battle of the Isonzo in October and the fourth in November and December. When Barasch opens his diary, they were behind the line in Komen. In the Austro-Hungarian order of battle the 106th Division was in VII Corps. On 8 February III Corps was given notice to prepare to move 'to another theatre', which was not specified, and it began to transition through VII Corps, which in turn took over responsibility for III Corps' sector. This hand-over probably explains Barasch's somewhat confusing account as to which corps he belonged at any one time. On 19 February he was reassigned to the 37th Landsturm Infantry Regiment in the 187th Landsturm Brigade, still in the 106th Division and placed eight days earlier in the front of the ruins atop Monte dei sei Busi, a feature 143m above sea level.

As a result of the departure of III Corps, the strength of the 5th Army shrunk by about a third, from 147 battalions to around 100 and its guns from 693 to 467. From 1 March, somewhat to his surprise, Boroević picked up warnings that the Italians were preparing another attack. Speculating on its purpose, some Austro-Hungarians would conclude that it was an outcome of the Entente conference convened in December 1915 to procure a coordinated effort across all fronts. They believed it was designed to relieve the German pressure on the French at Verdun. If so, it did not work. The so-called fifth battle of the Isonzo, which opened on 11 March, was not a major offensive by comparison with what had gone before or came after. The Italians lost 83 officers and 1,800 men, the Austro-Hungarians 483 dead and 1,500 wounded. The weather was bad, and the fighting broke up into a series of isolated attacks and counter-attacks. Although the Italians closed the battle down on 16 March, fighting continued, especially around Monte San Michele and along the western edge of the Doberdò plateau as Boroević sought to assert his army's control of the Carso.

Komen, 22 January 1916

I have been here since January 20th with the 32nd Landstrum Infantry Regiment. The latter is in fact stationed here in this small and dirty little town north of Trieste in the middle of the Karst limestone plateau of southern Slovenia. An encampment life in the full sense of the word.

25 January 1916, 3 am

A terrible hangover, cannot sleep. While playing cards in our officers' mess, I lost 100 Crowns, half the amount I had received yesterday from the accounts office as field support. A very dull soldiers' game called pontoon or *vingt-et-un*. I didn't even want to start playing this silly game, but had to for the sake of my comrades in arms. As is usual for me in games, I had no luck. I kept on losing and had the desire to win the money back. And so this altogether peculiar gambling bug kept me at it for six hours. The longer the game went on, the more I lost.

Now I have pangs of conscience that I was so weak and could not master this passion. I feel a limitless emptiness. I am in an enormously depressed state. This whole current frame of mind is in large part attributable to the circumstances in which I find myself. Indeed, I find myself living in a wholly new and unfamiliar world.

I have already been living in Komen (3 hours by car to Trieste), a quite small, rather dirty little town on the Slovenian Karst plateau, for six days. The regiment is encamped here. Not long ago we were four months in position in Doberdò and exposed to the most frightful artillery fire. We also had suffered huge losses so that out of three battalions only two could be said to be intact. I am currently with the 1st Battalion. With me here is a certain G.W. Korer from Prague, or rather a town near Prague, Klagsdochor. He is a clarion soloist. He is the one I played cards with today and who won the money off me. Actually, life here, relatively speaking, is still very good. We all have our own bed, which, in times like these, can be looked upon as a luxury. Our food is rather good, and we live a calm, ordered life. Of course, having said this, we must entirely refrain from having certain indispensable, absolutely necessary things, indeed, quite do without them. The digestive system has to get used to a totally new, primitive diet.

But not everyone can, as so many do, allow themselves to lead a much more comfortable, pleasant, and fortunate life. These are the favoured ones. To them belong all the General Staff officers that even this little place is swarming with. These are the ones that have been borne aloft by this war. They are continually being promoted, decorated with the highest honours, without ever taking up forward positions in the front line, without having done anything positive. But everything is handed to them on a plate. To the ranks of these gentlemen belong all the innumerable calculating and career-orientated officers, all the commanding officers of various institutions in occupied territories, also all those who have been assigned to military convoys. For them the war could go on indefinitely. All wars look after their futures and fill up their pockets in various ways.

Yes, I could even go so far as to claim that all these officers and doctors on active service are spared the war's heaviest blows. Of course, there are exceptions.

26 January 1916
A fine ride for pleasure to Reifenberg, a small town north of Komen, which is very prettily situated in a hollow in the hilly Karst country and overlooked by an old castle that covers a wide expanse of ground. The old, dirty, detached houses are scattered, many at a considerable distance from one another. In the surrounding area, on the slopes of the mountains and on the hills, isolated houses in picturesque locations form small hamlets. Here and there on a hill path, a lonely chapel can be found.

27 January 1916
Inspection of the regiment by the commander General [Svetozar] Boroević of the 5th Army to which this regiment is affiliated. In point of fact, the whole brigade, made up of parts of the 31st and 32nd infantry regiments, was inspected. The Archduke Josef, commander of No. 3 Corps, was also present as were many other officers. To this corps belongs our 106th Division, which consists of Brigades 110 and

111. Great excitement reigned everywhere before the arrival of these gentlemen. Poor and able-bodied elderly citizens were mustered here and subjected to all existing parade-ground manoeuvres, especially by the regimental commander, Colonel Jemisch.

7 February 1916
A very good travelling cinema show donated by a women's committee in Trieste for the soldiers on the Isonzo front has been in Komen for six days already and will stay for another two days.

Today there was a wonderful performance at which Archduke Josef, his wife, the Archduchess Augusta, and their son, a very young lieutenant, were present. The Archduchess, a fairly plump, elderly, not very attractive lady, who appeared today in military uniform with a Red Cross armband, is not one of those women who avoid male company. The Archduke himself comes over as a good-humoured, phlegmatic individual. There were also, of course, a great many officers present.

Immediately before the cinema performance I had been placed on regimental report by the regimental doctor, a Viennese general practitioner, Dr Abraham Feyering by name, for having gone yesterday, a Sunday, to Trieste without his prior consent. The uncooperative action of this gentleman was most upsetting to me. Certain escapades in wartime must be passed over in silence. Naturally, I had been issued with an overt order as, without this, one cannot know the source of the complaint. There was no great distance involved, roughly 20km, from Komen to Trieste. A journey of two hours with good horses. I had spent hours coming back in a farm wagon typical of the region in which one had to sit on barn boards stuffed with straw. The journey was very unpleasant as it was at night and quite cool outside. The way out was with a good wagon which I had come across quite by chance as far as Wahesina where I stayed overnight on Saturday and the signpost to which, for fear of enemy planes, was unlit. In Wahesina too it was quite dark everywhere you went. In Trieste the streets are also lit patchily … especially towards the sea, it is very dark. And all the premises that stand by themselves, like the F. K. Cafe and the Excelsior Restaurant, are dimly lit.

Sunday was a glorious, warm day on which it was possible to enjoy the finest prospects. During the whole of the day, exceptionally, no enemy plane was seen. Otherwise, they are a daily occurrence.

Those were fine hours that I had spent on the seashore, but the consequences were most unpleasant. I had to appear on a report for the first time in my unmilitary life and appear before Lieutenant Colonel Elacek, the representative of our regimental commander, Colonel Jemisch, who is currently on leave.

8 February 1916

Today in the mess at midday we had three gentlemen of the press as guests, a captain, the commander of a group that has its headquarters in Trieste, and two journalists in mufti. There are six gentlemen altogether in this group.

A car, two orderlies, always at their disposal. High wages, it goes without saying, and high decorations and for what? Because they undertake car outings here and there, all over, to places far away from the action, places they visit and then do there the most unthinkable things. Wherever they go, they could not be received and catered for better.

After such jaunts they return to Trieste in order to process their observations. Naturally, this takes up several days and once again they live the high life. They move into private accommodation in the best hotel in Trieste, the Excelsior. These are the chosen ones who, because of personal protection, can enjoy the best – what a shameful injustice! The war is made for people like these. They would like to draw it out for as long as possible. Just once they should be sent out to occupy trench positions and other men, who have had to suffer so much, should come to take their place to recover their strength. Anyone can churn out this journalistic rubbish. Of course, this is not what happened when they were with us. One has to look around first for friends in high places and protection with which one can do everything. Without them one can do nothing. Unfortunately!!

9 February 1916
During the midday meal today, there reigned in the officers' mess a terrible feeling of excitement. Quite out of the blue the grave news had reached us that we would have to take up our positions on the line early on the 12th of the month. We had believed, we were almost sure in fact, that we would be staying here for at least two more weeks. There are still troops belonging to the Imperial and Royal Army who have been in camp for six to eight weeks. Why should not the old army reserve that, before it set up camp, had spent four and a half months solid on the front line, not be able to enjoy the same rights? Why must we, after being in camp for only three weeks, to go back to the front to relieve troops (Hungarian Honveds) who have only been in position there for a month and this after six weeks of time out? And where are they going now? Back to camp in Komen. Lucky people! Where is the justice in this? Perhaps there is a justice, but one that we do not comprehend and cannot grasp. Be that as it may, this news came to us like a flash of lightning from a clear blue sky. And bad weather since last night. Till then it was such fine weather. And for the bad weather to come now, just as we are having to move out, cold and rotten with snow turning to sleet. Soon we will be seeing water and mud all over the place.

All those present in the mess wanted to hide their excitement and unease, but none succeeded. Our battalion commander, Major Seiwerth, was quite dismayed. He is the only actively serving officer in our midst, a very good-natured, intelligent, refined, well-educated, comradely 41-year-old gentleman, a man such as is seldom found among career officers. This man, who is a Transylvanian Saxon and is interested in all manner of things, though not much in military matters, and is much given to comfort, was nervous and anxious. He painted in the darkest colours the events that await us in the not-so-distant future, all the privations of life in narrow, dark, cold and musty caves from which one cannot stir the whole day long if one does not want to risk one's life. He was especially concerned that this news had been announced to us so suddenly and that, as a result, we had been unable to lay in provisions accordingly, and also that he himself had not been able to take leave of his wife, now living in Trieste to be near him. He is, of course, a very tender, indeed ideal, husband. His wife too is a very intelligent, witty, refined, and cheerful lady. They make a fine and dandy, harmonious couple, even though they are childless.

But there's nothing else for it. The command has been given and we must travel down this road. Therefore, the most urgent preparations have to be made. We must get used to this new idea forthwith.

But this comes as hard to those officers who have already been in the field for so long. Most are elderly people from the Third Reserve. All the officers on active service have disappeared from the regiment. Some have gone on leave without coming back, some have gone to hospital. This is easily done for those on active service. They need to be spared!! They will be needed after the war is over too!! These shirkers!! It's the same for doctors on active service. Out of three that ought to be here, two are off somewhere in hospitals and will be coming back. Many of the active ones have, as is more or less common knowledge, somehow come by posts away from the action and are living quite cosily and sporting high decorations.

A few days ago, an officer on active service, commander of the 2nd Battalion, the only career officer in the battalion, Captain Braun, who only because of the war rose to this rank so rapidly, disappeared to a hospital in Trieste, allegedly because of fever brought about by a suppurating tonsil. I was not a witness to it. He went of course to Trieste on a day out so as to be able to enjoy himself and that's where he stayed. If a Third Reserve or a Reserve officer were to dare to do that. That's how it is unfortunately! And we see all this and, as they say in Vienna, keep our 'trap' shut about it – 'It's wartime, it's a state of emergency.' Unfortunately, the latter has already lasted too long. Nineteen months of it now. And how much longer?! No one can answer this question.

It should be over with the Italians once and for all. Not long ago our Brigadier Major General Mack made some very interesting remarks in respect of this matter. He considers it possible that Italy, still in the course of this war, may turn against the *Entente Cordiale* and against France in order to seek reparations and join the Central Powers. In return it will get promises on the French Riviera. How much truth and substance there is in this I cannot judge. It's all very interesting anyway. We can expect anything from plausible, sly people. Now the most varied ways can be suggested leading to the peace that so many millions long for. Not everyone of course!! The guns should be silent for once. Mankind needs a rest.

So tomorrow, on February 10, at 8 am, we march out of Komen. Today at supper there was a general mood of being hung over. We are marching down the street that leads via Skrbina-Kostanjevica to Segetti to set up camp. Here we will take up our positions and get food. I find myself in a bad state of health. My nerves are badly frayed. My feeling of unease does not allow me to sleep. What will I have to endure in the days ahead? What will I have to live through?! Even the wildest fantasy scarcely comes close to the reality that those who have gone through it have experienced. If men like Grey, Kitchener, Poincaré, Salandra and their cronies could only feel the horrors of this war, indeed of all war, in their own hides for just a few hours, they would act differently. It is a misfortune for humanity that these murderers escape scot free.

10 February 1916
Today we left Komen. We went by way of Temnica and Kostanjevica to our camp at Segetti in cold and rainy weather. From Kostanjevica you can see for miles and miles, a long way over a considerable area. Odd shells could be seen exploding from here in the distance on Monte San Michele and odd bits of shrapnel bursting all over the place. Some time ago the Archduke Heir to the Throne [i.e. the future Kaiser Karl] took the opportunity to observe our own positions as well as those of the enemy from Kostanjevica. The command headquarters of the 3rd Corps is also here and to it once again is attached our Division 106.

I am encamped in a limestone 'crater' and housed in a little shelter made of boards that I share with a Dr Korer. Outside it is snowing a lot, getting more and more gloomy and cold. We are staying here until tomorrow. I have been ordered to take up a position at battalion command, that is to say: directly behind the line of fire. My young assistant and a stretcher bearer are going with me.

* * *

Today we haven't even had something warm to eat as our chuck wagon hasn't got here yet.

It was cold tonight in the shelter. Freezing. Unbearable. Apart from that, our neighbours, the 2nd Battalion doctor, Dr Beitelschneidts, a very young army doctor from Vienna, and his assistant, Medical Orderly Pessar, also from Vienna, played pranks to stop us from getting to sleep.

Today the medical inspection of the battalion must be held. As always, we were ready in next to no time. In the primitive conditions under which we have to work here almost nothing can be done. We can only make use of very simple medical supplies and this merely *ut aliquid fieri videatur* [Latin for so it may look like something is being done]. The number of these is very limited. Aspirin and not so much of it. Ipecacuanha in tablet form, tincture of iodine, tincture of amaral, aluminium oxide in vinegar, solid morphine, natrium salicyl. The contents of our medical chest end here. Apart from this there are some virtually unusable medical instruments, packs of bandages and petrol, the latter for cleaning the area around wounds. There is no room in which to put the patient in order to at least apply chest compresses when the patient catches cold, as so often happens here. Wretched surroundings for a doctor. Work is carried out here quite mechanically. It could be done just as well by an intelligent, experienced medic. The doctor here is like the fifth wheel on a wagon. And yet there are so many of them in our regiment. Five doctors and three medics. Two would be quite enough here to perform routine procedures of a more formal nature. The others could be made much better use of in the various military sector hospitals and behind the lines where, on the whole, there is a lack of doctors. But that's the way things are, and nothing can be said against them. We have to bow to *force majeure*. There is so much going on in this clumsy machine that constitutes our army. There are deficiencies and things that we could do without, even shortcomings, that future attempts at better organisation will need to consider and eliminate. In the meantime, we must bear with them.

* * *

After the medical inspection I made my way to the baggage train. There is a lot of activity everywhere. Preparations for departure are being made.

12 February 1916
So I am now in the so-called battalion crater in a small, cold, dark rocky cave in the middle of a rain of fire, shooting on all sides from the most varied, lethal, cruel, and deadly pieces of artillery. There is constant thundering and roaring, hisses, whistles, and bangs. Yesterday I travelled from Segetti to Marcotirei and at night because we were in danger of being shot at. From here we had to go further, that is to say: I myself, the battalion commander, Major Seiwerth and his aide-de-camp, Lieutenant Kamleki, accompanied by a specially seconded orderly. The second half of our way was very unpleasant with bullets flying all over the place.

Our regiment has relieved the 1st Honved Infantry Regiment of the 20th I.T.D. [Infantry Troop Division]. Already tonight there were some losses. A sergeant in the M.G.A. [Maschinengewehrabteilung – Machine Gun Section] was brought to me at half-past two in the morning with a broken upper arm. There was also a corporal with a contusion from a shell splinter in the area of his left eye with consequent loss of the eye.

* * *

This morning I visited with the major all our positions in order to carry out a general disinfection of E and F companies – codenamed Emma and Franz. From here I was able to observe the enemy's positions, in many places only thirty to fifty paces from our own. The trenches of our positions are very well constructed. We are here well protected from any misadventure. Work is still being carried out on the construction of our positions and on making the caverns habitable.

13 February 1916
Today, with the grey light of dawn, the enemy quite unexpectedly made an artillery attack with medium calibre guns on our positions all

along the front line. I woke up early suddenly at quarter past six and felt ill at ease. I didn't know at first what on earth was happening. A devil of a din from all sides at once, buzzing, thundering, whistling, moaning, groaning, crackling. All the music of hell. Everything is trembling. Ever new pieces of limestone are falling from the walls of the cave. We have the impression that not much more could happen and the whole cave will collapse, cutting us off forever from the outside world. There is great nervousness on the field telephone.

There are telephone calls being made in all directions and incoming calls from the most diverse of places. Franz and Emma are having to put up with a lot. It has already been reported that Franz's trenches have been badly damaged by shells in several places. Emma too is much the worse for wear from bombardment by foreign 'bears' (artillery). There is much use of the telephone in the 'steam' (our own artillery section). The din is getting louder and louder owing to the fact that our own guns are being deployed. This awful game of angry spirits has gone on for rather a long time, almost two hours. Strangely enough by way of casualties in our sectors, i.e. in our battalion, we hardly had any. Only two wounded men were brought to me for whom I had to make provision. Twice enemy shells of 15cm calibre struck the ground not far from our crater. One of them fell on a shelter for artillerymen right next to us. On the edge of our crater a 9cm battery is positioned. An artillery sergeant here was badly wounded. All of us were quite surprised that he actually survived. I had to attend to him under fire, which, given the extent and the severity of his injury, took a long time. Meanwhile, things calmed down more and more. Now the high command started to look for explanations to account for this attack. Not much could be ascertained. Perhaps these warning signs herald a new (the 5th) Italian Offensive.

14 February 1916

Once again, we have to change our positions. Tonight we will be relieved by the 43rd Hungarian Regiment that has been encamped for two months. We are taking up new positions in Doberdò. Along almost the entire front we are pushing forward. The 3rd Corps is being relieved by the 7th (Archduke Joseph).

First of all, we will be marching, and indeed tonight after 11 o'clock, to Mikoli where we will stay for a few days as a so-called divisional reserve, and then move on from there. The journey will not be pleasant as all these areas are constantly being raked by enemy gunfire. We must be prepared for the worst. Nobody here knows if he might be hit in the space of a minute by one of those highly diverse and cruel lethal weapons. Weapons technology has thought of everything. Trinitrophenol bombs, gas, mine-throwers, mortar of every calibre and every type of machine gun, shrapnel, and shells of the most varied calibres, etc., etc.

15 February 1916
Today we are already in Mikoli. Here I am housed with three other gentlemen in a small wooden shelter. This is a little village completely abandoned by its inhabitants and partly damaged through shelling, situated in the Valone valley on the road from Valkiščie to Iamiano. On both sides of the valley there are chains of limestone hills reaching up to a height of 250m. In the valley there are many places that have been completely deserted by their inhabitants and, in places, badly damaged.

This afternoon I had a little outing to the lake and to its sources beyond the well-built second line of defence.

16 February 1916
Today I had to go to Valkiščie for a distribution of gas masks to each of the men and the officers in the battalion, to be worn during enemy gas attacks and which can save your life in such cases. They serve as air filters containing chemicals that bond with poisonous gases (especially chlorine). I also got two for myself. In the afternoon I went to Iamiano, located on the road south of Mikoli. Here too none of the civilian population is in evidence. They have all fled. They left their homes to eke out a poor existence in foreign parts. All around there are no civilians. And this is as it should be, for here people are in constant peril of their lives. No one knows if he will be hit by some heavy enemy projectile from one moment to the next and die the most atrocious death. Everywhere the ground is deeply and extensively

pitted – a sure sign of shells that have fallen here. A few days ago in Iamiano, for instance, a shell scored a direct hit and killed forty-eight soldiers.

17 February 1916
Today I was at Lake Doberdò. The lake is approximately a kilometre long and totally covered with reeds. Its *y*-axis runs from north-west to south-east. Its edges are quite shallow. At the extreme north of the lake are its sources. Here too there is a 6HP strong pumping machine that pumps water from the sources into a reservoir which is then brought to the Cruihrib. From here it is taken further to the front.

* * *

North-west of the lake the plateau of Doberdò rises up with the village of Doberdò. To the north-east is Monte dei sei Busi. At a short distance from the lake's sources (circa fifty paces) runs our 2nd line of defence which, on one side, stretches out to the Cruihrib in the north, on the other, stretching towards the south, gives way to the Debeli. Further on towards the south the 2nd line of defence continues in front of Iamiano.

18 February 1916
Today as I awoke I had a sudden unpleasant surprise. Three shells fell quite near our shelter. I had the impression that everything was going to collapse on top of us. There was a roaring noise and shaking. We were all badly shaken. I got out of bed very hastily.

Shortly after this, several aeroplanes appeared in the sky – enemy ones at first, then ours. There was a dogfight between them which ended with one of the enemy planes crashing.

19 February 1916
Tomorrow night the battalion will have to leave Mikoli and take up a position (Sector 3 Doberdò). I was ordered to go with the battalion command and to stand firm there behind our positions. I have already made the most important preparations despite the great excitement

which was everywhere in evidence today. The Italian guns were hard at it. A shell burst in front of our shelter and two soldiers suffered serious injuries.

Towards evening a new piece of news reached me quite unexpectedly. I have been reassigned to a new detachment. I must now go with all due speed to join this camped south-west of Kostanjevica. This is the 5th Battalion of the 37th Army Infantry Regiment. After having gotten used to it here, I will need to adapt to different conditions elsewhere with all the difficulties that must be overcome wherever I go!!

I learnt this from the regimental high command in Valkiščie to where I had proceeded quite by accident.

Here too I saw today a very badly injured artilleryman. Both of his legs had been almost completely ripped off to the height of the last third of his upper thigh by an enemy mine. They were still connected to his body by thin cartilages. The patient was taken from his position to the 106th Medical Division Field Hospital in Valkiščie without having received first aid beforehand. On arrival the pulse was barely detectable because of the enormous loss of blood. Breathing started to become irregular and superficial. This state of affairs did not last for long and the poor man died. All attempts made to resuscitate him were quite hopeless.

21 February 1916

Yesterday morning I arrived at my new destination. I left Mikoli early at 8 o'clock and after a two-hour trek I came to the encampment. My way lay through Ferletti and Nova Vas and went to Kostanjevica. Nova Vas is quite a big place, completely abandoned by its inhabitants, and lies, for the most part, in heaps of rubble. You can see here everywhere the cruel effects of heavy enemy artillery. There are only small remnants of the church still visible. Enemy projectiles buzzed here over our heads today too. But this walk was most pleasant in spite of everything. It was a sunny, quite warm, clear day. The view was very spacious and varied. In front of us lay the so familiar chain of hills, starting with San Martino and going as far as San Michele after which there is the plateau of Doberdò. Somewhat further on in the background is the Monte dei sei Busi. In the far background, the wild, snow-capped, majestic chain of the Julian Alps rises in all its glory. I noticed on the way several trees completely covered in fine white blossoms. The wood of early spring.

* * *

Towards half-past ten in the morning I presented myself to the new commanding officer. He is a young man of prepossessing appearance – Captain Karlik. I also assumed my new duties.

The good thing about all this is that I have independent status here. My immediate superior is the divisional head, A.G. Brenner, with whom I have very little contact. With this transfer I have also been reassigned to a new brigade. I've gone from the 110th to the 187th – who knows how long I will be retained here.

22 February 1916

Today my battalion took up position in Sector I (Doberdò) for a total of six days. I have to stay encamped for another day. I have here in my sick room a number of sick people. On the 24th I will assign them to the doctor whose turn it will be to go to the aid centre, where I will still have to spend three days and three nights.

Today I spent the whole day very much in demand. During the medical inspection, which lasted from 9 am to 12 am, I had to deal with about fifty patients. Also, I had to give various orders concerning the time during which the battalion will remain in position. There were many things to complete. Most of it was in fact pretty much neglected as a young 3rd term medical student was given two months to carry out medical duties.

23 February 1916

The sky is overcast. It is raining continuously. The north wind is blowing and is almost impossible to bear. My small, board-built shelter affords me very little protection against the bad weather. The cold wind forces its way through all the innumerable cracks, as does the rain.

* * *

As the darkness of night fell the enemy artillery came into a state of animated activity which did not remain unanswered on our side. It was an almost uncanny feeling for me in that little shelter in the vicinity of which shells were yet again exploding.

24 February 1916
I left Kostanjevica around 5 o'clock in the afternoon and arrived at 7.30 pm at the medical centre in Doberdò. The centre is a dirty, low, wooden shack comprising three rooms. In the middle is the doctor's surgery itself and, to the right, living quarters for the doctor and padre and, on the left, the room for medical assistants and, at a pinch, for injuries that cannot be treated for whatever reason. This altogether quite poor and inadequate shack is located in a small and shallow crater and is surrounded on all sides by abandoned, shell-damaged houses. On the whole, Doberdò is abandoned and lies mostly in ruins. In the daytime it is empty of people. No one dares venture out. Venturing out of doors during the day is strictly forbidden by the military authorities. Enemy observers are located all around to report any movement to their artillery positions. Because of this, things get very lively here at nightfall. There is an influx of provisions and munitions, troops being relieved, an influx of sick and wounded to the medical centre and removal of same to the divisional field hospital, etc. Then, from all sides, down certain paths and streets, stream innumerable columns of pack animals and wagons to our positions bringing all that is absolutely essential for our front-line troops to thrive. What a massive undertaking this is. What enormous challenges have to be met by both animals and men. What a complicated exercise in logistics this wagon train represents. You cannot come close to imagining this unless you have seen it with your own eyes. If you have not seen these small, thin, weak horses, these really quite tiny, slow-moving donkeys, each carrying a big burden on its back, one, metal catering containers with warm food, another containers filled with water and another, whole sacks of refreshments and so on. There are long files of wagons laden with iron bars, iron plates, boards, barbed wire, ammunition chests. There are whole groups of them. Each group has its particular destination which it strives to reach. There are the most

diverse of difficulties to be overcome. There are a variety of dangers that threaten. All navigable paths at this moment are under enemy fire to render access difficult. Around 10 o'clock at night the groups within the columns have already arrived at their destinations. This is the time all have waited for impatiently and with longing, men as well as officers. Everyone can now quench their hunger and thirst. To each will now be doled out any letters they may have received. Each gets his ration of wine and tobacco. A time for recharging the batteries. And all this is performed by these poor, very much put upon, almost overburdened, undersized animals. What an incalculably important part they have to play in modern warfare. Could one imagine such a war without them? It wouldn't be possible. They keep the army at the front. And so many of them end up dead. And these poor, dumb warriors are not taken into account when the war and those lost in it are haltingly referred to.

* * *

In general, a very complicated, animated, multi-faceted, lively night life is played out that halts at daybreak to start all over when it gets dark again.

At the medical aid centre I met the colleague I have come to replace. Dr Marcella was hard at work looking after a badly injured patient. I took over his work immediately and liberated him. The work went badly to begin with, for here chaos reigned. Nothing was in order. A lot of people were just standing around. All over the ground were strewn rags and the remnants of bandages. No one paid much attention to keeping things sterile. It is, however, hard here to abide by the rules. But work can be organised in such a way that rules can be approximated to. I had with me in the basket packs of sterilised bandages and cotton wool, compound of mercury, carbolic acid, tincture of iodine, alcohol, petrol, mastisol, soap, rubber gloves, two sinks for hand washing, one sterilising bowl. The first thing is for everything to be put in its rightful place. I could not go on working like this. I shared the work out among the medics according to their intelligence. One, who had to wash his hands and sanitise them, just had to give me sterile bandaging, another had to help me with observing patients. Another had to give me disinfectant, etc. All unnecessary people, who were only in the way, were dismissed. The instruments I had with me were well cooked in a sterilising bowl in an oven. And now the work went forward swimmingly. Most of our patients were soldiers who had been badly injured as a result of exploding mortar bombs. The rest had lesser injuries as a result of rifle shots. Some knee injuries I put in splints. The area around each wound was first cleaned with tincture of iodine spread on with mastisol and then a dry, sterile dressing was applied. For deep tear wounds I also used Venibalsam. That night I had my hands full till 5 o'clock in the morning.

The wounded are transported on from here in wagons to Valkiščie and then to Kudilog to the field hospital of the 106th division. There are two pushcarts for the badly injured and two carts typical of the region for less serious injuries that take the wounded out of here. The whole night through these shuttle backwards and forwards between the medical aid centre and Valkiščie.

26 February 1916, 4.30 am
From half-past six last night to half-past four this morning, i.e. the whole night through, I have worked nonstop. There were a lot of serious injury cases brought to me. Many broken bones and extensive tear wounds caused by mortars, several shots to the head. There were about sixty of them that I had to attend to, one after the other. Many wounds had to be set in splints. Even now I am still quite tired out. This is the second night I have spent without sleep having to work incessantly. Tonight too the body count in this part of the front was rather high. Up until now, ten deaths have been reported. Among these is a would-be cadet of the 32nd Third Reserve Infantry Regiment, a nice young man with whom I spoke only a short time ago. The things we have to live through in times like these!!

At 5 o'clock in the morning I went to bed. The padre, alongside whom I live here at the medical centre, went to the military cemetery in Doberdò in order to bless the ten dead soldiers. When I woke up about 10 o'clock, this minister was already back and in a bad way mentally. He had witnessed a dreadful drama in the cemetery. Two shells exploded there yesterday and dug up many of the graves. Many of the dead bodies lay in pieces everywhere. A smell of decomposing corpses. Even the two just killed had been torn to bits.

Why hasn't society decided to build crematoria and burning sites for corpses? Especially in wartime. The living set out in the cruellest way to kill and maim, and this is permissible – but the idea of burning the dead to protect them from decomposition is one that they cannot go along with. This is unchristian, inhuman. Everywhere around here big cemeteries are laid out. In the cemetery in Doberdò 800 dead people have been buried up till now. Apart from this there are numerous mass graves in limestone craters. Everywhere you stumble over rotting and foul-smelling corpses. They can be trodden underfoot directly. This is more human than to burn them. What defective reasoning. What reprehensible madness. What short-sightedness.

27 February 1916

I had another sleepless night. The influx of wounded was indeed far less, but there was still plenty of work for me.

The padre left the medical centre around midnight and went to Kostanjevica. Another padre is coming to take his place for six days. He has carried out his duties. He must sprinkle water on each dead person, which is called 'giving a blessing'. To what a pathetic, comical, shameful role is the whole church with all its institutions condemned in this cruellest of all the wars known to history. She will not put off even for a moment her thick veil. She seeks with all the means at her disposal to hang on to her fine-sounding, meaningless formulas. The whole apparatus of empty phrases and sophistry is shored up with as much strength as possible, so that her weakness can be hidden. The representative of Christ on earth, the Holy Father, must sit there powerless on his high holy throne in Rome in that country of criminals and scoundrels and look on with a calm and unctuous face as the whole of Europe, country against country, ruthlessly murder, strike dead, rip one another apart in the cruellest manner with the most terrible and varied weapons of mass destruction. He cannot once speak out, does not even consider doing so, this apostle of universal peace and universal love on earth.

And what of his mission here on earth, what's happened to that?! And all the church's jurisdiction, what's happened to that? All the powers of hell, all the spirits of the dark underworld, all the devil's companions and fallen angels have broken loose and are playing their tricks with impunity on earth. Where are all your holy formulas, where are all your godly weapons, you 'All Powerful' Church, you Temple of Light, to banish this evil, to calm this storm? Where are You then? Are all these devil's disciples, men like Grey, Poincaré, Isvolsky, Salandra, Sonnino and all these baddies who rule us now stronger than you? Answer then! Free yourself once and for all from all your twisted logic, from the whole of that labyrinth of sophistry and meaningless phrases and confess the unadulterated truth. Make use of this opportunity of a great world upheaval, throw your thick mask aside, and consider. This will not help much though. You want to go on acting out your great comedy. You want to continue to hold humanity in your spell. It is certainly too easy for you, you cardinals, archbishops, bishops and whatever you are all called. At the cost of this short-sighted humanity you eke out such a fine, easy, pleasant, comfortable life. These people will not do anything for the sake of selfless love of truth and justice. When will mankind be able to see this, how long will it let itself be lied to? To many this whole apparatus is greatly to be desired. The great machines of state are helped in this way to prosper, are indeed preserved. The church is an important, great support to the state. It helps it to tame and train mankind, to make best use of it. It educates an individual within a state. They help one another. And mankind puts up with all this. Under the yoke of the church and the state people allow themselves to be soothed with empty phrases like 'love of neighbour', 'individual freedom', 'constitution', etc. and scarcely notice how much they are ruled by both. Freedom is out of the question – people are slaves in every respect. Who would dare to deny all this? Certainly not the church and all those gentlemen in positions of power, who sit in their comfortable apartments and manipulate the masses on all sides like a chess player his chess pieces. How many pieces does the latter sacrifice in order to attain his objective? Human life does not mean much to him. There are men to spare in the state. These he must sacrifice only in order to attain to what he considers to be necessary. Who has told him to treat the human life at his disposal so thoughtlessly?! This question can not even be asked. An order has been given and you must leave behind your home, separate yourself from wife and children, from siblings, neighbours, relations, go to far-off foreign parts, renounce all the comforts of life, all the habits that each of us has, live in holes and hollows, suffer thirst and hunger, be constantly in danger of losing your life and in the end give your life, die a hero's death. The order these gentlemen give is not a big deal. They know nothing of the terror of war. If they had to share in it just once, then they would certainly take care that the war was over as quickly as possible. Unfortunately, this doesn't happen. They continue to enjoy all their worldly goods to the utmost. They forge their plans. If these don't succeed, then nothing can be done about it. It happened and that's all there is to it. If the plans succeed, then the person who made them is showered with the highest decorations and honours. Did he ask the hundreds of thousands he sent to the battlefield for their opinion?! No!! Everyone must be a patriot; everyone must abjure all the dangers in favour of a 'hero's death'. And people witter on about 'individuality', 'freedom'. Yes! Church and State!! How much mischief both of them have on their conscience!

Tonight around 8 o'clock I will leave the medical centre and go to Mikoli. Regimental Doctor Hoitas of Division 157 of the 3rd Battalion of the Third Reserves will relieve me. I will be able to enjoy a bit of fresh air. For here one cannot even chance a few steps the whole day long for fear one might be spotted immediately in this shallow crater by enemy observers and attract shell fire. One has to lie in the dirty, dark, damp, close, smelly hole that bears the description of 'Trench Villa' and put up with the cold. This hole cannot be heated throughout the day so as not to give one's position away. On all sides guns crack, thunder, and chatter. From early in the morning onwards today there has been very lively artillery fire. Almost like the beating of a drum. On the one hand our own artillery pieces have been brought into play which are located in Valkiščie, Mikoli, Bonetti, on the main road and the west bank of Lake Doberdò. Their constant rapid, abrupt, angry fire on the enemy on the other side is not left unanswered by that very animated enemy. And his heavy guns are always firing over our heads. Some shells have fallen not far from the medical centre, which shares the appellation of the aforementioned trench. The description is most aptly chosen.

2 March 1916

I have been in Kostanjevica since last night. I left the aid centre trench on 27 February around 9 o'clock at night after Regimental Doctor Hoitas took over my duties. This journey from Doberdò to Kostanjevica was tiring and most unpleasant. I had a pack animal for my luggage and a horse at my disposal to ride on. It was a very dark, rainy, cold, windy night. You could barely see the person standing next to you. On the way I very quickly lost my travelling companions (both my assistant and the person leading my pack animal) and all my efforts to find them again were fruitless. I therefore had to travel on alone. I wandered about for a long time. During this inclement night I could find no one on the way to give me information. I finally arrived after midnight at my destination tired out, soaked through and frozen. I spent the next day in camp. On the 29th I had to leave again to go to Mikoli (Codename Hutteldorf), where my battalion is situated since last night. I had to go back along this path on foot, for during the day you are not allowed to ride here. It is forbidden. You could be spotted more easily by the enemy. It was raining heavily, and everywhere along the way, mud and water. About 10 o'clock in the morning I reached Mikoli where I had to do the medical inspection right away. Here I lived in a quite small, badly assembled, wet shelter with two colleagues, Dr Marcella from Prague, Assistant Doctor, and Dr Jung, Head Doctor. Any improvement on this dwelling was not to be sought. I stayed here most reluctantly, for this position was very insecure. Only yesterday an enemy shell struck the neighbouring shelter. Four soldiers were killed and eleven were wounded. I only spent one night in this shelter. On 1 March I had to leave Mikoli and go back to Kostanjevica, which I was loath to do because of the bad weather.

These three days (i.e. the 28th, the 29th and the 1st) were therefore very burdensome for me. I went through a lot. I should like to say just how much, if only briefly. I even tried to do so today, but I wasn't able to. I have fallen into a state of apathy from which I cannot tear myself away.

3 March 1916, 10 pm
Today eventually I had a restful day in Kostanjevica – in bed. I was able to recover a little from all the awful strains and privations of the last few days. The weather too was somewhat more favourable once more. The day was gloomy and cool, but it didn't rain. The enemy artillery left us alone for once. It didn't have much to say for itself for a change.

Early in the morning I held the medical inspection in the same hut in which I live in and in which my patients are housed too. About 10 am I went to the refreshment centre of the Red Cross where the sick and wounded of the Divisional Field Hospital are taken in the direction of Nabresina by railway. Here they are also served refreshments like tea with rum, bread and butter, bacon, etc. Today there were a lot of sick and wounded. Among others I came across a lieutenant who, during an outing to Trieste, caught a dose of syphilis. It was a married woman whose husband is away at the front who infected him with it. His consternation was that much the greater. He too is a victim of the war which has done so much to extend prostitution and has contributed to all the misery resulting therefrom. The number of people suffering from a venereal disease is mounting steadily. Whoever escapes from the enemy's methods of killing people and after months of a hard life full of danger in the field goes back to some great metropolis or home for a few days is liable to find awaiting him wherever he goes a new, dangerous, malicious enemy. Tiny, only visible through a microscope, but with dire consequences for him. This micro-organism is called Spirocheta pallida or gonococcus. The woman has caught it through and because of loose living, as an uninvited guest. But it does not stay in her only. She infects with it, if he is lucky enough to come back from active service, her lover, her friend, her sweetheart, her fiancé, her husband. Along with her so long and warmly wished and longed for love, she imparts this fierce poison.

3 March 1916

Early in the morning tomorrow I have to walk to Mikoli, where I will be spending four days with the battalion in the so-called divisional reserve. This going backwards and forwards constantly, and in persistent rain and wet everywhere, wears me out. If only one could at least stay in one place a bit longer, it doesn't matter where. Even in Mikoli, although the latter is constantly under enemy artillery fire. So many here have already suffered a hero's death. Everywhere you can see traces left behind by shells that have exploded in the shape of extensive deep furrows. Everywhere there are various large fragments of shells that have blown up. Apart from that the shelters here are for the most part very bad. Who is going to bother about making them better here? It is most regrettable that, up till now, in spite of this trench warfare that has already gone on for so long, so little has been undertaken in this respect. Only now are they starting to carve out caves, after we have already had several direct hits recently. And how slowly this work advances!! There are very few drilling machines at our disposal. And why is all this happening? Again because of defective organisation, because of the malfunctioning of high command. Because the leaders, the high-ups in the various decisive command posts are far too comfortable and never venture out to convince themselves of the need to oversee it themselves in person. They always live well away from the shooting and in comfortable premises to boot. In order to build these and equip them fittingly, even adorn them, everything that can be done is done. The others just have to 'be patient'. They 'have to suffer – there's a war on, you know'.

Today ran its course here in Kostanjevica without anything at all out of the ordinary.

8 March 1916

I am in Mikoli where the divisional reserve of the battalion is and this will continue to be the case until tomorrow evening when it will have to go to camp in Kostanjevica. Marching on from there will only take place once another battalion, which is already in position, comes to relieve it. This can only happen around 11 pm.

9 March 1916

So today we are marching to Kostanjevica to set up camp. The weather is still not favourable to us. It is raining constantly, and the north wind shows no sign of abating.

* * *

Today we learned something new. The 30.5cm mortar, which has stood here on the road through the valley of the Valone for some months now, is being moved from here. Where to no one knows. The Italians too have, according to the report of our artillery observers, removed their heavy mortars from this part of the front. Great preparations are to be found on both sides. We are on the threshold of significant events. Everything is in a state of flux. Everywhere various new measures are coming into operation. A few days ago all movements of personnel between Vienna and Trieste were suspended.

10 March 1916

Today throughout the whole of the day I have been very busy. And all of it with work that cannot provide the least satisfaction to us doctors. Matters medical are taken very little into account here. We only have to write a lot, to complete all the formalities. Firstly, a rather extensive medical inspection was conducted today. Hardly surprising. Tomorrow night the battalion is going into position again for six days. Everyone would like with all the means lawfully permitted to them to escape from all the hardships, privations and dangers that go with it. Everyone has had enough and feels that all this is more than they can bear. They are all at great pains then to lead the doctor astray and to lie to him. The latter must, however, take care that as few of the troops as possible go to hospital. He needs to be ruthless. He now needs to see his patients from a new, more military than human, viewpoint. The doctor's point of view must be left to one side. How many inner struggles do I have to endure every day during these medical inspections. Healthy people are of course the exception rather than the rule here. And all these sick, worn out, exhausted people I have to classify as fit for front-line duty. I am forced to do this by military regulations. I am playing the role here of a watchman and even, because of the large number of people trying it on, that of a detective. Nevertheless, I sent sixteen men to hospital today which bothered my commanding officer a lot. But they had to be sent.

* * *

Early tomorrow around 8 o'clock I need to travel to Hudilog to the 106th Divisional Field Hospital with Captain Karlik, my former commanding officer. He reported sick to me five days ago. Today, after examining him twice, I wrote him a prescription and he leaves tomorrow. But there is still one active serving officer in the battalion, Captain Kourat, who has now taken Captain Karlik's place.

Captain Karlik is an exception among all the serving officers I have known up till now. He is very energetic, intelligent, hard-working and has already been on active service for fourteen months. He has also achieved quite a lot.

And when will it be my turn?! When will I be able to return to normal circumstances?! Will I succeed in reintegrating myself? Here death can overtake you at any moment. Only today a few shells fell right next to my shelter.

11 March 1916, 11.30 am

Today I had from early morning onwards to work intensively in order to be able to carry out all my duties. First of all I had to hold the medical inspection around half-past six and wanted to get it over with as soon as possible. At 8 o'clock I had to travel to Hudilog with Captain Karlik. Despite the strain of all these efforts, I could not set off earlier than quarter past eight. I did not even have time to have breakfast.

A considerable number of soldiers appeared for the medical inspection – more than sixty. Each told me his tale of woe. All of them harboured an earnest wish not to have to take up position today. It comes as no surprise to me that each is driven to lead me up the garden path by fair means or foul, to deceive me, to lie to me and I need to defend myself against this in order, on the one hand, to be just and only send really sick people to hospital and the healthier ones to the front, but, on the other hand, not to come into conflict with the military authorities. It was a great inner struggle that I had to fight within myself. I had a lot to put up with. I had to give plenty of thought to the matter with many. They are all almost desperate that, in this bad weather, they have to march further and go through soaking wet defences where they sometimes have to stand up to their hips in water day and night and do this for twenty-four hours, six times over. They have already forgotten about the danger to life and limb from gas and shelling, etc.

I sent another twelve to hospital to the great dissatisfaction of the officer in charge.

13 March 1916, Aid Centre Trench (Doberdò)
I came back here about 7 o'clock this evening and started work almost immediately. The journey here was tiring. To begin with, it rained very hard and the paths were, for almost all of the way, under water. Then the artillery, especially our own, began a lively bombardment. It cracked and thundered on all sides. A dull-sounding racket. Guns of various calibres were used. The 15cm howitzer in the valley of the Valone near Mikoli and Bonetti. The 24cm mortar near Devetak. The small calibre guns of Cruihrib. The 30.5cm mortar in the vicinity of Kostanjevica. San Martino and San Michele came under fire. Shells exploded on contact with the ground, pieces of shrapnel flew up into the air.

14 March 1916
Today finally it was a clear sunny day. I had a lot of work to do all night. There were many badly wounded people to attend to. Someone came in who had been shot through the lungs with an extensive pulmonary emphysema that stretched out over half of the thorax and a corresponding half of the lower stomach. Several serious head wounds including two with prolapsed brain tissue and totally unconscious with an irregular, accelerated pulse. Fractures of the thigh, some elongated tear wounds due to landmine explosions. One puncture wound in the cervical spinal column who was already dying when he came in

and shortly afterwards did die. One person was dead already, brought in with a puncture wound to the head (point of entry: left temple, projectile: a piece of shrapnel to the occipital region under the skin), who had been a victim of friendly fire, a shot from our own artillery that fell short, as was told to me the same night by an acting company commander. Most of these patients were from the 31st Third Reserve Infantry Regiment in Sector III. In one company tonight out of 180 men only 70 were left. The rest of the company were either dead or badly wounded. All cover was wiped out here by enemy artillery fire. It was a hard night for us. I was able to go to sleep around 4 o'clock in the morning, but my sleep was disturbed by the constant blowing up and boring of the Aid Centre cave. Today I had a look at the drilling machine that is being used for the making of this cave and which is powered by compressed air. The high pressure under which this air is kept is generated by a 4HP machine which is housed behind the Aid Centre in a small shed. There's a very complicated attachment belonging to it.

* * *

10 o'clock at night. For two hours now there has been very lively artillery fire on our side against Monte dei sei Busi. The enemy has proved to be most active there during the last few days and has destroyed the biggest part of our positions in Sectors I (occupied by the 5th division of the 37th Regiment), II and III (occupied by the 31st Third Reserve Infantry Regiment). Everywhere there have been great losses in both dead and wounded. Probably more ambitious operations have been curtailed. Corresponding measures have been taken. Preparations for defence. Everwhere there is boring, digging, building, things being blown up. All this so as to dig oneself into the earth as deeply as possible and to protect ourselves here against enemy weapons. These cruel assistants to death, instruments to wage war of the most varied kind, mortars of various calibres (going up to 22cm), bombs (gas bombs, teargas, trinitrophenol bombs), hand grenades, flamethrowers that create the effect of awful devastation, machine guns, stink bombs, defensive grenades, etc., etc.

15 March 1916

The enemy heavy artillery are firing today most tellingly on our own artillery units, especially at Cruihrib. They are heavy guns mostly. Very large shell fragments are everywhere flying through the air over our heads. You need to be really on your guard to not be hit by flying pieces of debris. The latter are big and heavy. Much of the fire is directed against Doberdò. These shells exploded not far away from us.

* * *

Today they are working diligently in front of our Aid Centre. Things have been altogether neglected. It smells bad everywhere. No one has bothered until now to set things straight. There are rotting puddles of scraps of all sorts. I have finally today organised things. I have put the available bandage-bearers, medics, and assistant medics to work and instructed them to clean out everything, to dig a drain to drain off the water, dry the puddles and lay paving stones.

I have also taken some photographs of the aid centre as well as the village of Doberdò which I have visited with the padre staying at the aid centre. Here I photographed the church, which is completely destroyed, riddled with holes and partly without a roof. Right next to us a heavy shell exploded giving rise to a huge black column of smoke.

16 March 1916

Three nights and three days have already gone by since I came to the medical aid centre. Around 8 o'clock tonight I will be relieved, at which time I will need to march to Kostanjevica. This is, of course, a journey fraught with danger, for at this moment there is a lot of shooting. Especially infantry rifles are very much in evidence. Infantry bullets are flying about in all directions and particularly from the south, west and north. Enemy positions lie in the shape of an arc around the aid centre and especially around the whole area of Doberdò. South of here run the positions of Monfalcone, to the west those of Monte dei sei Busi and to the north those of San Martino and Monte San Michele. The infantry especially shoot off, from time to time at night, it varies, their various weapons, giving voice to an uncanny chatter. Also, other instruments of mass destruction, like mortars and bombs, chime in occasionally with formidable vehemence.

Relieving along the whole of this sector of the front has to be effected here at night. During the day you can't move if you don't want to run the risk of promptly being spotted by enemy observers, who are good at their job, and becoming a target. The enemy is naturally in possession of many high places from where he has a good command of the whole region and can keep it constantly under surveillance. It makes an uncanny impression whenever one during the day trusts oneself to go outside a crater. One is spotted immediately, and the length of stay is short and already there are shells buzzing, one after the other, in this direction. With nightfall comes a wake-up call. Then come columns of provisions with endless files of pack animals with cooking chests, meals on wheels, wagons with munitions and various wartime expedients. Troops are led to positions, while they are taken out of reserve forces. Further on, troops push back from their positions. These reliefs of troops take place regularly according to a certain guiding principle. The troops relieved are drawn back into a reserve for a certain time either as temporary reserves in the craters around Doberdò or as divisional reserves to Mikoli or army reserves to camp in Kostanjevica.

On all the streets, lanes and paths pulsates a very lively life. All of these are then full to overflowing. No wonder then that the enemy, especially at this time, displays the full extent of his firepower. During the day for the most part only the artillery batteries are fired. Of course, there are then the so-called short and long shots which accidentally hit places not aimed at and cause a lot of mischief. Then many a crater, when this is not noticed and observed, is heavily hit. In the last few days more than ten shells of various calibres have hit our aid centre crater. Various deep craters bear eloquent witness to this. All of these hits were within a short distance from our shelter, going on for twenty paces, and many a one could have easily hit our shelter and brought our lives to the cruellest end. It was a happy accident that our lives were spared. How often we need to marvel at all these happy accidents. The terrible sword of Damocles hangs constantly over our heads. And yet we are still alive. Here the shell or bullet went too far and fell behind us, there it went over our heads.

I have just received the list of fatalities for the last five days from this sector. Around sixty deaths have been reported from this division alone.

In the San Martino and San Michele sectors about 100 dead were buried in Devetak.

* * *

12 o'clock at night. I have just arrived in camp. I have retraced the way on foot from Doberdò to Mikoli, from whence I carried on on horseback. The way lay over Valkiščie and Oppacchiasella to camp. Oppacchiasella is a bigger place which, for the most part, lies in rubble and is totally deserted. Most of the houses are badly damaged and laid to waste. Everywhere you can see signs of shells that have exploded, the annihilating work of the ruthless enemy, the consequence of this wild, cruel war.

On the way here I encountered the 32nd Third Reserve Infantry Regiment (Novy nast), which has just moved into position in Sectors II and III, in order to relieve there the 31st Third Reserve Infantry Regiment (Eger) after a six-day occupation of these positions. The regiment relieved, which has suffered during these six days great losses (thirty-eight dead) is now going to Mikoli for a few days as a divisional reserve.

17 March 1916
What great joy today had in store for me. After such a long time I was able to take a bath. A rare occurrence at the front, two hours away from the enemy, to be able to bathe and do so moreover in such a good, pleasant, hot tub of water. It's a small, nice, well-appointed, quite modest bathhouse at divisional HQ. Yes, these high-up gentlemen strive with all means at their disposal to make their life pleasant and comfortable. They have the time for it. This too is their most important care. These high-ups spy out for themselves only safe places situated as far in the rearguard as possible. They have materials at their disposal that they

are able to push forward. But stop! Why scold them? I only have them to thank for being able to take a bath today. And what this means for someone, only those are in a position to judge who share with us our harsh fate, for days and weeks on end living in dirty shelters, sleeping in close, spartan, damp caves, having to make strenuous marches up to their knees in mud and water alongside us. This is a big event for someone like me. I feel out of the ordinary for once.

How hard it is though to come by things like this. It is at the disposal of the high-ups themselves first and foremost. They use it before we do. They need to have a leisure-time activity. They care not a fig about others.

I had a bath today then and was very glad of it. At 10 am the bathroom was vacant. And this was an opportunity for all these others to make use of. I learnt of it through my servant and went there. It takes about half an hour to get to divisional HQ. The latter is housed in a small wood in a well-protected place north of the camp – naturally, for these higher-ups spotless clean shacks have been erected. Everything is well maintained. And we see them walking about everywhere at every available opportunity. Generals and general staff officers and all of them with numerous high decorations. The latter, it goes without saying, are proportionate to the services rendered by them. All of them have an appearance which is reassuring, well nourished, good uniforms. Created to look good. Veritable *instrumenta dei*, who are called to lead, to command, to give orders, to be followed, to be representatives. The elect, the chosen few, who can rise to any challenge. It is incumbent on them. This goes without saying. The rest of us belong only to the ranks of that massively large, grey, uniform mass that makes our army such a complicated affair. Unfortunately, we have to take what comes. It's wartime. Duty calls. Our life is not as precious as theirs. If many from our ranks have died a hero's death, they can quickly be replaced by other new arrivals. None of us can perform such great deeds as these lucky beggars with their innate talents and capabilities. They've all completed military academy and are marked out as leaders. Their lives are very precious. They have a wholly logical mindset. It is interesting what these gentlemen are getting up to in these testing days (only a week ago bloody and terrible conflicts raged here in the sectors round

Doberdò and San Michele, the so-called 5th battle of the Isonzo). Today, for instance, I observed much. A brigadier general, kept an eye on from the moment of leaving his quarters, ate a good breakfast while a number of workers busied themselves before his shack. He gives out various orders, issues serious commands, and his home here is quite comfortable. It is to be wondered at that he now has at his disposal such a reservoir of patience and is able to think at all about such minor matters.

Another gentleman, the divisional commander himself, His Excellency K.L. [FML Ernest Kletter Edler von Gromnik commanded 106th Infantry Division], goes on amusing himself here with his dog and a fine, well looked after, ornamented black goat. His face bears no trace of the military commander's energy. He has a good-humoured, peaceable smile that speaks of perfect inner satisfaction and tranquillity. Perhaps it is because he can see with his sharp, far-seeing commander's mind's-eye into the distant future and discern already the great conquests of our arms. We are perhaps too dull and narrow-minded to be able to have an insight into the mysteries of a general's brain and to assign a true meaning to the contribution he makes to the war effort. Perhaps we need first to raise the level of our thinking to theirs in order to understand them better. And this is no easy task for someone.

Meanwhile, everything I have had occasion to see here has had an unpleasant and troubling effect on me. It was in stark contrast to the experiences, especially of my last onerous days, at the aid centre in Doberdò.

* * *

Today the wild storm at the front has abated somewhat. The artillery's firepower has left off. Probably it is only a short lull before the arrival of a new, violent storm.

Tonight my battalion is coming out of position (from Sector I – Doberdò) into camp where it will remain for four days. New, intensive work therefore awaits me.

20 March 1916, Encamped South-west of Kostanjevica
I am constantly very much called upon. This is already day three. The military doctor has to do everything he can. In addition to the unpleasant demands of medical practice, he has all manner of other things to attend to. There are gas masks to be inspected, to be fitted to each man and explained.

Delousing of all the companies to be carried out. Laying out for cemeteries, vaccinations of every description to be performed, reports to be made, reports on patients to be lodged, etc., etc. No wonder that I cannot find from early morning until evening any free time for myself. All this is enough to undermine anybody's nervous system. There can, however, be no counter indications. Orders need to be carried out.

If only we had every expedient at our disposal. We need to look around for a long time in various places, to cast around to describe, official forms and receipts fill in until we finally get something. Each authority wants to manage as comfortably as possible and yet do as little as possible. We are always sent from one person to another, until we are finally forced to lose patience. Today I had to go to the medical head of our division, Lieutenant A. Brenner, for disinfectant. He sent me back to the Divisional Medical Service of the 106th. There we learnt that the disinfectant is in Lokvica. Thither it was I had to be sent. Finally we got our disinfectant. And now for us to get the soap, the water, and the coal we need from various sources, we need to telephone around, to write off here and there, to send out medical orderlies. By the time we get all this, it will be late in the day.

Tomorrow at 6 am the delousing process in its entirety will begin.

21 March 1916
The battalion will depart tonight for Mikoli. A gloomy, rainy day. Tomorrow early I will need to march there myself. I will need to be doing my medical inspection there at about 9 am. Back again then in that poor, monotonous valley of the Valone with its bare flat hills and the numerous heroes' graves, the abandoned, ruined houses.

22 March 1916, In Mikoli

During the march from Kostanjevica to Mikoli I quite unexpectedly had something awful to endure. So as to be able to appear on time for the medical inspection I tried to make the way shorter. There I learnt for the umpteenth time that in this rocky, uncultivated, wild, trackless limestone waste such an undertaking was not so easy. Everywhere here you stumble over obstacles that are difficult to overcome. Whole heaps of stones, ravines, valleys, undergrowth, from which there is hardly any escape. And moreover wetness, water, and puddles after yesterday's heavy rain. I had to wander around here for a long time. I couldn't find a way out. Already I was bathed in sweat, added to which it was sultry day today too. I sought in vain for a way out. There was no one to see far and wide from whom I could have asked directions. A deep silence like that of the grave, only interrupted from time to time by the thunder of guns and shells going off. A quite uncanny atmosphere. Finally, I glimpsed at a distance a very bad Karst region footpath. Relieved and pleased, I strove to reach it.

This was the path that leads from Selo to Bonetti. Taking this path I can now get to the valley of the Valone. So, I go on further and then there opens up in front of me quite unexpectedly a splendid but really quite chilling panorama before my very eyes. The far-off flat mirror of Lake Doberdò, beyond that a part of the township of Monfalcone, and further on, the whole course of the lower Isonzo with its mouth and the hard-fought for and drenched in human blood chain of hills with their summits partly in enemy hands, partly in our own, and then, after that, the broad plain with all its towns and villages. All this lay at my feet, quite near to me. A piece of ground over which crueller events than ever had already been played out, are currently being played out and will be played out in future. A terrible human tragedy. Hundreds of thousands of people have been torn to pieces here, crushed, blown up and mutilated. It is a great cemetery with its innumerable heroes' graves swarming everywhere with shamelessly exposed corpses.

And all these things on this fair piece of ground were revealed before my very eyes in an instant. I was like someone intoxicated. I almost lost consciousness. I was as if rooted to the spot and could not stir from there. I stared and I stared.

Then a shell exploded almost on top of me. I woke up. And only now did I notice what a life-threatening situation I found myself in. This was the chimney of one of the highest summits here. I was visible to the enemy on all sides as if I had been on a plate. Everywhere in all these high places enemy observers are positioned. The distance as the crow flies from the enemy's lines amounted to 4km at most. I calculated it too. I was very frightened and uneasy. I wanted to run away. But it was difficult. I only had one way out. To run away as fast as possible. I did it too. And I started feeling more and more uneasy. I had to run like this for more than 10 minutes until I could finally conceal myself from the enemy and get further away. And I came across a stone tablet with the words: 'Beware of friendly fire'. It was a truly horrific place I had landed myself in this time where I found myself in extreme danger to life and limb.

* * *

5 o'clock in the morning. An enemy pilot appeared who, in spite of uninterrupted shooting from our small calibre guns (7–9cm), went peacefully on his way. These shots are always futile and can be accompanied by high costs. They only constitute a danger in terms of us losing our own lives through falling shrapnel. The plane was going towards Nova Vas and dropped two bombs there. I do not know with what consequences.

Around 9 pm it started to rain heavily again, to really throw it down. The sky was thickly covered with clouds. We played tarot till 11 pm: me, First Lieutenant Radumcič and Lieutenant Petrovič. The rain kept on falling. Pity those who are now in their positions, or on the way to their positions, or in front of their positions, the whole baggage train, all who must be suffering just now on such a dark, rainy night in this Karst region.

27 March 1916, 3 o'clock in the Afternoon
On the shore of Lake Doberdò. On the slopes of Cruihrib, a rather steep, fine-looking hill on the north-east shore of this unique and sizable Karst region lake whose waters spring up from the depths.

Enemy guns are continually making a racket. Their fire is mainly directed against the back of Cruihrib which is heavily occupied by our own guns. Blast upon blast, a long and low drawn-out buzzing that you could almost take for a heart-rending groan, sad plaints can be heard on all sides. Ever new explosions of shells, ever new clouds of smoke. Here fine, tender blue, there white, grey, or black. Our own guns are beginning to answer back. Towards Monte dei sei Busi it's kicking off where today too a very lively infantry action was fought.

When will all these hellish noises cease?! When will bestial, criminal, dull humanity have enough of killing?! When will the thirst of blood lust against peoples be satisfied? It's high time already!

Human resources, that poor cannon fodder, are already running out in the enemy's camp as well as in ours. From what poor cripples are built our brave armed forces. Old, rheumatic, sclerotic, heart-diseased, stomach-ulcerated, powerless, tired out men, fathers, even grandfathers, on the one hand; boys and youths, short, anaemic, still undeveloped, thin, undernourished, coughing and short of breath, on the other – these are our heroes in Doberdò, who are under pressure day in, day out, need to endure uninterrupted heavy bombardment and are compelled to hold out.

29 March 1916
Today the whole afternoon long the valley of the Valone, and chiefly the part in which our shelters are situated, was under heavy artillery fire. Thud after thud, explosion after explosion. Intense excitement. Unease and nervousness took possession of all of us. Everyone is fully conscious of the fact that it could be his turn to die at any minute.

Everyone is impatient. All around there are clouds of smoke, mist, flames, a rain of stones. In the air are enemy aeroplanes, including a very big double-decker with eight machine guns and 200kg of trinitrophenol. It's a case of everybody on the ground taking cover so as not to be spotted by the pilots. But where to?! The shelling never lets up. It goes on all the time.

* * *

News has just come in of the enemy's conquest of part of our trenches at Selz. A Bohemian regiment, the 102nd, had occupied this sector. And then they were driven out. Here there was heavy fighting, for the time being without success: reinforcements were called for. The 152nd Third Reserve Battalion were deployed there from the brigade of reservists in Doberdò. The 42nd Third Reserve Battalion of infantry is already awaiting the order to march in Mikoli. An energetic offensive is being planned. This is indeed a sensitive and important place in our line which needs to be won back.

* * *

My battalion left Mikoli tonight and marched into position. I am going again tomorrow to Kostanjevica for a day and will then be going to the aid centre in Doberdò.

1 April 1916
Owing to sudden displacements, only today am I going to the aid centre.

Yesterday I was in camp at Segetti. After long and hard work by 10,000 Russian prisoners and our own soldiers this massive, comfortable, splendidly situated camp has come into being where 20,000 soldiers can be housed quite easily. Here well laid out streets cut through the whole camp up, down, and sideways. Among the main streets are Krautwald Street, Grazer Street, Novara Street, etc. A faultless work of human hands. Two coffee houses managed by the military. A cinema. Chapels. Music. And all this in close proximity to the enemy who is only 14km away. It gives pleasure to see ten cans of tinned food, a bunch of figs, a salami sausage, and half a dozen delicacies.

3 April 1916
I went to the medical centre trench and arrived here on 1 April at 9 o'clock at night. For a fair few days now we have been having splendid weather. At the medical centre I met a colleague, Dr Lastovka, and a padre from the 31st Infantry Regiment, Reverend Luszczak, a Pole.

This time there was not so much work here. Yesterday during the day I visited the town of Doberdò. One must, of course, be very careful, for one can be watched here by enemy observers, who are, for the most part, on the heights of La Rocca. I was able to view in minute detail this time the whole town, which currently comes over as a big heap of rubble. It was a rather big, nicely situated, well-built town with long and wide streets. I also visited the military cemetery which, with its many mass graves, contains over 2,000 dead. This cemetery is well situated and meticulously maintained. A little necropolis. I took several photographs all over.

* * *

It has been relatively peaceful now for two days with a peace that set in after the most recent, violent fighting. Attacks and counter-attacks were undertaken here with great vehemence. The enemy occupied our trenches on Hill 70. It was then a matter of driving him out of them by all means necessary. In point of fact, it was a matter here of the greatest strategic importance. There was a lot of bloodshed. The 102nd Bohemian Regiment in particular sustained enormous losses. Reserve troops were brought in. During the night of 31st March to 1st April our artillery deployed heavy fire for almost two hours. But we could not attain our objective. Finally, our troops succeeded in digging in only eighty paces away from the enemy (i.e. from our own former trenches) and in securing the inviolability of our new positions.

* * *

3 April 1916, 5 o'clock in the Afternoon

A report from Adler Sector (i.e. Sector A: Monte dei sei Busi) and Biene Sector (Sector B) to the effect that they are being sorely tested by enemy mortars. These sectors are requesting cover – artillery support. And this was soon given. Heavy rapid fire from various locations was now commenced by our own side. These sectors are adjacent to Hill 70 (Selz).

4 April 1916

During this five-day period of being dug in we had altogether twenty-four men wounded and four killed. Among the former was a badly wounded lieutenant. The lieutenant in question was Lieutenant Demarchi, a young, extremely amiable person.

6 April 1916

At 9 o'clock in the morning several awards of decorations took place in our battalion. About forty men in the battalion were decorated. They included Falur Lulié (Quartermaster's Assistant), an intelligent, good man from Spalato in Dalmatia who held the post of a high official there in the Austrian office of Lloyds. It was Archduke Josef, our present 7th Corps commander, who hung on each one his medal. Also present were Fieldvicemarshal Kletter, our divisional commander (I.T.D. 106) and many other senior officers. This decoration ceremony concluded very ceremoniously with a military march-past.

We were issued new orders today as well. The battalion, thank goodness, will now have to leave the plateau of Doberdò. As soon as the day after tomorrow it will no longer form part of the 7th Corps and will become a unit in Corps 16. Preparations are already underway. Everyone is looking forward to going to the Tyrolean mountains and to leaving behind the hell that is Doberdò.

This pleasure, unfortunately, will not be granted to me. I have just learned that I have been ordered away from the battalion as from now. I must stay with the division. I must now leave behind all my dear comrades. I will once again be transferred and placed in a new situation. And why? Because Staff Doctor Brenner, a man whose ethics stand on crooked and weak foundations, expects it of me. This immoral medal-chaser who, on the one hand, misses no opportunity to make life difficult for the doctors in his charge, even to harm them, nor, on the other, to conjure up some new decoration for himself. This feeble-minded, stupid, divisional HQ sycophant and flatterer, this coward, who hides behind the backs of others, is nowhere to be seen, but is always boasting about his heroic deeds. He is a scoundrel who is just there to oppress the division's poor doctors and have them transferred to one place today and another tomorrow. A thoroughly immoral individual. An actor who uses every means to cover up the darkness of his soul. But this he does not always succeed in doing – he rarely does it, in fact. He is too mentally defective for that, too stupid. A dirty parasite who only wants to make use of everyone.

I had a real fight on my hands with this 'gentleman' over my transfer. Nothing helps. Tomorrow I will go to him again to ask him for representation in his report to the division's medical officer of health. The latter is Senior Staff Doctor Stehlik, a really nice man.

And when will all this be over? The whole of this war itself? When will I once more be out of this fix? This whole system of bureaucracy that grinds all of us down. This malignant growth of officialdom which is destined to weaken the whole of the state even further.

Big troop movements. Reinforcements are steadily being brought up. Preparations are everywhere being made in abundance. Everyone feels there is something in the air, that they are standing on the threshold of very great and decisive events. Will they be a long time coming? Many people go as far as to believe that we will go on the offensive. Is this even a possibility? Are we not quite simply too exhausted after all the carnage that the war has wrought so far?!

7 April 1916
This afternoon I was with the division's medical officer of health, Colonel Dr Stehlik, to whom I have set out my case. He did not, however, give me the answer I wanted. I was sure I would have to stay behind and await a new posting from this gentleman. My battalion commander too, Captain Conrad, acted vigorously on my behalf at divisional headquarters but all to no avail.

I have already made the appropriate preparations for my departure. I was most dissatisfied about it, yes, for a short while almost unhappy even. And then I suddenly had the unexpected, pleasing news that I had to march off with the battalion anyway. This on the command of the medical officer of health. A truly gratifying piece of news which changed my mood completely in an instant. This must have come as a very unpleasant surprise for Lieutenant A. Brenner, of course. It came to him like a slap in the face. At today's evening meal everyone was in high spirits – we even had music while we ate. Our farewell supper to

Doberdò. A genuine life experience. None of us know what lies ahead. But we've all had enough of Doberdò. Tomorrow we march off at half-past seven in the morning.

8 April 1916
At approximately 8 o'clock in the morning we marched out of Kostanjevica. Quite a warm day. A path deep in dust. We marched via Wojscica-Komen to Kraina Vas. Roughly 23km away. Our distance from the high plateau of Doberdò increased more and more with each step and therefore our happiness did too. We aren't even thinking where we will eventually end up. Just a long way away from Doberdò.

We are leaving behind now that bare, highly rocky, grey, fissured, totally barren, inhospitable, trackless Karst waste for ever more pleasant and attractive areas where everywhere spring in all its splendour meets us laughing. What blessed and unaccustomed silence. What godly peace came from everywhere to meet us.

More and more we are getting away from shots and the fire of hell. We scarcely want to believe it ourselves. We are finally out of life-threatening danger. We are marching along in a happy mood now. Our good Dalmatians sing merry soldier songs as we march. Heat, dust, thirst, all the strains attendant on a long march, mean nothing to us. You almost want to laugh out loud. We finally arrived at about 5 o'clock in the afternoon in Kraina Vas. Here we had to await further orders.

At 8 o'clock at night I was continuing my journey with two other gentlemen: Lieutenant Colonel Radomcić and Lieutenant Tollveh via Dutowié to Sezana by car, and from there on we were to proceed by train to Laibach. We got there too late and had to stay overnight in Sezana in the Hotel Central.

9 April 1916
Departure to Laibach.

10 April 10
At midnight we travelled back to Kraina Vas.

11 April, 7 pm
The whole battalion marched off to Dutovié where we boarded a train! At about 9 o'clock our very long and packed train set off. We still didn't know what our final destination would be. Each of us had a go at guessing. One person thought this, another one, that. Görz [now a town in north-east Italy, Gorizia], Oslavija, Tolmein, Trieste and so on. All of us were really curious to know where destiny was leading us to. Our route took us through Laibach and Villach. In Villach we stopped for three hours. I took advantage of the opportunity and had a look round this small, unprepossessing but well-situated town. We still did not know where we were going to go. But we soon found out.

Chapter 2

Tyrol

Introduction by Hew Strachan

Over Christmas 1915 the chiefs of the general staffs of Germany and Austria-Hungary reviewed their options for 1916. When acting in collaboration in 1915, they had reversed the situation in Galicia, pushed Russia out of Poland and taken charge of the Baltic states. That autumn and winter, thanks not only to German cooperation but also to the entry of Bulgaria on the side of the Central Powers, Austria-Hungary had finally overrun Serbia. The Serb army was evacuated to Corfu and thence to Salonika, forming part of an allied front in Macedonia from early 1916. The effects of these successes did not stop there. By allying with Bulgaria and clearing the Danube, the Central Powers opened the direct route to Istanbul, enabling them to supply the Ottoman army on the Gallipoli peninsula and completing the defeat of the Entente in the Dardanelles.

However, the options which in early 1916 the chief of the German general staff, Erich von Falkenhayn, chose for Germany and Conrad von Hötzendorf selected for Austria-Hungary took them in divergent directions. Strategic cooperation was forfeit, with neither trusting the other and both developing plans without fully informing his partner. On 21 February 1916 Falkenhayn opened a limited offensive on the western front by attacking Verdun. He was convinced that Britain was the hub of the Entente and that, as a sea power, it could only be broken if its principal continental ally was also defeated. For Conrad, neither Britain nor France was a major consideration. The Habsburgs' enemies were closer to hand and, with both Russia and Serbia under the cosh, he decided he could turn defence against Italy into attack. His plan was a typical display of operational bravura, which looked imaginative on the map but would be much harder to implement in practice.

In May 1915 both Austria-Hungary and Italy had treated the northern sector of their joint front as secondary. The Alps provided Austria-Hungary with a natural line of defence. It pulled its limited forces back from the frontier, so enabling it to concentrate its strength on the upper and lower Isonzo. For Italy, the going in the mountains would be even tougher than on the Carso, nor was it likely to achieve its political objectives. The Italians waiting to be redeemed from Habsburg rule lay more to the east than the north. Conrad's plan for 1916 was to reverse this set of assumptions by exploiting the opportunity which the weighting towards the Isonzo had created. Southern Tyrol formed a natural salient as it followed the line of the Dolomites south-west to Trient (or Trent) and on to Lake Garda. The mountains screened the valley of the Etsch which provided a route to the south along which he could assemble an army to strike the rear of the Italian armies facing the Isonzo and cut their lines of communications. The operation was dubbed *die Strafexpedition*, 'the punishment expedition'. Its deep roots in Conrad's animosity towards Italy were updated by the need for vengeance following the betrayal of 1914.

To execute the attack, Austria-Hungary formed an army group for the first time. Placed under the command of Archduke Eugen, with Alfred Krauss as his chief of staff, it consisted of two armies, the 11th and the 3rd, commanded respectively by Viktor Dankl and Hermann Kövess von Kövesshaza. Divisions and guns were brought in from Galicia, but owing to Falkenhayn's objections not in the numbers Conrad wanted, and from the lower Isonzo. The withdrawal of III Corps from the Carso in February had been the beginning of a major shift in units which were redeployed behind the arc of the south-western front via Laibach, into the interior of Austria, and then fed into Tyrol from the north. On 6 April Barasch's battalion was withdrawn from Doberdò and placed in XVI Corps behind Gorizia. By the time it reached Tyrol it was in I Corps – commanded by Karl Freiherr von Kirchbach auf Lauterbach – in the 3rd Army.

Conrad had hoped that the thaw would be sufficiently advanced to be able to attack in early April but the weather worsened, and the offensive was postponed until 15 May. Despite the delay and the mounting intelligence of Austro-Hungarian troop movements which had been evident since late February, Cadorna refused to respond to the threat to his rear. The 11th Army, which was on the Austro-Hungarian right, led the way and achieved early success as it broke through and thrust south-east towards the plain of the Veneto. The 3rd Army, on its left, kept I Corps in reserve ready to exploit success where it came.

Barasch tells us that he was now part of the 21st Mountain Brigade. It had been formed from a Landsturm brigade and, when it arrived in the Dolomites, was exercised hard so that it became accustomed to the lower oxygen levels and steeper terrain in which it found itself. The signs of spring and the magnificent mountain-top views on clear days, when combined with the troops' growing fitness, clearly raised the morale of both Barasch and his comrades. The reports and then evidence of victory after 15 May added to the mood. As the advance achieved its initial successes, I Corps, comprising the 34th and 43rd Infantry Divisions, was fed into the battle, on the 3rd Army's right, so marching with the 11th Army on its left. Barasch tells us that the 21st Mountain Brigade was disbanded on 25 May but leaves it unclear in which unit his battalion was now serving. As he was in the front line in early June, it seems reasonable to conclude that it stayed with I Corps.

In the early morning of 27 May the whole of I Corps was committed to the capture of the Asiago plateau so as to enable the army group to break out of the mountains across the plain in a south-easterly direction. Casualty evacuation in mountain warfare was even harder than on the Carso. Barasch says that the nearest properly equipped hospital was at Brunech in the Puster valley (and today in Italy). Even further to the rear, the university hospital in Innsbruck was a centre of excellence and a reserve hospital had been established at Bozen (today Bolzano), but all three were too distant for swift treatment, and the routes to them for the most part lay along steep tracks and then mountain railways. Forward units in the Tyrol therefore needed to be more fully equipped and better staffed in order to be able to treat patients in the field. Brigades, rather than divisions, became the treatment hubs. Each had its own complement of three doctors, as well as integrated medical and transport establishments. At battalion level, the number of stretcher bearers was doubled and stretchers had to be hinged, so that the wounded could be carried vertically up and down steep inclines. Barasch reckoned each wounded man needed a team of eight to carry him and sought to set up a relay system so that the stretcher bearers would not waste too much time carrying empty stretchers on their return journeys.[1]

Falkenhayn reckoned the offensive in south Tyrol needed twenty-five divisions. It was never strong enough for the task which confronted it. Conrad wanted eighteen divisions but had fifteen. Germany's and Austria-Hungary's offensives, Verdun on the western front and the Trentino in Italy, had left them exposed to the Russians on the eastern front. At the beginning of June Brusilov broke through in Galicia, forcing the Germans and the Austro-Hungarians to break off their attacks and shift troops eastwards. Each tended to blame the other, and Conrad in particular was reluctant to give the enemy any credit for the outcome. However, his attack had already begun to lose momentum in late May. Cadorna, albeit belatedly, moved 180,000 troops west from the Isonzo to form a new 5th Army. It was enough to check the Austro-Hungarians on the Asiago and to block their exits from the mountains. The *Strafexpedition* reached its high watermark on 12 June. I Corps launched its last major attack on 15 June, but it was checked the following day. By 30 June Archduke Eugen's army group had fallen back and taken up defensive positions.

---

1. Biwald, *Von Helden und Krüppeln*, Vol. 1, pp. 59, 68–70; Vol. 2, pp. 392–3, 408–9.

13 April 1916
On April 13 at 7 o'clock in the morning we reached Frati during a festival. From here we carried on via Busen and Bozen to Lana-Burgstall. Here we alighted from our train around 1 o'clock in the afternoon and marched via Gargazon to Vilpian. In this place we found accommodation. It is located in the splendid valley of the River Etsch.

We are attached here to the 21st Mountain Brigade, 1st Corps and 3rd Army (Kövess).

28 April 1916
We only stayed for two weeks in Vilpian. During this time I had, of course, to take part with my battalion in a mountain training exercise marching via Schlaueid to Molten (1,133m high). Apart from that we had an inspection by our army commanders, His and Her Excellencies Kövess and Kövesska [Hermann Kövess von Kövesshaza]. These fine days went by very quickly for us. I undertook almost daily, in the company of certain comrades, excursions that took in the surrounding area. I spent one day in Smerau. We visited sometimes the beehives further out in Mals (I myself, Lieutenant Swabensky and Lieutenant Colonel Radomcić) where we made the acquaintance of the castle's owner, Mr Carli, and his daughter, Helene. Here, in the splendid park, we spent some lovely hours.

The three of us also rode to Payersburg, of which only a small part is well maintained. For the most part it is in ruins. At present it belongs to a family of winegrowers (Malpaka). Then again we spent an afternoon in Prossian, a big village in the mountains high up. On our travels we came next to Wehrburg, then to Fallburg, both well maintained and partly lived in by castle staff. In the distance we also saw the Zwingenburg. All the time that we were here we had very good weather.

For three days now we have had a new commander, Lieutenant Colonel Theumer. Today we are marching. Only at half-past one in the afternoon will we board a train in Lana-Burgstall. The order came through today at 4 o'clock in the morning quite unexpectedly. Energetic preparations for our departure must be made. Where we are actually going, none of us knows. Each of us is eager to guess. Each of us is very curious.

29 April 1916
The train took us via Bozen, Buxen, Franzensfeste and Brunech to Olang. We are now in the valley of the Puster over 1,000m above sea level. We were quartered in Lower Olang and our baggage train in Middle Olang. Because of the difference in height the climate here is much rawer than in the valley of the Etsch. What an enormous difference in the topographical layout and vegetation. The vine no longer prospers here. Those sun-kissed laughing hills with their heavy burden of vineyards that come to meet you everywhere are not in evidence here.

The Rienz flows here, a tributary of the Eisack that pours itself into the Etsch.

30 April 1916
Today at half-past seven in the morning we have to leave here again and march to Niedersdorf, a place 15km from here in the direction of Toblach.

1 May 1916
Since yesterday at noon we are in <u>Niedersdorf</u>, a fairly big, well-situated place in the valley of the Puster. The idea was that we should go to Monte Viano from here, from where the enemy is firing on Toblach. Each of us would have been well satisfied with this wartime decision. Unfortunately, we again got the command tonight to march out. Tomorrow at 5 o'clock in the morning we must go to Brunech. We have about 25km we need to put behind us.

1 May 1916
Almost midnight already. I can't get to sleep. At the moment I am very nervous. Actually, the whole of my nervous system is in a constant state of tension. I can hardly believe that an equilibrium will be able to re-establish itself. The most varied of thoughts are going through my brain at random and the most varied feelings are all mixed up in me, discomfort on the one hand and longing on the other – these are the bottom lines in my mindset. Longing for something tender, incomprehensible, hard to define.

2 May 1916
We are on the march from Niedersdorf via Welsberg to Brunech. We are even having a little rest on the other side of Vercha, a very small locality. This for the second time during our march. The first time we stopped at the Windschirm Guesthouse. Here I took a photograph. The soldiers on the march resting with their officers in the foreground with the Anthalzer valley and the place called Anthalz in the middle ground and the mountains in the background. The weather was most favourable. A cool and calm day. The Rienz accompanies us with its dull and mysterious rushing noise. The birds are singing prettily. The woods are standing there, dumb and blessed in all their splendour. Deep peace reigns both far and near in the valley of the Puster. An untroubled and idyllic picture. We could almost forget all the horror of this dreadful war, all the nastiness and cruelty which is being played out not so far from here, up there in the snow-covered mountains.

5 May 1916
It's three days today since we set out from Brunech. We only stayed there one night. Already, on the third day of the month, early in the morning, we marched out. Our route lay this time via Montal and Zwischenwasser to St Vigil, a village situated at a height of over 1,200m. Here we are housed in the Monte Sella Hotel.

6 May 1916
Life in St Vigil is truly pleasant. You feel the war here very little. Undisturbed, peace reigns over this place and over the whole romantic surrounding area. All you can hear is the rushing and splashing of the St Vigil stream. It hurries towards the Pustertal to join up with the Rienz with the help of the Gaderbach. To the south-west a splendid panoramic view stretches out. Huge, snow-covered, untamed, silent giants rise up in the Dolomites to which the eye of every newcomer turns. They close off the valley at this point. To the north-east the valley narrows and deepens. Hardly a kilometre away from St Vigil is the village of Montal. All these places were very popular with foreign tourists during peacetime and, for this reason, everywhere there are guesthouses and hotels. I share a most agreeable room with a balcony

here with Lieutenant Sowabensky in the Hotel Monte Sella [converted to a hospital for officers during the First World War]. If only we could enjoy this peace here for as long as possible. Unfortunately, we will soon have to go from here. We have to go back to the Keves 3rd Army. In the meantime, I want to make good use of my time and after surgery hours undertake daily excursions.

7 May 1916
Today we marched out of St Vigil at 4 o'clock in the afternoon to go to Tamers. We're staying overnight there to leave at 6 o'clock tomorrow morning for Pedern. From there, mountain manoeuvres for one day to take us as far as Fodara Vedla (1,991m) where our two lines are. From there back to St Vigil.

9 May 1916
Yesterday at 5 o'clock in the afternoon we got back from our mountain manoeuvres. The weather was bad. It was raining. There is still a lot of snow. At Fodara Vedla the frontier sector deputy commander, Lieutenant Colonel von Barth, was waiting for us with his adjutant and explained to us the positioning of our lines. What with the murky weather and all, we could not see very much. Monte Cadini lay clearly visible in front of us. It is occupied by us. We could also observe the area around Monte Cristallo. The latter, for the most part, is in enemy hands.

After the climb down we stopped in Pedern to rest for a couple of hours. Here we took in supplies. From here we marched on to St Vigil.

* * *

A photograph of Lavinores with a great snowfield in the background. In the foreground Rita, our St Bernard, whose job it is to seek out a patient and lead our paramedic to him.

* * *

Today a new unhoped-for command came from the frontier sector vice-command. Our companies have to leave St Vigil, partly to go to Pedern, and partly back to Fodara Vedla and Stuva in order to stay there for a time. Battalion staff officers will stay till further notice in St Vigil. I am still awaiting orders. I don't know where I'll be sent. The battalion is scattered. We can't know what might happen here from one minute to the next. We are constantly up in the air. We need to be ready to march at all times.

* * *

About 4 o'clock in the afternoon I undertook a short excursion. I went to Soleneid and from there to the Grand Joch (1,655m high). From here I was able to overlook the splendid, untamed valley of the Gaderbach. A clear, sunny, warm day. Before me, beyond the valley, a long chain of mountains with extensive permanent snowfields.

10 May 1916
I travelled to Pedern by car to carry out my duty as a doctor there. There I took some photographs. (The Little Fanes Alp, the Col de Ru and the Tamerswand.)

About 3 o'clock in the afternoon I travelled to Brunech for the purpose of procuring medical supplies. The former is a tiny, neat but very dull little town in the valley of the Puster on the River Rienz. I stayed overnight. The following day – i.e. 11 May, I went back to St Vigil in Enneberg.

13 May 1916
At 10 in the morning we (Sowabensky and myself) left St Vigil and rode to Pedern and from there via Val a Salata to Stuva (1,695m) where our frontier sector HQ is encamped. It was a rainy day. On high ground it has snowed a great deal. We reached Stuva about 4 o'clock in the afternoon. The camp was built by Bavarian troops who have been defending this frontier sector for months. [The German Alpenkorps, trained for mountain warfare and commanded by the Bavarian general, Krafft von Dellmensingen, had been sent to the Tyrol front in May 1915.] All the barracks here are very well built.

There was a bathing shack in which I was immediately able to take a tub bath. A fine and comfortable barracks adjoining the officers' mess where we sat down for an evening meal. About 11 o'clock at night we took leave of the company and proceeded to our barracks.

14 May 1916
The whole night through I was unable to fall asleep. A hard, makeshift bed that it was not easy to get on friendly terms with. Rather cold as well. And my nerves that have already lost so much of their power to resist. Nor is it any wonder.

* * *

How beautifully the little birds are singing in the wood today. As if they didn't have a care in the world. They are twittering and trilling all around and do not allow themselves to be disturbed by all the ugliness that has been enacted in this vicinity for months now.

I have just got back from a pleasant time out with Medical Assistant Dr Lechner, a general practitioner from the Salzkammergut. He is a good-natured, jolly man. Apart from me, Lieutenant Colonel Radomcić (a high school teacher from Ragusa) and Ensign Mrazek (a Viennese lawyer) were also present. Outside it is raining steadily today. All the mountains roundabout are covered in dense mist. The damp cold and the mud are a source of discomfort. About half-past seven I shall go again to the mess.

11 o'clock at night. I have just got back from the mess. We had some fun there tonight. We sang a lot and laughed a lot. On this occasion it was more agreeable than usual as we spoke less about war-related things and duty than is normally the case. A lot of this is probably due to the fact that today is Sunday, and, because of this, we have had beer again, which all of us have looked forward to all day long. Also, our frontier subsector commander was less excited and distracted than he usually is. (His name is Lieutenant Colonel von Barth of the Imperial Rangers.) His adjutant, Lieutenant Colonel Wodenensky, did not try once to lay aside his workaday countenance.

The battle sector commander, Captain Irlweg (at the same time battalion commander of the 68th Third Reserve Infantry Battalion) has not been able to find time enough or opportunity to develop his plans for defence and attack. He is, by the way, an intelligent and energetic man. He is always on the look out for new ways of frightening the enemy, of leading him astray, of making out that we have enormous power on our side. He is always talking about barbed wire barriers and roadblocks with which he hopes to effectively baulk the enemy's way forward. He already has the Order of the Crown *Signum Laudis*, but this is not enough for him and will not suffice for the long years of peace still to come.

The padre was playing this time as he always does, and as all the other members of his profession do, the role of the innocent, chaste, holy knight.

Dr Lechner was, as always, cheerful. He is a great drinker, and it is all one to him what form the alcohol takes which he is offered. He drinks beer with as much gusto as he does wine and rum, laughs incessantly, and keeps a cigar in his mouth as he does so. A really nice man.

Artillery Major Artaria, a distinguished old gentleman, tells us, from time to time, tongue-in-cheek jokes. He is from Vienna. He possesses an art dealership on the Coalmarket.

Ensign Mrazek spoke a good deal as is his wont and raised his glass diligently. To put it in a nutshell, it was fun in the mess for once.

Many gentlemen have remained there. They are carrying on drinking and playing cards.

Outside it is still raining. When will it brighten up? I'd like to go out.

15 May 1916
Today I was at Monte Cadini (2,363m above sea level.) Very fine weather with a clear view. I got a very good overall view of the whole of the beautiful Ampezzo valley with the charming, daintily meandering path through the Dolomites and the greenish Borte Stream running alongside it, the long ribbon of Cortina d'Ampezzo further out towards the south and a place called Zuel. The latter in a southerly direction.

In the south-east the Fiammes lifts its head, obscured in front by the small Monte Pezzovica. On the latter is a fine hairpin bend which leads to the enemy's so-called Pezzovica battery. In the south-west there is the huge, wild Tofana Massif (over 3,200m high) with the little Col Rosa in front of it. On the latter another hairpin bend is visible which leads between Col Rosa and Monte Pezzovica to enemy batteries and on which is situated the ruined castle of Peutelstein. Our army's high command left the whole of this area right from the start of the war voluntarily to the castle's heir. We have fallen back on our present positions. These are Monte Cadini, San Pauses, Il Fallè, the area round Fanes.

16 May 1916
We are on the way from Stuva to St Vigil. Having a little rest in the valley of Salata. I am sitting in the middle of a one might almost say endless, undulating snowfield. The snow in places is up to 5m deep as a result of sliding avalanches. In front of me, coming in from the south-east and south-west, tower the jagged, steep, silent, wild giants of the Dolomites. In the foreground loom the Lavinores and Monte Cadini. Further back are the Cresta Bianca and Col dei Stombi as is the jagged peak of Monte Cristallo. In the distance big guns are thundering incessantly. Our offensive was due to start yesterday. Already today we had news of victories. We learnt of them during the midday meal in Stuva. In the region around Laorine 2,500 prisoners were taken, 15 guns and 30 machine guns captured. Fifty officers too were made prisoner.

18 May 1916, In St Vigil in Enneberg
What a really good afternoon I have just had! A hot clear day. The whole of nature is bursting out all over hereabouts. All the broad, fresh, green, fragrant meadows, the many small and high-up lushly wooded hills, all the mountain huts, small and simple it's true, but gazing proudly down at you from on high and then the hollow-sounding, intensely rushing mountain springs.

I had a walk along the path marked out in red which leads to the Kronplatz, a mountain which is over 2,000m high. I only got halfway

Portrait photograph of Dr Isaak Barasch.

Lea Barasch Mehlsak, Dr Barasch's mother.

Pages from Dr Isaak Barasch's diary, written in German.

A formal studio portrait of Dr Isaak Barasch and members of his family, 1914. He is seated on the right. Standing next to him is his younger brother, Leon Barasch. Seated on the left is his sister, Klara, and behind her is their cousin, Dr Schilem Jung, an attorney who will later marry Klara.

Moses Mehlsak, Dr Barasch's father.

Dr Isaak Barasch with his cousin, Dr Schilem Jung, on his father's estate, *c.* 1910.

Dr Barasch (with the small letter x over his head), 15 January 1912. On the back of this photograph he wrote: 'Photo taken during a clinical lecture in the new 1st medical clinic of Professor Carl von Noorden. It was the day of my practical.'

A photograph taken in a studio in Vienna, 24 December 1914, the date of the famous Christmas Truce. Dr Isaak Barasch, in civilian clothes, is seated next to a close friend or relative in military uniform. On the back he writes in Polish in a light-hearted tone: 'If you follow our example you will be Austria's best son.' He signs it I. Mehlsak.

Dr Isaak Barasch standing in front of the army field hospital in Grassaga, November 1917. 'We are already in the fortieth month of the war and the men just as much as officers have had more than enough of this wicked war', he wrote at the time.

Dr Isaak Barasch wrote on the back of this photograph: 'At "Makuči" medical help centre, Me, Medical Orderly Sadek and a not seriously wounded ensign in December 1916.' In the diary on 21 December 1916, Morning, he writes: 'Today I will be relieved of my duties at the Makuci medical centre and go (with the whole battalion naturally) to Ossegliano.'

Dr Isaak Barasch standing on the extreme left with a group of officers.

A group photograph, 17 December 1917. Dr Barasch is not present in the group. In his diary around this date he writes about his efforts to build a bathhouse for the soldiers.

Dr Barasch, second from left, with fellow soldiers in front of a coffee house. The sign is in German.

Dr Isaak Barasch seated in the centre of a group of medical officers in Grassaga, 1917.

Dr Barasch on a well-deserved break from his military duties.

Dr Isaak Barasch on a sea trip in the Kvarner Gulf of Fiume (now Rijeka), April 1917. On the back of the photograph, he writes: 'With Dr Gauss, Garasey his daughter and her fiancé.'

Dr Barasch's younger brother, Leon (standing), on the Italian front, 1918.

Dr Yoel Chaim Mehlman, Dr Barasch's brother-in-law, another family member who enlisted in the service of the Austro-Hungarian army, on the Russian front. Dr Mehlman and wife, Helen, immigrated to New York and took the diaries with them after Dr Barasch's death.

Dr Isaak Barasch's gravestone in the Jewish section of Vienna's Zentralfriedhof cemetery, the largest in Europe's.

and contented myself with the splendid view which I had from here over St Vigil, Montal, the little groups of houses clustered round them and the mountains. Here I lay down in the grass. Various flowers (the purple gentian especially and, in addition, a purple primula and the yellow first flower of spring) adorn in beautiful patches too numerous to mention all the meadows in which everywhere goats and sheep are grazing. In the fields women are working busily and each one is wearing a small straw hat on her head, which looks quite comical. The men all had to go off to war and leave all the work to the women.

20 May 1916, 3 am
Today I'm not sleeping very well. I preferred to light the candle nearby rather than gaze into the darkness. In the deep stillness of the night I can hear the noise of the close, quickly rushing stream that with the thaw of spring carries off more and more meltwater out of the mountains towards the valley of the Puster in the direction of the Rienz. It is coming down now to more peaceful and calmer regions. Perhaps it has been forced to see up there the sad drama of war during the thaw, this dumb witness. Yes, they're going at it hammer and tongs there. Our offensive is in full swing and has already until now a fine list of successes to its credit. After yesterday's court report we have already in this short period taken more than 10,000 prisoners, captured more than 60 guns and several machine guns. We have gained a lot more space to breathe in. Our main force falls back on the line that links Mori, Marco, Zugua Torta, the northern slopes of Monte Santo, Monte Maggio, Campomolone, with what hopes, what expectations.

25 May 1916, After Midnight
A great change has come over our battalion. Our battalion commander Lieutenant Colonel Temner was today ordered away from us. Also, our battalion no longer belongs to the 21st Mountain Brigade as this has been disbanded. I don't know what will happen to me in the next few days, to where I will be directed. Perhaps to Stuva?! We live in a constant state of uncertainty, and this is what poisons our life here so much. For my part I have gone through enough already in this war. I would certainly not be able to put all of this into words. All the

events great and small. All that I have had to witness and go along with. It might well be high time for people to give it a rest. We could quite easily take one of the innumerable gentlemen who have so far been spared participation in the war and who away from the front are leading a comfortable, even luxurious life and have them serve at the front. They too should get acquainted with the pleasures of waging war …

How monotonous, grey, and dreary life is here in this remote piece of earth between high mountains. We are here quite cut off from the outside world. We move in such a narrow, dull round of duty rosters, live constantly in the gloomy workshop of war, hear of precious little else other than attacks, patrols, prisoners, dead and wounded, etc. I have had enough of all that. It's high time that I could breathe freely again. For the time being unfortunately I have no such prospects.

3 June 1916
A few days ago something changed in the battalion. Our Lieutenant Colonel Temner was relieved of his duties as battle-sector commander of Frontier Subsector X (Marmolata). Its seat is in Arabba not far from Corvara. The oldest officer of rank in our battalion, Captain Konrad, has taken over the command. He is in Fanes as battle-sector commander of G.U.A. 96. I myself will now have to go there as the greater part of our battalion will be leaving Stuva for Fanes.

* * *

Not long ago our battalion suffered some losses here. There were four men wounded and two killed in 20 Company at Croda and Ancona in one night. The enemy, that is to say, tried to attack Peutelstein from Croda. They failed in this. Three times they tried it and three times 20 Company beat them off and were lucky to sustain so few losses.

* * *

Afternoon
This whole way of life here poisons me, kills me, robs me of all my joy in living, saps all my strength completely, actually brings me to the point of despair. The bad weather only adds to my problems, this constant rain we have been having for days now. Not the slightest let-up. We are completely thrown back on our own devices. There is no warm or sympathetic person that we could turn to at a pinch. No noble or sympathetic soul. If only I had something to do that could bring me inner peace. I have been feeling for days and weeks now a limitless emptiness. I am quite alone. My other comrades, who are still here, have it better. The company of stupid, unintelligent, dirty farm girls, with whom they spend all of their free time, is enough for them. They are quite satisfied with it. They visit all the outlying places just to seek out new girls. I can't do that unfortunately. I therefore admire their ability to sit and chat with them for hours on end. I prefer to live in solitude rather than make such overtures.

I am, by the by, an odd person who cannot easily adapt to new situations. Apart from that, things here would be fine. The place we're in is a beauty spot. The only things missing are a society in harmony with it and a serious occupation to pursue.

After two days I am going from here to the mountains. A small change would perhaps be as good as a rest for me, for a while at least.

4 June 1916
Outside it's raining more and more heavily. All the surrounding mountains and hills are totally submerged in thick mist. Likewise, the mountain huts that are strewn everywhere hereabouts, singly or in small groups. Only here and there, out of this thick white, grey veil, a church tower looms. I need to stay in my room where I can deal with all my correspondence.

I have also written to a man I got to know in Vilpian and who has aroused my greatest interest. This is Lieutenant Colonel Scholz, the well-known Viennese painter, a very interesting, idiosyncratic person. He is the same age as I am. A very modest, undemanding, introspective, self-controlled man who feels quite ill at ease in his officer's uniform. He holds a high office. That is to say that he commands a small detachment of workers and has to keep the streets and bridges in order, a truly edifying occupation for such a high priest of art. Is it not a miserable misuse of this man's talents to use him for work like this? I pitied him.

Today I'm sending him the following letter. I hope he'll receive it. Probably he is still poste restante in Meran.

> My Very Esteemed and Dear Scholz!
> Do you still remember me, for it was granted to me, approximately one month ago in Vilpian after such a long, futile, wartime existence, the chance to spend a highly poetic hour talking to you that lifted my spirits?! You told me at that time truly fine things. I saw clearly how all this beauty sprang forth out of your innermost depths as you talked about painting and high art to me. This was a view of life arrived at through fine, tender feeling, highmindedness and hard work in which I was able to feel so much that was great and elevated. I often think about all this. Unfortunately, it was not vouchsafed me to listen to you more frequently. Orders called you away from Vilpian the following day and I too had very soon to move on. It would give me great pleasure if you could write to me just once. I further harbour the fond hope of being able to see you back in Vienna once again after this awful war is over. Cordially yours. I wish you all the best. An unpretentious comrade. Fieldpost Nº 601 on 4 June 1916. I have addressed the letter to poste restante in Meran.

5 June 1916

Adieu, you fair St Vigil! With your good Monte Sella. Adieu, you broad green meadows with all your enchanting splendour of bloom. Adieu, all you little villages up there that gaze trustfully down into the valley. Adieu, all you proud hills. You rushing streams and fragrant pine forests, adieu!! I am taking my leave of you. Farewell, you pious Latin populace with your language that is incomprehensible to me and may you diligently cultivate your fertile open fields. And you, old rattling watermill, whose sound is everywhere audible here. Today I must separate from all of you.

I must go on to the mountains, obedient to the call of the hour.

My bundle is lying there already tied up. Tomorrow at dawn I have to march away from here.

I'll see you again in the course of the war. And when the war is once over and fate in the meantime has not snuffed me out. If the bloodletting stops and I am still among the living, you'll see me again, fair St Vigil, and then I want to enjoy all your splendour unmolested.

It's 2 o'clock in the morning already and I can't get to sleep. The god of sleep has been quite cruel to me for some days now. I don't know how it came about that I forfeited his favour. He is a most capricious god. My wish is that I could get in his good books again. Then I could, if only for a few hours, forget about these tragic times and this awful war. How good this would make me feel. Alas!! This won't happen.

6 June 1916
At 7 o'clock this morning the three of us left St Vigil (me, Mandolfo and Temo) and proceeded to the Fanes barrier. All three of us were on horseback. The weather was dreadful. It was cold. The sky was covered in heavy dark clouds. It started very soon to rain cats and dogs. In Pedern we consumed a modest breakfast and had our horses fed and watered. Shortly afterwards we continued our journey. The rain became ever more driving and unrelenting. In Little Fanes we stopped more than half an hour so as to be able to eat our midday meal. It soon began to snow heavily. An unpleasant, damp, and cold snowstorm that lasted a long time. We went on further via Gross Fanes to the Fanes barrier. Here you can hear an intense thunder of guns. The enemy has of late engaged us with lively fire. Today four men were wounded by enemy gunfire.

7 June 1916
Today <u>early I received the news that I have been appointed head doctor with corresponding rank as from 1 May</u>.

Today our own artillery as well as that of the enemy opened heavy fire throughout the afternoon. The enemy also attacked at several points. Especially Croda d'Ancona and Il Fallè. Il Fallè stood for many hours under heavy fire whereupon the attack made by enemy infantry stopped. The attack was turned away by our 17th Company under the command of Lieutenant Colonel Rossi. There were considerable losses on both sides. On our side sixteen men were wounded, four killed.

At the Fanes barrier this afternoon a sapper was badly wounded. A shot to the head with brain prolapse and resulting loss of consciousness. I saw to him but have not the slightest hope of him staying alive. The Italians also sustained losses today (inflicted by Company 18). They ended up with five dead, among them a medic who took a shot to the head in front of our barbed wire and fell down dead. The latter came into our hands and was also buried by us.

Reinforcements were brought up.

8 June 1916
Early. I have just been woken up. I am experiencing a general dull feeling of discomfort, exhaustion, and overall fatigue. Late at night we left the mess. For purely social reasons I stayed till almost 2 o'clock in the morning with the others. One is almost obliged to keep one's comrades company and for them sitting in the mess, breathing in the stale, close, smoky air of this tiny shack, empty chitchat, drinking sour red wine and smoking gives them a lot of pleasure. And I, of course, have to tag along with them, which I am always quite reluctant to do. I cannot do otherwise. The number of messmates was small last night so my sudden disappearance would have left a gap. Among those present were Captain Konrad, our battle-sector commander, who takes the greatest pleasure in staying as late as possible. His adjutant, Lieutenant Colonel Mandolfo, me, our quartermaster Ensign Temo and a first lieutenant of artillery, Dr Weiss, from Budapest, were also there. There were besides four officers from Standschützen (one major and three first lieutenants) who cannot be taken into consideration socially as they are rather unintelligent people who belong to the lower classes (pub landlords, farmers, chimney sweeps even). They feel this and soon draw back from involvement. [The Standschützen were raised in Tyrol and Voralberg from men aged over 45 and youths under 16 and were formed in 30 battalions to guard rear areas in Tyrol; they mustered about 40,000 men.] We, therefore, make up only a very limited company here. Going for walks, reading, and writing give me far more pleasure.

Yesterday afternoon I was in our battle-sector trenches in the front line. Three to four lines have been built here one behind the other with barbed wire obstacles and barbed wire blocks. I was surprised at how much work has gone into building running trenches and shelters up until now despite all the great problems that topography, climate, and nature itself constitute for man here in the mountains. For a certain time to begin with there were Bavarian Alpine troops and then, in their turn, several of our own select groups of soldiers. Each brought to this work the best they were capable of. Once the enemy succeeded in breaking through here. Bavarian troops were driven back over the Limojoch. These positions were won back by our troops, however, and well defended too. And how well these positions have been built up here and how flawlessly maintained. All the forests here in the valley have delivered their quota of building material. The immaculate shelters for the men are hard by the running trenches, so that a man does not even have to leave the trench. And then officers' shelters – excellent villas made out of wood. And the many other fine barracks buildings which serve as munitions depots, kitchens, and chanceries. A whole new world in this otherwise unfriendly land. Man has understood how to tame nature. The trenches between the steep, rugged, wild wall of Il Fallè and Monte Vallon Bianco well to the fore, far from the splendid Fanes waterfall, together make up the so-called Fanes barrier adjoined by the Trabenanzes barrier which likewise belongs to our battle sector. Here is our Company 20 with Lieutenant Colonel Kourtier as their commander. These positions are really uncomfortable since the enemy can dominate them from above and can, in addition to that, fall upon us in our rear through gullies.

Yesterday a substantial enemy patrol dared to come quite close to our positions. It was driven off leaving five of its members dead before reaching our trenches. Some of them were wounded too. The dead had to stay where they lay because of the heavy fire. At night the enemy succeeded in taking four of them away. The one left behind we could still see today, face to face, in a crouching position. There are a lot of missiles flying around. The two big guns housed in two caves on Col Rosa spit out constant fire from their hellish, murderous maw. The rattle of machine-gun fire on both sides. Here and there the rifle fire of infantry assaults. And in the middle of it are our sappers, quite at home, working. They are putting up bridges, felling trees, building new shelters. It's a strange business, all of this.

9 June 1916
A short time ago a man was brought to me who had been badly wounded. It's another sapper. They are more at risk from danger than others since they cannot always find cover in their various occupations and are seen more easily by the enemy. This poor man had sustained a very serious wound. A shot through the face with its point of entry at the left temple and its exit point through the bridge of the nose on the left. A high level of oedema in the right eye, especially on the eyelid. I saw to him most carefully. I have, in view of the prevailing conditions hereabouts, a rather spacious medical centre. I am also sufficiently well equipped with bandages and medicaments. These things are not always so easy for us to obtain here. A rather large expenditure of energy is required for us to get something. We have enough money for all sorts of things, but there is always, I'm afraid, a lack of medical supplies. Thrift takes pride of place. One needs to know how to tackle those in positions of power.

Arrangements to ferry the wounded elsewhere leave a lot to be desired. They have to be carried on stretchers all the long way to Pedern through mountainous terrain. Each wounded person will be carried away from here by eight men who constantly relieve one another. At the same time, a request is received from Pedern by telephone that another eight men be sent. On the way to their final destination the latter take the wounded man and carry him further while the original team of eight go back. This is a really complicated way of doing things and it takes a long time until the wounded man finally arrives at a well-equipped hospital. This is, of course, in Brunech. Badly wounded cases are sent there in pushcarts from Pedern.

Today one man was killed in our trenches who was buried in the nearby cemetery.

We stayed in the mess tonight for a very long time again (till 1 o'clock at night). We played tarot and chess.

10 June 1916
Today is a cold, rainy day. Here and there the enemy tried to approach our positions during the course of the day but was repelled. The sound of a dull, long drawn-out roar up in the mountains, the thunder of enemy guns. Our guns too were not silent.

Towards evening it began to snow.

If the statements of odd deserters are anything to go by, the enemy wants at all costs to break through here so as to be able to get to the valley of the Puster. On our side there was quite a lot of excitement.

1 June 1916
The enemy is bringing up ever new reinforcements. He obviously attaches great importance to achieving success here. He is undertaking attack after attack. Yesterday he succeeded temporarily in penetrating our defences near Rufiedo.

Today enemy detachments again overran our positions in Croda d'Ancona. But very soon they were driven back.

On our side counter-measures were devised. New guns are being brought up. A 30.5 mortar to Pedern. Two 10cm calibre guns in the Fanestal. Only men are in short supply. We need them but don't have them. We are in a grave situation right now.

14 June 1916
Today I was on sentry duty on Monte Vallon Bianco (2,684m). The climb up lasted about two-and-a-half hours, the descent taking only half an hour as I was able to slide down very fast on the snow.

From up here you have a view of the Tofana, part of the Travenanzestal, and the whole of the Fanestal with all the mountains round it.

This sentry duty at altitude (ten men) is designed to secure our positions in the valley of the Travenanz against enemy attack in our rear.

15 June 1916
Around 10 o'clock in the morning, i.e. after my surgery, I proceeded to our positions. I stayed there all day. It was a day of lively enemy

activity. San Pauses and Malga were both under fire. The enemy shelled these positions with heavy artillery. There were constant explosions of shells and shrapnel. Great clouds of smoke, here black, there greyish blue, spread out on all sides. A dull sound of thunder. An echo in the mountains. As if these dumb, proud giants wanted to express indignation that people dare to disturb their holy and eternal rest. Here and there heavy shelling fell on positions in Il Fallè. But our guns too did not stand idle. They held under a barrage the positions of enemy reservists in order to prevent any action on the part of the enemy's infantry. All of this I could see quite clearly from our own battle-sector trenches. Even the latter were not spared. They came under heavy infantry fire. The bullets whistled and buzzed all over the place. Also, yesterday part of our running trench was destroyed as a result of heavy artillery fire.

16 June 1916
A sad piece of news. During yesterday's attack by the enemy two of our officers were killed. Lieutenant Colonel of Artillery Sommer and an ensign.

18 June 1916
I was once again on sentry duty on the slopes of Monte Vallon Bianco.

23 June 1916
Today I was on Col Becchei (2,730m) in our gunnery position. An 8cm field gun is deployed here, which has, in particular, to keep under fire the guns in caves on Col Rosa and, in addition, Frammes, the enemy camp on the Firenzesattel and Pontalto. From here we have a broad, very rewarding view.

Our way lay next from the valley of the Fanes in a north-westerly direction to the lake at Limojoch (2,157m) and from there north-east over a well-maintained hairpin. Far away to the south-west the Marmolata glacier lay before me. More in the foreground, the small, dark, awesome, blood-drenched Col dei Lama ridge. And also the Siefsattel. Both of them burial grounds for tens of thousands. Both dumb witnesses to the cruellest and bloodiest of struggles. In great numbers and with a huge expenditure of force the enemy mounted attack after attack at this point. He wanted to break through in order to have a shortcut to the Pustertal railway. Our side, however, offered strong resistance accompanied, of course, by an enormous number of losses. The pretty valley of the Lagaco allows one a glimpse of those mountains that rise up a long way off in the background.

3 July 1916
Today I went to Monte Castello (2,809m high) to another of our gunnery positions. Here and there are two Gem field artillery pieces housed in good, deep caves hewn out of rock. One of them has its sights trained on the observation platform (belonging to the enemy of course) on Tofana I. These are guns with a very old operating system, the accuracy of which leaves a lot to be desired. I stayed up here for about two hours and a storm set in quite unexpectedly, heavy rain, hail, and a cold wind. I spent this time in the officers' shelter in the company of the commanding officer, a lieutenant of artillery. About 6 o'clock in the evening, when the storm had blown over, I started the descent of the mountain. Now I was able to observe the splendid chain of the Zillertaler Alps in a north-westerly direction. In the south-east lay the three Tofanas, the ravine of the Travenanz and so on.

Before my climb up I visited, on the Gross Fanes Alp, the group commander of artillery for this sector, Lieutenant Colonel Kostner who, in civilian life, is a big businessman from Innsbruck. I stayed for lunch. I took a few photographs as well. This high, broad, ancient mountain is beautiful, surrounded as it is by numerous fissured, jagged peaks. Through the narrow valley of the Lagaco one can view Sivelea far off over the Marmolata glacier. At least one can breathe much more easily than in the narrow clefts of the Fanestal where one cannot move without feeling exposed to the danger of being spotted by enemy observers on Col Rosa. One feels safer here.

A few days ago on the 25th of last month I was with Lieutenant Colonel Flick, the commander of the 1st Alpine Detachment. I spent a night in his really pleasant, rather cosy, well-situated shelter in the narrow gorge of the Travenanz on the bank of the wild, roaring Travenanz stream at the foot of the great, rugged, mighty rock walls of the Tofana Massif. On one side, Monte Vallon Bianco and, on the other, the summits of the Furcia Rossa and the tower of the Fanes. The following day I visited, in the company of Lieutenant Dr Bartscher, the highest lookout post in this sector on Tofana III. The route naturally presents many difficulties for the mere tourist and requires heads that are not subject to dizziness. Here we were shot at efficiently by enemy lookouts. Our repeating rifles answered them back with rapid fire. A hell of a racket. Shots whistled past us. None of us were injured.

4 July 1916
Today I learnt that, in accordance with Royal and Imperial Army decree number 93, I have been decorated *Signum Laudis* (as a mark of distinction) for my efforts at Doberdò.

9 July 1916
There has reigned here from early this morning a great deal of excitement. We have received a most disturbing piece of news. Our positions at the 'Forcella della fontana negra' (Black Fountain Pass) fell during the night into enemy hands. This happened in the sector directly appertaining to us (viz. the whole of our right flank in the Travenanz sector). Their commander, Captain Baboka, was wounded in this action and taken captive. This was an event that could have far-reaching consequences for our battle sector. The danger of being attacked on our right at the so-called Travenanz barrier is quite serious and even frontally (Firenzesattel), from the rear and from above (Lorto). They are already thinking about eventually surrendering this position. Today there is vigorous shooting. The Varga gunnery on Col Becchei di Sopra has received the order to fire on the Forcella della fontana negra. The gunfire constantly rolls and thunders over our heads. The enemy does not rest either. He sends us pieces of shrapnel. They explode high up over the valley. Somewhat haphazardly reinforcements are being brought up on our side.

And all this has happened just today on such a splendid, clear, sunny, warm, beaming day in these marvellous, awe-inspiring natural surroundings which everywhere offer their ripeness so copiously. Oh, you ungrateful, brutal, short-sighted, impotent, and yet so conceited humanity. From your tiny anthill you dare to climb to dizzy heights from which you must fall down.

13 July 1916

For roughly ten days there have been delays with the post. All letters have been held back in Innsbruck for a long time. A great many of them have gone missing. Each of us feels this very acutely! The writing and receiving of letters and cards is one of the pleasantest pastimes life has to offer. Today there was no post for me. Not even newspapers.

* * *

About 10 o'clock at night there came to our command HQ the quite unexpected and unpleasant order to advance a company of the 5th /37th to the Wolf-Clauvell Hut on Hill 1780 in the enemy held part of the Travenanzestal. The enemy is making efforts in the Col de Bois to attack the Bavarian so-called Frighteners. The company must be placed there while a serious action is in full swing in the sector commanded by Lieutenant Colonel Flick.

Early tomorrow a company of Tyrolean *chasseurs alpins* from Stuva are to come to reinforce us. [Bavarian and Tyrolean (i.e. Austro-Hungarian) troops trained in mountain warfare. The Tiroler Kaiserjaeger were an elite in the pre-1914 army. In December 1914 both Bavaria and Wuerttemberg raised ski units for mountain warfare and they were consolidated in Germany's Alpenkorps in 1915, which served on the Italian front. It went to Romania when the latter entered the war in September 1916 but returned to Italy for Caporetto in 1917.]

Towards midnight our Company 20 left to join the fray. The enemy means business with our elevated positions in the Travenanz area. He is also engaging in some very lively activity in front of our positions in the so-called Travenanz Barrier. There he is working diligently day and night. Preparations are being made. Saps are being constructed. Here and there our guns are trying to disturb the work. But it is coming on there in leaps and bounds. The thought of giving up our Travenanz positions is being pondered more and more.

14 July 1916

It is becoming ever more dangerous and ever more troubled here. Today two enemy artillery shells hit a shelter close to us. And when will it be our turn? For some time now our life has not been safe here.

15 July 1916

For the whole day it has intermittently snowed, hailed, and rained. Add to that uncomfortably low temperatures which one must feel all the more keenly as, during the day, one is not allowed to have a fire in the shelters. The resulting columns of smoke could betray the exact location of our camp to the enemy observer on Col Rosa. It's a bleak life we have to live. In addition, you can still constantly hear the explosions of enemy heavy artillery shells which occasionally land quite near to you. Then you forget completely about the cold outside. You feel icy cold inside.

Today we had two guests for lunch: Lieutenant Jugoneck Neumann, a Viennese gentlemen, and Lieutenant Colonel Erlsbacher, an Innsbrucker, the latter's Christian name being Lavinore or Herengist. He is the brigade's expert on Alpine matters. A man who constantly goes for walks in the high mountains and can take in his stride all the physical demands made on him as he is quite familiar with them. He has been staying now for a few days in Gross Fanes and now has the task of extending our elevated positions from Monte Castello via the twin peaks of Casale and Furcia Rossa as far as Monte Vallon Bianco. These places are now very important since Forcella della fontana negra fell into enemy hands. Formerly these high ridges were largely unoccupied. Now half of our own Company 17 is up there. God knows what people there have to put up with what with the cold and the snow and the rain, having to manage without shelters and without winter equipment to boot. This was only asked about and has been a long time in coming. Has mankind not yet had enough of all the awful evil that the war has conjured up? Can it not make an end of all this misfortune? It scarcely bothers to do so! It cannot come to a decision to do away with it. All this lies in the hands of individual consciences – and of unscrupulous individuals whose own interests take pride of place. Their ruthless personal ambition enslaves humanity and lets it bleed. And *Homo sapiens*, that cowardly creature, calmly puts up with this, accepts his fate and suffers in silence.

23 July 1916
Up until now we had unsettled weather. The sky is for the most part cloudy and the air distinctly cool. It rains, hails and snows very often. This morning was an exception, bright and fine. The sky today was clear, a deep shade of blue and we could at long last warm our limbs in the hot sun. This was a real pleasure for us. But it didn't last for long. Already in the afternoon thick, dark-grey clouds rolled in. They heralded the approaching storm which was not long in coming. A heavy downpour mixed with hail.

Now I am very busy in building a house for my patients. Of course, here in mountainous terrain, directly behind the front line, this is fraught with the greatest of difficulties. Building materials must, for the most part, be transported in by pack animals from Pedern. This is going to be a blockhouse (i.e. made from trunks of trees split in two and not from boards) capable of holding thirty beds. At the same time a bathhouse will be set up for the use of officers and men. Likewise, a delousing unit.

27 July 1916
I am really tired and stressed out now. I have had to work all through the night and was therefore unable to sleep. Several men were injured by the explosion of a hand grenade in the Travenanz barrier trenches and four, badly. An upper arm fracture, then skull and facial injuries with extensive tear wounds and contusions. It is not easy to work in the confined space of the medical centre under these miserable conditions. Added to this are the uneducated, clumsy, unintelligent paramedics that military regulations require to be here. Nothing changes. Step by step we must confront the greatest difficulties. Although we have been here for a year in our static positions, nothing is being done to alleviate the pain and suffering of the sick and wounded. And how much could have been done during this time! Many lives could have been saved. Nobody thought to worry about it. With us everything happens only because it has been ordered to happen. There is an overall

lack of initiative. And orders come down from high command, those gentlemen who lead a cosy, comfortable life well away from the front and who know very little about actual conditions here. They don't trust themselves to come out for once and see things for themselves. It is certainly much pleasanter to live in Brunech away from the shooting and have everything reported to you. Everywhere the same bureaucratic inertia, the same indolence.

How much I have had to fight for with all these gentlemen until I got all the necessary means to build the new house for the patients. You have to beg around until you get some boards, some rolls of corrugated roofing, or a saw. Here you must daily send off four audio-messages with requests and justifications. And this to the utmost displeasure of these gentlemen whose peace and quiet you disturb by so doing. Without these interruptions they could carry on their lives well away from the war. They don't need them.

It was even harder to get workers. I had to work for the most part with men who were only slightly sick. We have no more manpower available. Nearly all is at the front. There are, of course, among them many sick, weak, old people. What little remains comes from worker units. These are out and out sick people (tuberculosis, catarrh, heart defects, bent over, hunchbacked, deaf, etc.). They can't do anything. Add to this their miserable food which completely undermines the state of their already endangered health. They are literally starving, literally beggars, suffering from a lack of bread. In the morning they get black coffee, for lunch soup, which is nothing other than hot, dirty water and then at night scraps of vegetables in very small helpings along with black coffee. Very little bread. On this a poor sick man is supposed to live and carry out decent work. This is impossible, of course. Most of them want to queue up for food since they are better catered for when they do so. They make use of every opportunity to rejoin a squadron and report back to the front. They are only kept here with great difficulty.

A truly sad picture of our society here. It really is high time to put an end to this dreadful war. Now politicians must give up their ambitious aspirations. Unfortunately, they feel the war very little. They have no idea what this war is actually like. They behave quite soberly and coldly with only an eye on their own interests.

Yesterday marked the second anniversary of our waging of this war. How much longer must this inconclusive struggle between nations go on? There have already been enough victims for mankind to bear, going on for 7 million dead just in Europe during these two years. And then these imponderable phalanxes of the crippled and sick people. Immeasurable treasures have gone up in smoke. Poor humanity for putting up with this! How cowardly you are! Where are all your high ideals? Where is your love of liberty? Where are all your freedom fighters? They're all phrasemongers, nothing more than that. You allow yourselves to be enslaved and led astray so easily.

31 July 1916

Quite a restless night tonight. In the neighbouring sector the enemy's heavy artillery thundered incessantly. The enemy means business in the Travenanzestal which, since the conquest of the Col de Bois, he has singled out to hold under heavy fire. Here, in the immediate vicinity of the Col de Bois, we succeeded yesterday in taking eighty-three prisoners, among whom were eight officers. Tonight we escorted them through the Fanestal to Gross Fanes, from whence they were immediately transported on. Both officers and men were chained and roped to one another. This happened as a result of orders from above so that they would not take to their heels on the way. The prisoners belonged to the 7th Alpini Regiment, Company 79 thereof, from the battalion of Captain Bakou, who was himself one of the prisoners. He has been slightly wounded. They were all without exception strapping youths, lads impeccably equipped. The officers, once we were in the Fanestal, were catered for. We behaved towards them in a strictly distant way. None of us reached out to shake hands with them. They devoured a really large amount of bread with jam and butter. After they had finally eaten their fill, we gave them cigarettes. About 5 o'clock in the morning they had to further wend their way.

At half-past six in the morning I proceeded with Lieutenant Colonel Mandolfo to Gross Fanes. There we met up with the captive officers again with whom I gradually got into conversation. Three of them were from Udine, one from Milan, and the rest from Belluno. For the most part they were reserve and third reserve officers. According to what they were saying, the enemy is constantly suffering enormous losses of officers as the latter must always precede their men. They themselves had only been captured owing to an error on the part of their commanding officer. He gave this company the order to advance in the conviction that another of their companies had completely encircled one of ours and that the latter had therefore no choice but to surrender. This was hard by our own positions. Two enemy machine guns also fell into our hands.

At about 10 o'clock I came back to the Fanestal and there I was already awaited by a huge crowd of patients. I began my surgery immediately and it lasted till 1 o'clock. I was very much in demand. This is an extensive sector, occupied by two battalions. Besides, sick people come to me from Gross Fanes, Travenanz, and various artillery units. Very little is available to me by way of equipment and only two medics, one of whom has gone away on leave.

1 August 1916, 1 o'clock in the Morning
Until now I was busy at the medical centre to which were delivered two dead and two wounded. One of the dead men had suffered a shot through the skull from an infantry rifle, the other had received a serious injury from a shell to the chest. I had both buried immediately. I gave the necessary attention to the wounded whereupon they were carted off or rather carried (as ever, eight men carry one wounded) to Pedern. Apart from this, I am waiting for a third injury case reported to me by Company 20.

2 August 1916
Today through a telescope (22 times actual size) I looked at Il Zurlong, the Cresta Bianca, and the Schönleitenscheid, all mountains which, with the exception of the last one mentioned, have been occupied afresh by the enemy. And what an enormous and admirable show unfolded before my very eyes. What vivid and idiosyncratic liveliness there is in these high, wild, quite barren, jagged, inhospitable mountains. Above all on Il Zurlong. There is a cave containing an artillery piece next door to a second cave. A truly mysterious piece of work! What an enormous amount of work has gone into it, what immeasurable quantities of

work, material, and make-do-and-mend expedients. How many difficulties to overcome before such a work is knocked into shape. Yes, the Italians are the true unsurpassed masters of the art of fortification, which, unfortunately, as far as we are concerned, is not up to their high standard. In this respect we cannot compete with our enemy. For this reason we ourselves must suffer very much. Besides, everywhere with the enemy there is an unflagging initiative and resourcefulness in direct contrast to our stinking indolence. With us something will only be undertaken and constructed when the activity and actions of the enemy compel it to be done. The enemy is everywhere only lacking in the perseverance needed to bring his work to perfection. And this is the only thing that we can count ourselves lucky for. But let us leave all these considerations to one side. We'll keep on hearing all the things that I have seen there. All these numerous fine, big barracks and shelters at dizzying heights. What a huge sacrifice in terms of manpower is involved so such things can come into existence. Not everyone can appreciate this. Only he who has tried it already can build here in the mountains, produce something. And all these artfully constructed paths and hairpin bends which everywhere wind and twist. One must have seen all this with one's own eyes, otherwise it cannot even be imagined. And how many people I saw here (Italians, of course) who, either alone or in small groups, in broad daylight, were in various directions quite cheekily running up and downhill, most of them laden down with building materials. Busy as ants.

On the extremely straight-up summit of the Fiammes I also clearly perceived the enemy observer at his viewing tripod. He is observing the Stuva sector.

And yet, despite all this work and expenditure of energy, the enemy has not been able to achieve during the war so far (for over a year) any more substantial success. This is certainly not due to us. The reason lies with the enemy himself. He does not make use of the opportunities that come his way at the right time. And there is certainly no shortage of opportunities for him to seize on. He never tries to make the most of the successes that he has already obtained.

Chapter 3

Gorizia

Introduction by Hew Strachan

On 23 September 1916, Barasch was still in Brunech, the site of the hospital behind the front in Tyrol. Two days later he was back on the Isonzo. His diary is concentrated on events and locations within his own immediate and personal experience, rarely mentioning the wider context of the war and the big events that punctuated it. In most cases this narrowness may be no more than the result of ignorance but his lack of commentary on turning points on the same front is striking. While he had been in the Alps, two more battles had been fought on the Isonzo, the sixth in August and the seventh between 13 and 17 September. The Italians gave the sixth battle a different title – the battle of Gorizia, because they captured the town – or what was left of it – on 8 August. Barasch's diary is silent for most of August and September. Only on 2 October did he record that the old Austro-Hungarian positions – Oslavija and Podgora, both forward of Gorizia, and Gorizia itself – were now in Italian hands.

In December 1915 the Entente powers had agreed at Chantilly to coordinate their offensives in 1916 so that they attacked the Central Powers simultaneously from east, west and south. The Brusilov offensive in June and the Somme offensive in July were reflections of this strategy applied to the eastern and western fronts. Although Cadorna's fifth Isonzo battle in March was set against the background of the Chantilly plan, it was the sixth battle in August which was really designed to follow through on Italy's obligations to its allies. By mid-June Cadorna realised how the Austro-Hungarian offensive in Tyrol had given him an opportunity on the Isonzo. Because he could cut across the short cord from southern Tyrol, whereas the Austro-Hungarians had to make their way back through the mountains and take the long way round to the Isonzo, he could redeploy more quickly. Moreover, Boroević's 5th Army had been reduced to nine divisions. Only three brigades had returned from Tyrol by the time the Italians attacked, not least because most of the troops released from the Asiago plateau were urgently required in Galicia to stop the Russians.

Cadorna disbanded the 5th Army he had created to meet the attack in Tyrol to reconstruct the 2nd Army. By 4 August he had completed the concentration of three armies along the Isonzo front, giving the Italians a superiority of three-to-one and in some areas twelve-to-one. He threatened both the front's extremities, with a demonstration from Monfalcone in the south and sustained artillery fire at Tolmein in the north. As a result, Boroević could not be certain of Italian intentions. In the event, the main thrust came in the centre and – unlike the fifth battle of the Isonzo – had a clear geographical objective commensurate with the means available. Monte San Michele was in Italian hands by 7 August and Gorizia was taken the next day. On the morning of 9 August Cadorna believed he had the opportunity for a breakthrough if he attacked with energy. 'Time is of the essence', he signalled on 10 August, in the hope that his 3rd Army could take the high ground on the bounce.[1] In focusing on the heights, he lost the opportunity to follow the valley of the Vippacco (or Wippach), a tributary of the Isonzo, eastwards. The next day he ordered a general advance along the whole front, from Tolmein to the sea, but by 16 August Cadorna realised that he had to stop, build up and then start again. Although he had lost over 21,000 dead and nearly 53,000 wounded, the capture of Gorizia lit up the Italian war effort – and in Falkenhayn's judgement prompted Romania to join the Entente.

Cadorna was now committed to a sequence of methodical and limited advances, known as the seventh, eighth and ninth battles of the Isonzo, which lasted from 14 September to 4 November. Their logic, timing and sequence all bear comparison with the Anglo-French offensive on the Somme, even if historians have tended to see the latter as one continuous battle rather than as a succession of related attacks. Cadorna's aim was to take the Carso, so that he could come from the

---

1. Luigi Cadorna, *Mémoires du Général Cadorna* (Paris, 1924), p. 224.

south at the high ground which overlooked the town of Gorizia from the east (Barasch was able to look down into its streets on 17 October). Italian progress was slow, blunted by worsening weather and the need to reposition and re-lay artillery after each short step.

Barasch served in the area encircling Gorizia during the eighth and ninth Isonzo battles. Even when he was not in the front line, he was never fully out of the battle zone. Austro-Hungarian losses over the three battles, from mid-September to early November, have been put at over 9,000 killed, 43,000 wounded and 23,500 missing and captured.[2] Trying to work out with whom Barasch was serving is not easy, and he seems to have been moved around according to need. On 10 October, he refers to the third battalion of his regiment being captured at Sabotino, north of Gorizia, in August, so implying he was then in a different regiment from the one with which he had served in Tyrol, as it had then not yet returned to the Isonzo. On 23 October, he was ordered to the 3rd Battalion of the 85th Infantry Regiment. On 24 November he was the doctor of the 75th Landsturm Battalion and six days later 'we are going back' to the 4th Mountain Brigade. The 5th and 4th Mountain Brigades were both in the 58th Division which held the sector either side of the Rosental, the valley which led from Gorizia eastwards to Laibach. It and its brigades had fought in all the Isonzo battles, but its partner division in XVI Corps, 43rd Schützen Division, had been brought from Galicia to Tyrol in March and was moved to the 5th Army on the Isonzo in early July. The 43rd Schützen Division held the ground on the 58th Division's left down as far as the line of the Vippacco, both forming XVI Corps under the command of Wenzel Wurm. Between September and November the corps suffered total losses of over 20,000 killed, wounded, sick and missing.[3] The pressure from his seniors on Barasch to keep soldiers at the front, given the shortage of men, was understandable.

By mid-December he was out of the line and on 21 December the battalion was allowed a week's rest, just in time for Christmas. Barasch would not return to the front until October 1917. In his absence

---

2. Amédée Tosti, *L'Italie dans la guerre mondiale (1915–1918)* (Paris, 1933), p. 211.
3. *Österreich-Ungarns letzter Krieg*, Vol. V, Beilage 33.

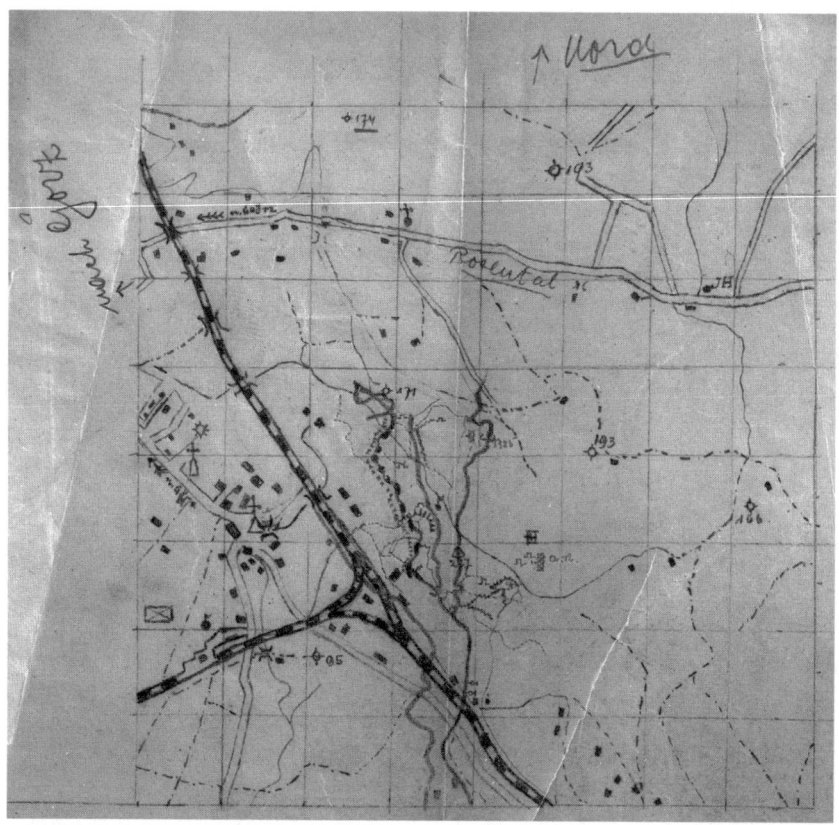

Map drawn by Isaak Barasch found in the pages of the diary.

Cadorna launched two more offensives on the Isonzo. The Entente plan for 1917 was effectively more of the same: coordinated attacks from west, east and south to put simultaneous pressure on the Central Powers. Lloyd George, who became the British prime minister in December 1916, was convinced that Austria-Hungary might crack before Germany and agreed that Britain would provide the heavy artillery to enable the Italians to attack. Sir William Robertson, the chief of the British imperial general staff, persuaded Cadorna to use the guns by May, so that they could be returned in time for the British offensive on the western front later in the year. Cadorna planned to attack on the Carso first and then to switch to the Bainsizza plateau, north of Gorizia. He hoped to pull the Austro-Hungarians first in one direction and then back in the other, leaving him free to deliver the decisive blow on the Carso. If that did not work, and Boroević was not persuaded to strengthen the Bainsizza plateau, he could win there instead and then push southwards to the Vippacco.

The tenth battle of the Isonzo began on 12 May 1917 but Boroević held both north and south of Gorizia, and the battle was closed down on 5 June. The eleventh battle opened on 17 August and this time – although there was fighting along the entire Isonzo front – the Italians put their main weight to the north. Boroević withdrew from both Bainsizza and Monte Santo, having been persuaded by the new emperor, Karl, to abandon strong fronts for defence in depth. He also lost Monte San Gabriele, but then regained it. The problem for the Austro-Hungarians was that they had not much depth left – either territorially or in terms of manpower. Although Cadorna's army had suffered 166,000 casualties in a month of fighting, Habsburg losses were comparable – and to observers looked increasingly unsustainable.

25 September 1916

Today we are already in Lapenje, in the area around Gorizia, at the foot of the Trnovo Forest. We were still in the valley of the Puster, in Brunech, on the 23rd and already today we are in the valley of the Vippacco. Tomorrow we will march forward further. If only we could be allowed to break ranks for two or three days. We are constantly on the move.

28 September 1916

I am in 'Ma Mokrim' at the foot of Mounts San Daniele and San Gabriele in a small, dirty, almost empty farmhouse which, only a few days ago, was hit fairly and squarely by a shell. Here is the so-called collection point for the wounded to which I have suddenly been ordered for the time being. The house is being overlooked by the enemy so that no light is allowed to be shown at night. It comes across as quite uncanny here in mountainous terrain directly behind the front line to build such a complex – hardly anybody here can really imagine it. First of all, I had to look around for workers. I turned to various command centres and asked for one or two additional workers to be allocated to me. This without success. Everywhere heard the same thing. 'We only have a few workers ourselves and we need to use them for more important jobs than the building of medical centres.' Yes, these high-up and comfortably off gentlemen in various command centres do not have the slightest understanding of the huge importance of such establishments. They sit far away, well to the rear, and have no notion of how things look to us here. And, as to the final fate of the sick and wounded, they don't give that a second thought. They are there for the most part to use the war to their own personal advantage, to sit as far away from the actual shooting as possible, to weigh themselves down with as many decorations as possible, to organise their lives as pleasantly and cosily as possible. These gentlemen never take the opportunity to take such medical centres into account and therefore, they don't bother about them. And the same is true for medical officers of health, doctors on the general staff whose sole occupation is to sit in their offices and to scrawl as many orders as possible which will never be followed. And, fortunately, they are not even worried about them not being followed. Only there needs to be a lot of writing done. Despite all my efforts, nowhere was I able to find a worker. Therefore, I had to recruit some of the only mildly ill patients in my care for these jobs. These were, for the most part, people afflicted by catarrhal conjunctivitis, slightly ulcerated feet, abdominal and intestinal complaints, skin rashes. These people did a lot for me.

And now there's the acquisition of tools and all sorts of building materials to think about. How many times I had to telephone around, apply for things, requisition things, appeal for things, beg even till the sapper in Pedern deigned to send me something and until in the end, I had all the necessary boards, beams, wooden frames, doors, windows, all the corrugated roofing, pipework, kettles, and ovens ... In order to bring this all about, I had to expend a great deal of time and energy. I even fetched a saw myself and had the slightly sick patients turn out boards and wooden frames. And finally all this bore fruit. Everything was made ready. We were able ourselves to enter the building. The work was done diligently. Till late at night. Now everything went quickly to plan. A building came into being after the second was built and very soon everything was ready. To my great joy and satisfaction, the sick and wounded were able to find in this new establishment reliable and appropriate accommodation.

Unfortunately, I was not lucky enough to stay any length of time in this new Fanes barrier field medical centre so as to be able to work for the benefit of the sick and wounded and reap the reward of such huge efforts on my part. Someone else came. He was a young, inexperienced doctor, a Bohemian by the name of Dr Krčmar, and I had to hand everything over to him. This gentleman deigned only to record his satisfaction and appreciation of the finished article. He was unable to grasp how it had been possible under these conditions to bring such a thing into being. It is an establishment in which each sick and wounded person can be treated as if he were in a proper hospital according to the principles of modern medicine. And each of us will be able to measure what huge importance and significance this has for us here if he only considers how difficult it is to transport patients in this rugged terrain. Yes, this is at times impossible for days on end because of rain or snowstorms, especially in winter, and not only that, but each patient must be carried for over four hours by six to eight men until he arrives at his final destination in Pedern, the sector's military hospital.

This field hospital covers an area big enough to contain fifty beds. It is a solidly built blockhouse, situated on a rise, hidden from the enemy by the back of Monte Vallon Bianco. It consists of four sickrooms, a waiting room, a first aid room that is light and spacious and fitted with all the necessary furnishings and which is, moreover, used as a storeroom. The medical centre includes the bathhouse and three rooms adjoining: the boiler room, the officers' bathroom, and the men's bathroom and, lastly, the delousing room. Near to the medical centre a second blockhouse has been erected that contains the patients' kitchen and the patients' laundry.

I have, for all of these achievements of mine, benefited from the appreciation of the high-ups. First of all, a border sub-sector form singing my praises and soon, on top of that, a divisional command letter praising me accompanied by a decree. The high-ups never economise on the distribution of medals (war decorations). But they are starting to be more careful. To begin with they want to keep them for themselves. Not only the ones who deserve them receive them. Only to those who have fallen in action are they not withheld. Each of these is always awarded one posthumously, sometimes even a high one. Men as well as officers. The bestowal of the decoration happens very quickly, is even wired. Decorations intended for the living always go astray until a commission is agreed upon. The commission passes from one command centre to another getting higher and higher, everywhere adjusted upward, and assessed, always by gentlemen who have not the slightest inkling of the achievements and the personal worth of someone. Hence, it goes without saying, the quite unjust distribution of decorations for valour, hence the deplorable state of affairs here. All the gentlemen who live a quite serene and comfortable life well away from the front line have their heroic chests richly adorned with these decorations, while those who are constantly risking their lives and have to endure all the stresses and strains of real warfare have to wait a very long time until they are awarded, here and there, such a decoration. What a glaring injustice there is in this respect as well.

If only it were to hapen only once! Unfortunately, it occurs time and time again. If the exact number of times it happens could be counted, people would find it difficult to accept.

That the organisation of our sanitary arrangements leaves a lot to be desired in every respect the following case bears eloquent testimony to and serves to show. The day before our march out of the Fanestal I had delivered to me from the adjacent battle sector in the Travenanz Ravine a badly wounded member of the 2nd Alpine Detachment thirty-seven hours after being injured and in a quite hopeless condition. It was the Rifleman Reichenegger David who had been the victim of an explosion. First aid had been administered to him by the inexpert hand of a quite young medic and the poor man had to spend thirty-seven hours lying on the ground, under fire, in the most inadequate conditions, to endure the most painful torments and to wait until he could finally be moved. This is how well things are regulated here. He could have been moved just as easily the previous night. But nobody bothered about it. Special, quick-acting bodies should be set up for this kind of thing and not everything entrusted to a totally inexperienced medic. It should have been the duty and the business of medical officers of health to regulate this. Such crimes lie heavy on their consciences. These gentlemen can hardly move inside their offices due to their living the high life and their large number of medals. Apart from that, their expert knowledge and medical experience are moot points. They were always and even more so now during wartime just scribblers and scribes. – And on these men's shoulders unfortunately rests the whole regulation of our system of hygiene. Besides they are, for the most part, poltroons who never venture out.

So, after thirty-seven hours of excruciating pain, the poor, badly wounded man was delivered to me at the medical centre on the 22nd around midnight. I went to work on him immediately. It took me more than two hours to attend to his many severe wounds in the manner each warranted. First of all, there was the matter of a singeing of the left cornea and the left cheek (second-degree burns). Then there was a deep pressure wound to the area of the right lower jaw with the loss of two teeth. There were multiple pressure wounds of varying size to the right kneecap. Complications had set in with the latter.

There was a swelling and inflammation of the knee joint and the area round it with a bad smell of gangrene and the emergence of blisters. On the skin palpable crepitus was perceptible. There had been more than enough time for a gaseous phlegmony to develop. Nothing much could be done to counteract it. Under the skin very deep pockets had sprung up everywhere. A sad state of affairs to be sure. What agonies I had to go through myself. This was indeed a heart-wrenching sight for me. Apart from that, there were numerous pressure wounds and burns to both lower legs. I did everything possible to make sending this person on to Pedern easier. I immobilised the knee joint with a splint. Having stitched all the wounds needing surgical intervention, I administered a generous injection of morphine. I also administered an anti-tetanus jab. The patient's pulse was already short and frequent with a high temperature. Around 5 am I sent the patient on. At the same time I requisitioned an ambulance in Brunech which was only given grudgingly. But as long as you have the gift of the gab you can get these things. What happened to him afterwards is unknown to me. At all events, this case cannot offer much satisfaction to a doctor. At best this can end with the loss of a leg.

* * *

On 22 September, after midnight, we left our place of sojourn. Over the fine, narrow valley, over all the newly wrought paths, over all the many huts and shelters, over all the high mountains all around lay a thick, fresh, soft, blindingly white covering of snow. It snowed for two days without stopping. Just before our march out the weather brightened up. It was really cold outside to the point of freezing. We marched with the battalion. Very many fell behind as it was too strenuous for them to march for such a long time with full packs over this mountainous terrain. They had to follow on slowly. About 5 o'clock we came into Pedern. Early in the afternoon we were taken from here on lorries to Brunech and boarded a train there early the following day.

Shortly before our march I climbed to the summit of Monte Vallon Bianco, from where I could take my leave of the giants of the

Dolomites. The climb up was very strenuous and above the level of the Furcia Rossa many places scraped against me most unsettlingly. But all in all, it was a pleasant climb. A narrow, tiring climb is made safe in these dangerous parts by rope and crampons. Already the Bavarian Alpencorps started to work there last year in order to install a machine-gun post. They even built a shelter high up on a small ledge. During the winter all this work had to be abandoned because of the huge amounts of snow and the danger of avalanches. Only in June were we able to embark on further building. There is still a lot to do. Apart from this a good and accessible path for pack animals going from Mount Castello over the tops of Cavallo and Furcia Rossa has been blown up. What people have to put up with here. It almost borders on the impossible for them. Lieutenant Colonel Erlsbacher from Innsbruck has done us all a very great service.

From the top of Monte Vallon Bianco I had a tremendous panoramic view of the Dolomites.

29 September 1916, 11 o'clock at Night
At the 'Ma Mokrim' medical centre. I went without an evening meal today. One was not brought to me from the supply train, I don't know why. I am hungry as a consequence. It's a hunger I can't satisfy with bread as I don't have a piece of bread on me. I must therefore be content with a cigarette I rolled myself. To top it all, it's raining heavily. And the guns are thundering on every side. Here can be heard our own guns firing off and there, the explosions of enemy heavy artillery. I'm sitting in my godforsaken, dirty, empty, uncomfortable little house by candlelight and awaiting the arrival of the wounded. And this little house is under fire from the enemy. Only a few days ago it suffered a direct hit from a shell.

30 September 1916
A dull, grey, cold day. A large number of patients appeared during my surgery hours. I had to examine them under the most primitive conditions and treat them too for the most part. Not many of them needed to be sent on. What torments I have to suffer with all these sick visitors. Most of the people who appear at these times are weak,

undernourished, struggling to cope and tired, afflicted by the most varied of aches and pains. One cannot with a clear conscience call hardly any of them healthy and yet, I must, for military reasons, pass many of them as fit for duty and let the weak person have one to two days off after which he will have to resume his duties and only send those who really are sick and debilitated off to hospital. It can now easily be gathered from all this in what an unpleasant situation the doctor, especially an honourable and conscientious doctor, finds himself. We have to stick to a plan.

Today much fun was had here. 'Ma Mokrim' stood for more than two hours under enemy heavy artillery fire. Hundreds of high-calibre shells, shrapnel, and grenades buzzed through the air and exploded, one after the other, with the utmost vehemence. An unprecedentedly demonic music of hell it was that I had to listen to as I was quite close to it. The explosions took place for the most part at a short distance from the little house in which I had performed my duties as a doctor. Fortunately, the little house was spared.

1 October 1916

I have a headache, a general feeling of weakness, constant nausea, lack of appetite. The topsy-turvy lifestyle of the last few days, especially the cold, badly prepared, unappetising meals, is what is responsible for this. Our food is cooked for us in the supply train in a place called Lokvica [south of Gorizia] from where it is brought to us twice daily by pack animal. And how long we then have to wait before we actually get it. The day before yesterday I had to go without my evening meal completely as, by mistake, mine did not turn up. Is it not obvious then that, under such circumstances, we cannot hold out for very long and finally, sooner or later, must fall ill?

Today I had to send away my Ensign, Jovan Lazarevič, because of an acute intestinal catarrh with fever, to Divisional Hospital 58 in Ossek.

2 October 1916

A truly fine, clear, sunny, feel-good Indian summer afternoon. The war is raging far more than on dull, misty days because of the see-for-miles uninterrupted view. Objectives can be made out better on both sides. The roaring of aeroplanes is constantly audible in the air. Sometimes it's our own planes, sometimes the enemy's. The so-called anti-aircraft guns spit fire from their metal throats against the latter. Shrapnel explodes high up in the air far away or close to the aeroplanes and leaves behind a reddish-white here, a purely white cloud there. The former we cause with our shrapnel; the latter is down to the enemy's shrapnel. Actually, hitting the target is as rare for us as it is for them. That is to say that what we are up against here are the almost insuperable difficulties in determining the distance from us and direction of a moving plane. It's pure luck when one succeeds in bringing down a flying machine with an anti-aircraft gun. For the most part it's about the demoralising effect on your adversary. The only thing is that we ourselves run the risk by shooting at these planes of having a shrapnel casing or a heavy lump of iron fall on our heads. And the usual consequences of this one can predict very easily.

But you forget very quickly this show in the sky when you notice, to your horror, that a heavy mine or a trinitrophenol missile has blown up not far from you with a howling noise that drowns out everything else. Soon there ensues the 2, 3 or so metre high development of broad, black columns of smoke, one after the other. Large clods of earth and lumps of rock are thrown up a really long way into the air. Big iron splinters rush with enormous speed out of the eye of the explosion. Many of these, falling down, single out a victim.

If only you knew where you could flee to. Wherever you choose to turn the same cruel tragedy plays out. A roaring sound that makes the ground tremble. All you can do is to wait for these things to die down. Perhaps you'll be spared this time. It's all at the whim of pure chance. On the other hand, what good does it do to be spared today if one of these things catches up with you tomorrow? One has to come your way sooner or later. They're dancing around all over the place here. Everywhere you see their traces: deep and wide craters.

I have just received the news that Castle 'Ma Mokrim' in which our brigade command is housed has been hit. Two people have been badly wounded.

Everywhere here caves are being hewn out of the rock. In our old positions in Oslavija, Podgora, and Gorizia we had already built good ones. These the enemy has been sitting in for weeks now. And the new ones that we are going to move into first have to be built. Day and night intensive work is being carried out. What these poor infantrymen, sappers, and workers have to do to keep going. And the food is wretched. Our helpings are more and more restricted. Hardly surprising then that the number of sick is on the increase. Especially intestinal catarrh and rheumatism.

* * *

Unfortunately, our whole system is a very faulty one. Things are never provided for or prepared in advance. Only that is done that absolutely needs to be done at that moment. These long months have certainly given us enough time to build our second line of defence as it should be built. We had to reckon in advance with the possibility that our first line of defence could be lost here through the tremendous efforts of the enemy to break through at this point. We could have prepared for this eventuality very well. Unfortunately, very little happened here during these long months. One could almost say that nothing happened. Only now are things being energetically worked for with a corresponding loss of human life.

There are no plans for a medical centre for the St Caterina sector, which our regiment has occupied. One needs to be built there as quickly as possible. For the time being, however, we don't have enough building materials or workers. It's something that needs to be addressed. Otherwise, we'll wait a long time for one to appear.

* * *

There are no end of mice and rats in this little house. They're gradually starting to race one another. I'll wager that all the small animals in the surrounding area are playing their part in this. An unbearable hurly-burly. I admire the fact that, in spite of these hard times of war, animals still find the necessary urge and free time to do this. They are dragged by the war into sympathy with other creatures. Their whole future has become uncertain. Every day robs large numbers of new victims of life. Arbitrary bombardments are not fussy. They do not ask who is guilty and who is innocent. Whoever gets in their way will be torn to pieces. But what do all these mice and rats that never leave me alone want of me? As if they had got together to conspire against me. As if they wanted to revenge themselves on me.

But I'll work out what needs to be done. Of the many cats which are running around here, abandoned and ownerless, I will take just one or two to help me out. They'll sniff out the rodents immediately.

3 October 1916, Morning
Today things are running amok. Several shells exploded quite near the medical centre. One only a few paces away from here. Another hit the little house next door which, fortunately, was unoccupied. Perhaps the next one will hit the medical centre. But we must keep a cool head and wait quietly.

* * *

Evening. About 5 pm the enemy commenced heavy artillery fire against Castle Cronberg ('Ma Mokrim') and the medical centre. The castle once again suffered a direct hit which resulted, thank goodness, with only one man wounded. High-calibre shells exploded without a break right next to the medical centre. Among the sick and wounded who were waiting to be taken on by the next transport available, as also among the helpers, a great hullabaloo broke out. Everyone ran from there in all directions and instinctively looked for a wall to shelter them. Nowhere could a place to hide be found. Not the slightest thing had been provided. Always with us as little as possible is done to provide for the well-being of doctors and the sick and wounded. They are always the last people to be considered. What a scandalous state of affairs!! First of all caves are hewn for the command quarters. The doctors can wait. The medical officers of health in the rear do not need to bother about us. Their hide is not on the line. They lead their predictable lives well to the rear where nothing too serious can happen to them. They never trust themselves to go out. And those other gentlemen, the brigadiers, divisional commanders, and so on, do not have an inkling of the enormous significance and the importance of the role that well equipped and half-way secure medical centres have to play. Only in such can a doctor give appropriate and suitable expert help to a patient. Only in such is serious medical attention thinkable. But there is no question of this being the case in the present deplorable climate. We can only attend here to the most pressing needs and not always that. With us this is always the case. The whole rotten sick system and a lethargic bureaucracy are responsible for this. There is an overall lack of initiative, of a desire to work and of the ability to derive pleasure from work, of a sound and firm resolve, of a goal-orientated unified striving, of a strong will. This is true of the whole engine room of state, in which the nuts and bolts cannot and will not pull together. Every wheel, every axle, everything, even the smallest screw goes its own way. Only the cold external form is there, the inner substance is lacking. And our biggest cancer it was and is and remains that the outward appearance is always everything for us, plays the biggest part, has an exclusive right to be regarded as important.

Can all this still change for good? It's hard to say beforehand. The basic principle is already lacking, the natural, superable drive to great, inward-dwelling, strong life in common. It would need a miracle to happen.

* * *

11 o'clock at night. A violent attack by enemy artillery on a part of our trenches in the St Caterina sector. Immediately our own guns, which are positioned here all around the medical centre, opened up with heavy fire. The guns there chattered and cracked, thundered and rattled. A roaring noise that made everything around us tremble. Gleaming and flashing on both sides. Hundreds of flares danced in the air, glittered and glimmered in long rows. A truly hellish pursuit. It made me get out of bed double-quick. I got dressed in an instant. It was impossible to put up with staying in the room. I ran outside.

My orderly sent for my seven bottles of plum liqueur so as to be ready for every eventuality. But this disgusting devil's music did not last for long. It soon stopped. Unpleasant, even gruesome surprises like this in wartime, in this theatre of operations in particular, are not rare – I could almost say that they are a daily occurrence.

4 October 1916
The same melodrama was enacted today as well. Our medical centre stood there under the usual heavy artillery fire. This time it was mostly high-calibre shrapnel, many of which burst directly over our roof. The enemy means business then with our shack on which the Red Cross is clearly visible. He falsely assumes that there is something more here. Shells in all probability will follow the shrapnel and then things could get really serious. He was surely aiming at the house with the shrapnel.

Unfortunately the new medical centre isn't ready yet. Work cannot be speeded up on it as the necessary building materials and workforce are not available. Today, for example, I asked for 100 boards and 15 rolls of roofing. I got only 50 boards and 3 rolls of roofing.

5 October 1916
A gloomy, rainy day. Since early in the morning we have been hearing in the distance a persistent, fierce, dull thunder. The enemy has been all day keeping long parts of the more southerly Karst plateau under steady, heavy bombardment. But he has been giving us no rest either. We are everywhere being made aware that the enemy's artillery is far superior to ours. A very large number of new, good, accurate guns, ammunition that performs faultlessly, careful observation. Also, they have at their disposition many 30.5cm Skoda mortars.

* * *

For a few days now I have really had nothing to do here. In the morning my surgery takes place. Thirty pitiful figures appear in soldiers' uniforms. In one or two cases some kind of illness is involved. Based here, however, I can do nothing other than send them off to the

Division's Hospital in Ossek. A medic as green as the grass, even a well-trained intelligent medic could only do as much. What a wretched role for a doctor in such serious times when, further in the rear, there are oodles of work. Most of those who appear during my surgery hours are cheats and shirkers. A policeman could certainly perform his duties here more competently than a doctor. Many of these people are quite weak, undernourished, too young, inexperienced, or too old, worn out individuals, all of them tired of the war, yet, according to the harsh military regulations currently in force, all passed as fit for military service. What am I supposed to do with them as a doctor? It annoys me and makes me ill that I have to perform such a demeaning task. What can I do? On the odd occasion I believe their unfounded complaints, now treat them, now shout at them and have them punished. I only have a few simple remedies at my disposal. These don't really help. The most important thing for these people is, failing sending them to hospital, is to leave them at the very least for a few days relieved of their military duties. I make full use of this last solution. This whole silly farce is played out on a daily basis. My own health is undermined by it. After this tedious, barmy carry-on comes the midday meal. The latter is naturally quite unpredictable.

Sometimes the pack animal arrives with the officers' meals earlier, another time it has to be waited for for a very long time. My orderly has to fetch my stone-cold and not very appetising food for me. Not much of a feast, is it? We must eat out of bowls, of course. The idea of plates is out of the question. In the afternoon I must deal with any paperwork: reports, more reports, official forms, reports again. A most sedentary, aimless, idle existence. And why am I kept here? I am totally superfluous to requirements here. My place should be somewhere quite different. There are too many doctors here, most of whom have nothing to do and are bored. Elsewhere doctors are in short supply. Again, a defect, a sin of faulty organisation. We have too many doctors in front-line positions and therefore not enough in backward-lying medical institutions. Doctors on the general staff don't understand how to organise things as they ought to be organised. They don't allow any doctor to leave the front line. The more doctors they have in forward positions, the more calmly they are left to their own devices to lead their own lives. In our regiment alone there are five doctors and six paramedics. What an excess of manpower. For all the functions that need to be performed here, two doctors and two paramedics would be perfectly adequate. But medical officers of health, those dull-witted scribes, cannot see this!

We doctors at the front are in the worst position we can be. There is talk of conducting some kind of exchange. But this doesn't come off. Hundreds of young doctors have been sitting in hospitals away from the front line since the beginning of the war. They could for once enjoy the pleasures of front-line service. We should have the right to be used in a genuinely medical capacity. But for this to happen we must be well connected and carry recommendations. Without these it's no go. We never reach our goals here by honourable ways and means. Injustice, immoral stagnation, indolence and corruption wherever you go.

* * *

3 o'clock in the morning. Sleeplessness has been a veritable torture to me these last weeks. My nervousness is on the increase. Physically I am rather run down. I feel in general very bad. Problems with my intestinal tract.

It might well be time to report myself as sick. But I'm afraid to do this. I want as much as I possibly can to avoid those military hospitals where general staff doctors look on every sick non-serving officer, particularly doctors, with the greatest distrust. They look upon them, irrespective of how long they have been in the field and the quality of their service, as cheats and swindlers. They give no credence to any of the statements and complaints made by the patient. They are for the most part police and army officials, not doctors. It's a different story again for serving officers. They are entitled to privileges. They must be spared. What an upside-down and twisted logic! How can one speak of logic where these gentlemen are concerned? As long as this situation stays the same, I'll put up with things here. I don't want anything to do with these gentlemen.

6 October 1916
Midnight. My heart is still beating quickly. I had an unpleasant shock. I had scarcely fallen asleep when I was abruptly woken up by a fierce racket. Bang after bang, flash after flash, right next to the medical centre. Shrapnel exploded above it. I got dressed quickly, ran outside, looked for the second doctor on duty, Senior Doctor Scheck. We both fled to a room on the ground floor. We were not, of course, protected there against a direct hit, but it was better than being on the 1st floor. Fortunately, this time as well, despite heavy fire, we were not hit directly by a shell.

7 October 1916
Also, this morning the enemy peppered us soundly with fire. He sent us over fifteen pieces of shrapnel. A powerful explosive device hit the gutter round the roof of our house. Another destroyed the gravestones of the nearby cemetery. Two dum-dum bullets fell into our so-called operations room. And we still have to stay here as we have nowhere else to go for the time being. Now the other medical centre will be built quickly. Of course, we ourselves will have to see to it. Towards midday things got calmer. Now we can make a start with the digging of graves in the cemetery. Early today six dead bodies were delivered to us from the trenches. The cemetery is getting bigger and bigger. New graves are appearing there daily.

10 October 1916
Today things are going badly for us. Since early in the morning the Karst plateau is under the heaviest of bombardments. The earth is trembling and quaking. There are ghostly wails and cracks. One could almost believe that all the evil spirits in the underworld have sworn to do away with suffering humanity. It's an inferno that not even a Dante could find sufficient words to describe.

At the medical centre there is a great to-do. All of us are running around like headless chickens. Hundreds of shells and bits of shrapnel are exploding on all sides in the vicinity of the house.

I have just learned that Senior Doctor Jung was wounded a short while ago. A piece of shrapnel hit his left forearm and broke the bone.

How much I envy him. If only something like that could happen to me.

11 October 1916, 4 o'clock in the Morning
I am already in Bonetti. Yesterday at 8 pm I left the medical centre attached to 'Ma Mokrim' (Cronberg) and marched to more forward positions. At around 10 am I was already up there in Bonetti with all the battalion's staff officers and the battalion too, naturally. This battalion has relieved the 2nd Battalion of our regiment and taken up position in the St Caterina sector. What awful positions these are. Especially those on the left-hand hill which Lieutenant Colonel Petar Radomcić has moved to with 19 Company. There are hardly any running trenches and no cover on this so very exposed hill constantly under heavy fire. We can expect very large numbers of casualties here.

I am lying down in a dog-miserable wooden shelter in Bonetti North. This is the medical centre here. A quite small, low, dark, windowless wooden shack in which one can hardly move. Built onto a house which serves as an ammunition dump. Hand grenades, explosives, ammunition for machine guns and so on are stored there in large quantities. Right next to the medical centre. The ideal location for an ammunition dump, isn't it? A cold shiver runs down your spine when you remember just where you are here. And those bloody shells are screaming and venting their spleen all the time. For the last two days especially we have been under very heavy bombardment. The so-called 8th Italian offensive is underway. The enemy is developing heavy fire against all our most forward positions, all our streets and paths to the rear and all our troops held in reserve. I am living on very unstable ground here. Continuing to stay at this medical centre is quite impossible for me. I'll look around tomorrow for another shack. Perhaps I'll find one that's more happily situated.

11 October 1916, 3 o'clock in the Afternoon
Heavy enemy artillery fire is going on without respite. A devilish music reminiscent of a permanent hangover continues to resound through the air. All sorts of pitches from the deepest base to the highest alto, collections of chords, dissonances. All sorts of noises, howling and

groaning, wailing and lamenting, rushing and rattling, whistling and hissing, thundering and cracking, all these things combined in an unprecedented, dreadful mishmash.

The ground on which we tread is blood-soaked. In the first days of August this year our regiment sustained enormous loss of life. This was during the time we lost Gorizia and all its adjacent villages, when we had to move to new positions away from the front line. Our regiment also lost many prisoners during that period. The whole of the 3rd Battalion was captured then on Monte Sabotino. And how many others there were that were made prisoner in other places.

12 October 1916
Today the enemy calmed down a bit. Nevertheless, it is altogether unnerving here. Everywhere you go you see the malicious features of death's ice-cold mug. He has taken up residence here unmolested and his blood lust is merciless, insatiable. Daily he rips out the hearts of new victims to accompany him to the realm of everlasting darkness down in Hades. Hundreds and thousands of them. Each clod of earth has been rooted up by enemy shelling. Everywhere there are deep and wide craters. All the houses have been destroyed.

Everywhere you see only rubble and ruins. You dare not venture out of your shelter. In your tiny, dark, inert and damp hole you must sit, brood and wait until your turn comes round, until you too are blown up and your medical centre along with you. All that needs to happen is for a shell to burst with your name on. So many shells fall hard by the medical centre on a daily basis, 30, 20, even 10ft away. The next one could hit this wretched stupid shack that bears the name of medical centre. And this is because, like most of the medical centres we build, it is exposed and unprotected. Even an infantry bullet could quite easily penetrate these paper-thin walls. There is no cave in the vicinity in which, in the event of a bombardment, one could go in order to be safe. We are completely in the hands of blind fate.

There are, in fact, two caves and very good ones. Both of them belong, however, to group headquarters, ten minutes away from the medical centre, a really long way off in terms of the conditions that prevail here. You could be hit fairly and squarely by a shell just making your way there. And to move the medical centre there is not a good idea either as to carry the wounded and injured there every time would mean going out of our way to get there.

So, you must squat here and be ready for anything, even the worst. There is never any alternative for us. So little attention is paid to the lot of doctors and the sick and wounded. If our commanders can protect themselves, they are satisfied with that. And the divisional medical officer of health, Dr Fautl, never goes out. This short, amiable, plump, always good-natured gentleman sits in divisional headquarters in Ossek and is very difficult to tempt out. He certainly has no desire to expose himself. There are already shabby hordes of military doctors to do that. If one is lost, there is always one to take his place.

13 October 1916
I have had a blinding migraine throughout the afternoon. Hardly any wonder either. I hardly slept a wink all night. First of all, there were several wounded delivered to me. I had to go to work on them. Some of them were badly wounded. Head injuries, lower limb fractures. All as a result of shelling. I attended to them most conscientiously, despite the primitive conditions in which one has to work here. Besides just falling asleep at all is difficult.

* * *

Tonight I started building another medical centre more securely situated, more comfortable and more hygienic. In the morning I traced a plan of this place for an engineer. It is about 400m away from the present medical centre in a small, narrow gorge next to the so-called Bonetti Path. I had a look round for workers. Only eight men were assigned to the task who will, during the night, prepare the area for building. Tomorrow early the building work itself will begin. The building will be a hut 7m long and 2.75m wide. It will need to be made ready as quickly as possible. Perhaps even as soon as tomorrow night. To stay here, in the old medical centre, is out of the question. I also suggested that the excavation of a cave be started immediately.

This will happen as well. In all likelihood it will be completed within fourteen days.

Then the other doctors will be happy too. They will be there at the finish. To undertake something on their own initiative, for that they are too lazy and too lacking in energy. They have sat about here for such a long time and have undertaken nothing. If they had had an order to do something it would certainly have been done. But who can issue an order? Perhaps the general staff doctor who does not know how things stand here. Sending on the wounded will be much easier too. It will no longer be necessary to follow the upper Bonetti Path, which lies under a heavy bombardment, but the lower, which is under less scrutiny, less shot at and a lot shorter. Apart from that, the path is always visible from the gorge. The new medical centre will be 400m nearer to our trenches so that the bringing of the wounded to the medical centre will be easier and quicker. What a horrible oversight it is that until now this hasn't been done. Once again, it is our indolence, our laziness, and our faulty organisation that is to blame. Another crime that our high command have on their conscience. They are there to give orders. They should, at the very least, do that. In order to be able to issue relevant orders, one must be acquainted with the situation on the ground. And that needs more courage than our chief medical officer is capable of.

14 October 1916
This morning I was again outside in the gorge in which I am having the new medical centre built. Unfortunately, I have, for the time being, too few building materials at my disposal. I have asked for the rest to be sent. Today was a really beautiful, clear, sunny, hot day. In the afternoon I had two badly wounded patients. One had broken his thigh bone and had second-degree burns in several places on his body and on his face. This was the result of a mortar bomb blowing up. The other, who had been affected by the explosion of a shell, had several contusion and pressure wounds and a broken thigh bone himself.

15 October 1916, 4 o'clock in the Morning
Sleeplessness is torture to me. I have by dint of such long-lasting and strenuous front-line service become highly strung. The most diverse, disconnected, strange thoughts come into my head willy-nilly. I should like to drive them out. But so far I haven't succeeded. In my hard, quite low, and very narrow bed I twist and turn from one side to another and adopt every thinkable position. But still I can't fall asleep. I have banged my head with this constant moving around against the cold, damp, rough stone wall. My state of health is going from bad to worse. I am always getting weaker. My rheumatic problems are drawing attention to themselves more and more. It's high time I reported sick. But I would have to go to so many hospitals and be examined by so many doctors. No! I fear it like the plague. I don't want to do it. I'll wait.

16 October 1916
Today it's been raining heavily all day. A night as black as pitch during which even things in our immediate vicinity could scarcely be made out. In addition, a heavy downpour and a cold wind that chilled one to the bone. In my shack it's raining in. It's already quite wet inside. I'm freezing. The wind is coming in through the cracks in the joints of the boards. And yet I am pleased that today I can stay indoors, that I don't have to march anywhere. That would be terrible. What is the poor gang of workers to do who must bring building materials down here tonight from 'Ma Mokrim' twice? Down these bad paths, churned up by shells and soaking wet through? This is a huge sacrifice on their part. I couldn't begin to do it myself. Barbed wire, sandbags, 'Spanish riders' [knife-rest wire entanglements], boarded-up bits, etc. And they have to do all this in the most horrendous darkness in rain, wind, and cold. These poor men are sacrificing much. Almost superhuman demands are being made of them. And they're not being fed enough. All of them are suffering from hunger pangs. They are eating raw chestnuts by the kilo to still their hunger, which naturally causes them to get sick. Not once do they have enough bread. Wartime rations are decreasing all the time. And supply officers and rationing officials are doing alright from it. They are ruthless. They care very little about the

poor people here. The most important thing for them is filling their stomachs and their pockets.

17 October 1916
Today we have high visibility again. From the high point that we occupy we have a panoramic view. A splendid picture is painted here before our very eyes. First of all, the town of Gorizia with its many houses, its church towers, the old castle, looming up on an eminence and dominating the whole town with its numerous suburbs and further away its collection of outlying villages. Many of these houses in the town, and even more so in the suburbs and villages, bear the all-too obvious signs of the shells that have fallen here, of the pieces of shrapnel that have exploded. Of many that is all that can be seen here, and there are large heaps of rubble; of others only a few walls are still standing; on others the roof is missing; on many the walls are irregularly peppered with holes. For miles around during the day you cannot see a single living soul. Everyone and everything, people as well as animals, have crept into various holes and dare not venture out. This is as true for us as it is for the enemy. The earth here is undermined and furrowed. Everyone and everything has to stay hidden so as not to betray their presence to the enemy. Only towards nightfall do things and people start to move about. Then, out of running trenches, holes, caves and quite low, hidden wooden shelters, people and things can emerge. Then commences the bringing-up of building materials, ammunition, food, and troops who will eventually relieve other troops.

The Isonzo flows majestically with its many bow-shaped meanders down to the sea. You can also see the sea from here on clear days on the edge of the horizon as a delicate silver-white stripe. Northwards and eastwards from the town extends a wide plain which, in the north and in the south, is surrounded by undulating chains of hills. Everywhere are vineyards, orchards, cypresses and chestnut-tree hedges, fig and mulberry trees. All this uncultivated, not looked after, devoid of human habitation. The owners had to leave all their worldly goods and wander off, maybe homeless and hungry, to other unfamiliar areas. One thing you find a lot of here, many large military cemeteries as well as scattered single graves. Everything all over this region speaks eloquently of the bloody, violent, countless struggles, battles, attacks and counterattacks, all the killing, anger and destruction that have been going on here for more than a year now.

18 October 1916
Today I finally moved into the new medical centre. I had so much to do there all day just getting things straight. I am so pleased that I've finally managed to get out of that rickety old shack. Here I have at my disposal an indeed tiny, but at the same time bright, dry, and pleasant space for myself. The bandaging room can be used for a variety of purposes, bigger than the previous one, quite friendly and welcoming. Apart from that I have in addition a small room for my medical orderly. Tomorrow I will start work on the building of a second small hut for my medical assistants and the patients. Even the cave will be diligently built.

Today I had nothing to eat for the midday meal. It was not brought up from the supply train. Why this happened I don't rightly know. According to what I have just been told, this will go on being the case. We will get our food only once a day and that in the evening. With time we will learn to be satisfied.

19 October 1916
Today two enemy fixed air balloons are clearly visible from here. These are elongated balloons in the shape of a Knackwurst whose task is to observe the movements of the enemy. Such a balloon stays suspended for hours at some fixed point in the air and looks down your throat to your stomach. As anyone can easily see, this is not a very appetising prospect. But with time you get used to it and in no time at all you start to not even be aware of them being there. You come to terms quite quickly with a lot of things here. The observer stationed in the balloon naturally chooses a vantage point from where he has the best view of his adversary. It goes without saying that we too use this type of balloon for the same purpose.

* * *

Today too I did not get my midday meal again. Quite fortuitously I still had some tinned food with me. With this and with real chestnuts, which I am now consuming on a daily basis in increasing quantities, I helped myself. A truly unpretentious lifestyle, isn't it? Now I am waiting for the evening meal for which, however, I have lost my appetite. The tinned food didn't do me much good today.

20 October 1916
A blustery, icy cold north-east wind has been blowing today since early this morning. Being in the shack is unbearable. One is freezing cold here. And one is not allowed to light a fire as the rising columns of smoke could give us away immediately. One must slowly get used to the cold because, as the autumn wears on, the north-east wind blows more and more frequently getting stronger and stronger.

Tonight we will be relieved of our duties. We will then proceed to the reserve positions in Cronberg ('Ma Mokrim') where we were ten days ago and where it is even more uncomfortable than it is here.

It is night. Outside the wind is howling and shrieking pitilessly. The north-east wind is blowing increasingly violently and intensely. Added to that, it is very dark. I am waiting for the arrival of a second doctor who is due to relieve me. It's Senior Doctor Colonel Weidinger who will come to replace me. Then we will march through this miserable weather not fit to let dogs out in and over these bad paths. One of those cycle-race stage winners or rearguard dandies or one of those elegant, idle, indispensable gentlemen should come here just once and go on this march with us, live under these conditions, get to experience all these hardships. All the shirkers and army suppliers, countless numbers of whom there are away from the front who have used this war quite long enough to feather their own nests, should come here and experience it first-hand for once. These bloodthirsty hyenas have all got rich at other people's expense, have raised themselves up to the status of being millionaires. This whole great horde of rogues and swindlers, who have used the state quite unscrupulously in these times that are so hard, now belong to the ranks of cigar-chomping capitalists with money to burn. And they have always been spared all the difficulties, dangers, and efforts of the war itself. They are very important away from the front line. They get to make further use of the state that employs them. They must get a return on their investment. They are exempt from military duties. The rest of us, who were not allowed to 'shirk', have to drink our poisoned chalice to the dregs. We are handled quite ruthlessly. What an injustice!?

21 October 1916
Yesterday towards midnight I got here through this lousy weather not without a lot of difficulty. In that pitch-black night I couldn't see my hand in front of my face. And, just to round things off, a storm that tore innumerable big branches off trees, carried off roof slates from many a house and blew down many small huts. And that excuse for a path, on which you kept falling down into a fresh, deep shell hole, were always encountering deep and wide puddles, coming across badly positioned milestones that you were stubbing your toes against because you couldn't see them, and stumbling time and time again over loose stones and rocks. And a damp cold to make things even worse.

So I was finally glad to arrive in that house that was already familiar to me, in which still only a week ago the collection point for the wounded was housed and which, because of the continuous artillery bombardment, had to be moved from there. It feels uncannily cold in the treatment room. Many panes are missing from the windows. A strong wind is blowing through incessantly. How strange all this looks. It was good that I found a couch on which I could rest. Naturally I had to satisfy my hunger first. Otherwise I wouldn't have been able to sleep. No midday meal today either. Now I'm waiting for the food my orderly has gone to fetch for me. Unfortunately, when it came, it was stone cold and I had to leave it even though I was very hungry. Hardly had I spent half the night and today in this hole than I received a new, quite unexpected order to proceed to a neighbouring position, to a different battalion, the 3rd Battalion of Infantry Regiment 85, in order to replace their doctor who has gone on leave. I was most indignant at this lack of consideration. I, who had only just taken up one position, must now transfer to another in this still filthy weather. The medical officer of health has decreed it. He doesn't know what it means to live here and to have to go through all this. He doesn't experience any of this in Ossek. You are almost at a loss to know what's coming next. You never quite know what's expected of you.

25 October 1916
The weather has not been clement for quite a few days now. Today it's raining cats and dogs. I handed in an application to the army command post with a request, after such long service in the field, to be allocated to a hospital away from the front. I doubt if this will happen though.

31 October 1916
Since last night I have been sitting in Bonetti North in the group command centre with the so-called group reserve. I spent the night in a small, doorless, wooden shack on a stretcher for injured patients. It was very cold there. And it goes without saying that I had no good opportunity to sleep. It was a good thing that it didn't rain; otherwise it would have been full of water in there. Early in the morning I looked around for another shelter. I managed to find one, a small, quite-low, damp, cold, and dark cave in which I now propose to live. Here it is even more uncomfortable than yesterday's shack. But you are much safer. Today they went at it hammer and tongs all day long. Our own as well as enemy artillery kept the whole region under heavy fire.

2 November 1916
Today our battalion received a quite unexpected and disagreeable order. According to this order the battalion will march out of here at 6 o'clock tomorrow evening and proceed to the Rosental. Here it will remain for the time being in the Alla Baita gorge close to Villa Starkenfels.

Yesterday in the Rosental during the day the Italians conquered Hill 171. Perhaps it's important to us to win this back.

We are about to move out. The sky is covered in cloud and it's dark. The enemy is keeping under heavy artillery fire all of the path that we must use to march along. It won't be a piece of cake to march there. On the way we'll stop of course at the church of 'Ma Mokrim' to eat in the open air.

3 November 1916, Morning
We have been camped out in the open air since 11 o'clock last night on the eastern edge of the Panowitzer Forest. The original command issued to us was altered during our march to 'Ma Mokrim'. In our HQ there is an overall atmosphere of nervous tension and excitement. We did not, as was originally intended, eat at 'Ma Mokrim'. We had to keep on going. The pack animals with their load of food and drink naturally came with us. No one was able to give us precise orders. All we knew was that we had to go to the eastern edge of the Panowitzer Forest where we must link up immediately with the command centre of the 5th Mountain Brigade in Frühling. About 11 o'clock at night we were standing on the very spot itself. Fortunately we have hung on to the good weather. But it was cold and damp everywhere. Here we ate and had a rest, in the forest itself, on the ground. My sleeping bag only on this one occasion was of great use to me. Nevertheless, I could not sleep all night for the bitter cold. Apart from that, artillery fire was throughout the night uncommonly active. Our guns, which were positioned at the edge of the wood, sent over hundreds of shells that dropped on the enemy's positions. The whole wood trembled with the noise of the bombardment. The enemy held all our own positions from St Catherina extending to the plain of Prestau to the heights of the Panowitzer Forest and then on to the Rosental and the valley of the Vippacco as far as the high plateau of Komen and even beyond this to the sea under heavy artillery and infantry fire. Hill 171, which we had lost the day before yesterday, was won back whereat we took 700 prisoners, but afterwards we lost them again. This hill is situated on the south-west edge of the Rosental.

4 November 1916
We are still on the eastern edge of the Panowitzer Forest as a so-called divisional reserve. Tonight we all, both officers and men, had a roof over our heads. We found in the vicinity of where we are some already erected shelters standing empty. Apart from that, yesterday in the course of the afternoon, we caused roofs and tents to be put up. Old boards and roofing material lay around in adequate quantities. All these things were collected, and the work was carried out diligently.

We did not, of course, have access to proper tools. We could only use our bayonets.

Today we are having a really cold and gloomy day.

5 November 1916
Since 11 o'clock last night we have been in Baita in the Rosental. At 7 o'clock in the evening we left, on the grounds of a sudden order, the eastern edge of the Panowitzer Forest. In good weather we marched down the road that goes via Aissovitza to Gorizia as far as Baita. I am sitting for the time being with my medical orderly and my medical personnel in the collection centre for the injured, the chief of which is a serving officer and regimental doctor, unfriendly and not well initiated into the mysteries of medical science. There is a very big influx of dead and injured here.

Today has been a gloomy and rainy day. Today too a large number of fatalities were brought here, officers as well as men. They are busy now digging mass graves for them. There are still today 145 in the cemetery precincts awaiting burial, 26 of whom are Italian. The remainder, our own dead, belong in the main to the 2nd Hungarian Third Reserve Regiment and to Dalmatian Regular Army Infantry Regiment 23. What a hair-raising impression the sight of all these terrible victims of this horrible war makes.

5 November, Evening
Outside the weather is getting more and more inclement. The rain is steadily increasing in strength. It's raining in in all the rooms. It is cold and wet in these large, empty, old rooms. Our own as well as enemy guns are thundering away without a break. How sad things look in the room that I have. A nightmare is burdening my breast and constricting my breathing. My heart beats uneasily. I should almost like to cry out and weep in my despair. No trace anywhere of zest for life or hope. Gloomy thoughts dominate my mind and my ego. I should like to chase them away, but I am unequal to the task. They torture me endlessly.

I only have one great wish. For all this to be over once and for all. By whatever means it takes. It doesn't matter how as long as all the suffering stops. Because it can't keep going on like this. My willpower has weakened to nothing, my zest for life has vanished. Can you wonder at that? If only one could describe and express all this, clothe it in words, all that we have had to live through here. Happy the man who has been spared it. He doesn't even know the actual meaning of that one word: War. He cannot even begin to imagine the terrors it contains. Neither does he know what tragedies are being played out there a thousandfold on a day-to-day basis. Nor does he understand what a great shame, what an immeasurable disgrace this war is for the whole of Europe, for so-called European culture. (How can one still speak of culture? It's just an empty and meaningless word now.) Such a man has never had the opportunity to look into the real essence of human life, to see man before him naked and unadorned, without all the superfluous phrasemongering and all the conventional claptrap about culture, as only here such things can be seen.

* * *

The so-called 9th Offensive [i.e. the 9th battle of the Isonzo] is now in full swing. The enemy has latterly breached our positions at several points and taken them on the ground by a concerted infantry attack after a softening-up process set in train by an artillery bombardment. Hill 234, San Grado, Marna, Lokvica, and Kostanjevica are now in enemy hands. We suffered great losses through this in terms of human life. What will happen in the days to come, none of us can predict. We are, in any case, confronted by important events on this front.

6 November 1916
Today the artillery fire has abated somewhat. It threw it down with rain all night. And this morning as well. In the afternoon the weather brightened up a bit.

Tonight I got new orders, the upshot of which is that I have to march to a more forward position early tomorrow with my medical team and equipment. Namely, to the hunting lodge next to the road.

11 November 1916
Since 7 November I have been in the hunting lodge in the Rosental. The weather during all this time has been extremely bad. It has rained torrentially without let-up. It has also rained heavily into my room, so that the roof as well as the ceiling are both in a mess. The house had already been hit by shelling prior to my occupancy of it.

14 November 1916
After the sudden dropping off of the irrefutably short 9th Italian Offensive, lasting only a few days, but involving an enormous expenditure of artillery and infantry, it became relatively peaceful again. Few were the successes that the enemy could point to. On the high plateau of Komen he succeeded in occupying some of our positions by way of Faiti Hrib up to and including towards Kostanjevica. We sustained enormous losses (dead and wounded) as a result, but the losses sustained by the enemy were incomparably more. Whole heaps of bodies are lying around there all over the place which, because of the hostilities, cannot be buried.

For a few days things got much quieter. The day before yesterday and yesterday enemy planes were up to mischief. Last night a plane dropped two bombs on our camp, one of which exploded not very far at all from the medical centre.

Tonight there was more intensive shooting. An intensive artillery and infantry bombardment on both sides. Many shells and pieces of shrapnel exploded close to the medical centre, so much so that I could not stay here with my medical team and had to seek shelter in the cave. Here we waited for a few hours until the firing died down a bit. In this instance there was an operation underway undertaken by our infantry in attacking some of the enemy positions on Monte San Marco (171). The enemy was surprised by this and driven out of his second as well as his first line of defence, whereupon we availed ourselves of the opportunity to take 400 enemy soldiers prisoner. There were very many dead and wounded on both sides, but more on the opposing side. A Bohemian battalion belonging to the 28th Infantry Regiment brought about this minor success.

22 November 1916

Up to and including the evening of the 17th I stayed with my medical centre in the hunting lodge where I was relieved by the Head Doctor of the 3rd Battalion of the 23rd Third Reserve Infantry Regiment, Dr Tommaseo, Baron of Lazzarini. The latter is an Italian from Albona (in Istria) and was for a few years employed in a hospital in Tunis.

I went from the hunting lodge with my battalion to Ossegliano for so-called rest and recovery. The next day the whole battalion were deloused at Divisional Health Headquarters in Ossek. Unfortunately, the weather was terrible. First of all, a sirocco and then heavy downpours that went on day and night. Men as well as officers were able to relax a bit and recover from all the stresses and strains of the last few weeks. Unfortunately, the window for rest and recovery is too short. We are only allowed to remain here for seven days. No later than the evening of the 24th we must go back to front-line positions and this time to San Marco, south of 171, a very unpleasant and dangerous place, which was betrayed to the enemy by deserters. On the 19th of the month five officers, among whom was a serving second lieutenant by the name of Jedlička of the 24th Marching Battalion of 37th Third Reserve Infantry Regiment under the command of Captain Weinberg, went over to the enemy. As luck would have it, they were not sufficiently informed about the conditions that they had only a short time ago left behind them in the field.

23 November 1916

Today all four company commanders were outside in the positions that we are to occupy tomorrow night in order to get an idea of them. They are in a very bad state of repair. There are no shelters whatsoever there for the men. They will have to stay during the whole of the posting period, i.e. for seven days, in the open air regardless of the rain and cold. There they will have to work like men possessed rebuilding the positions and creating caves. And the catering won't be any good either as the way forward, because of the bad paths under enemy observation, is a very arduous one.

172   *The Mountain War*

Today a cold and blustery north-east wind blew all day long. The rain stopped accordingly.

Tomorrow, the 24th, at 8 o'clock in the morning, we will, on the occasion of the imperial succession, officers as well as men, swear an oath of loyalty to the new emperor. The white-haired old monarch, Franz Josef I, has died and the until now heir to the throne, Archduke Karl Franz Josef, now ascends to the throne as Emperor Karl the First.

29 November 1916
Since the 24th we have been in position in San Marco, south-east of Gorizia. Here I have taken over from Regimental Doctor Fuschmann of the 75th Landsturm Battalion [Landsturm – Third Line Reserve of the Austrian army]. He is an army doctor who, even at the beginning of this war, was serving as a captain in the field and had reached the grade of Honved 4 [Honved – Defender of the Fatherland in Magyar].

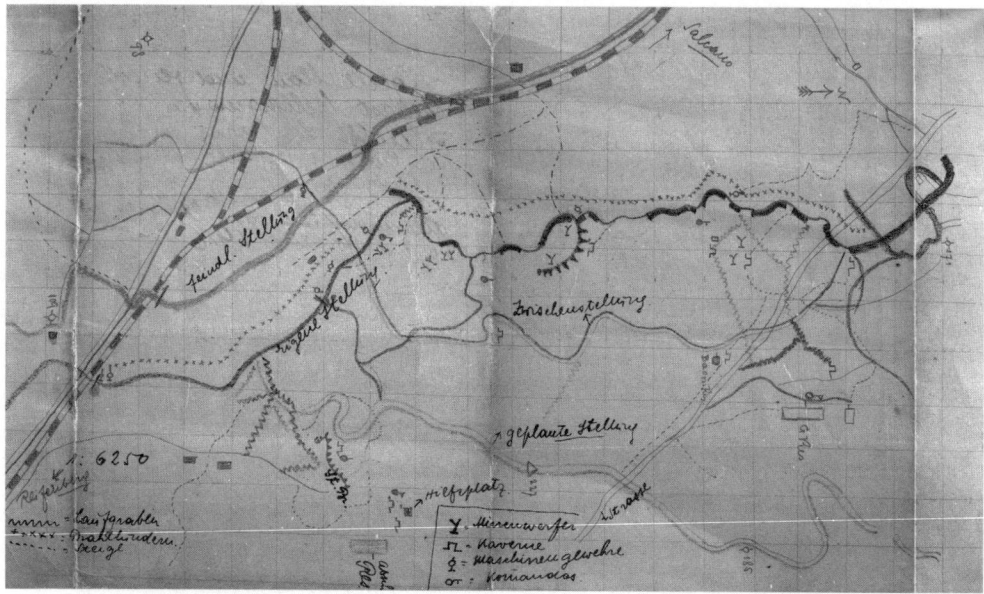

Map drawn by Isaak Barasch found in the pages of the diary. North is to the right. In Salcano, now Solkan in Slovenia, the Solkan Bridge over the Isonzo River was blown up by Austro-Hungarian engineers in August 1916, but was re-built by the Italians in 1925–7.

30 November 1916
This evening we are to be relieved by the 96th Croatian infantry regiment, which suffered huge losses in the 9th Italian offensive. Only three weakened companies were left out of the whole of the regiment. After a short period of restoration, supplemented by a battalion march, we are again taking up a position …

We are going back to be with the 4th Mountain Brigade. Today we are going to Ossegliano. [Ossegliano is present-day Ozeijan, a suburb of Nova Gorica (Slovenia) and Monte San Marco (227m) is also in Slovenia being one of the elevations of the Vippacco (now Vipava in Slovenia) valley/Wippachtal between Ranziano and Monte Sabotino that lent its name to a military sector ('Sector San Marco') during the First World War. The Italian army's biggest success would take place in November 1916 when they captured Hill 171 near Monte San Marco.] Our period of being dug in here was very unpleasant. There was a lot of shooting there and, apart from that, the shelters and the catering were awful. To top it all off, the weather was bad as well.

9 December 1916
Since the evening of the 7th we are once again back in position in St Caterina. I am there in the fairly good and comfortable medical centre built by me about three months ago. I spent both the first night and the second night almost without sleeping a wink, working, bandaging the wounded. Several people were badly wounded with multiple, compound fractures for the setting in splints of which a great deal of time was required. Even before I arrived, many people had been dropped off there

What with the incessant bad weather, the wet and the damp and wretched cold, we suffered very much. If only we could get warm just once during the day. But this we aren't allowed to do. Faiti Hrib, which was captured by the enemy during the 8th offensive, looks down on us early in the morning. It gives you the willies. With all these bad conditions army catering both for enlisted men and for officers is lousy. Everyone suffers from hunger. The outdoor kitchen comes only once a day, i.e. in the evening. The food is badly prepared, cold and there really isn't much of it. All those gentlemen who bring up the rear and fill their stomachs as replete as they fill their pockets see to that. Quartermasters, assistant quartermasters, commanders of convoys and whatever else they're called. A disgusting, black-market gang of common parasites, who quite ruthlessly make use of the infantryman and the infantry officer, poor as mice anyway, who have so much to go through in the front line and who live in the utmost danger. Right at the back of our battalion is Lieutenant Vetar, a customs official from Ragusa, who likes the war a lot. He is the commanding officer of a convoy. He has such a good time of it here that he never once wants to go on leave because 'time is money'.

A second such person is Mr Leopold, a quartermaster. A third such person Lieutenant L. Anton, an official with Lloyds in Spalato. Sometimes there was a general feeling that the latter, because of a recurring chronic inflammation of his middle ear, should be invalided out. He, however, doesn't want to be. It goes without saying that he prefers to be here. Patriotic elements probably come into it with him as well. And there are still other people that I don't even want to mention.

A day before we marched away to take up our positions, i.e. on the 6th, the [Austrian] Home Defence Minister, Major General [Friedrich von] Georgi, inspected us. For this purpose we had to march on the evening of the 5th from Ossegliano to Cernice where the inspection took place. The gentleman had not trusted himself to go any further. With him was also present the commander of the 5th Army, Major General Boroević. Apart from them the commanding officer of our own Corps (the 16th Corps), General Wurmfeuer, the head of a division, was also present.

21 December 1916, Morning
Today I will be relieved of my duties at the Makuči medical centre and go (with the whole battalion naturally) to Ossegliano in the so-called R & R zone. Here the battalion will remain – when nothing prevents it – for seven days. To take my place at the Makuči medical centre the medical head of the 37th Division of the 2nd Army, Lance Corporal Assistant Doctor Stannoch will come, who, until tonight, is stationed at the St Katharine Medical centre. This morning I went to visit him there and found him in a really bad way. During the night

two large hand bombs had hit the medical centre, one of which was so heavy that I couldn't even lift it. The latter fell in the doctor's living quarters and also destroyed the floor. Fortunately, the doctor was at that moment lying on his bed of wooden boards at the diametrically opposite end of that really tiny room. Because of this he remained unharmed. Only the aftershock of the intense explosion did not go away. People's lives continue to be in the greatest danger.

21 December 1916, Afternoon
I just received a fine piece of good news. I am finally being discharged from the regiment and going to the Reserve Hospital in Fiume. This is what the submission of my application almost two months ago has led to. There will now be a well-deserved, most favourable change to my whole lifestyle. I will be able once again, after a long and difficult time, to lead an orderly quiet life. I will once again be able to have an opportunity to practise as a real doctor. I am hugely pleased by this news I have waited for and yearned for for so long. I shall therefore in the next few days be taking leave of this regiment in which I have had, especially of late, to endure much unpleasantness, even career-wise, in the shape of our battalion's commanding officer, Captain Karlik, a short, sly, conceited creature, who, for reasons unbeknown to me, has made life difficult for me everywhere I go. He is a man who moves heaven and earth just to get his orders from the Crown. Towards his subordinates he is totally ruthless, sullen, unfriendly. And his second-in-command is Lieutenant Mandolfo, a weak, hesitant, yielding type of person. Yesterday I had an unpleasant set-to with the gentleman concerned. I expressed my opinion, of course, well within the framework set down by military rules and regulations. On this occasion he levelled the bitter reproach at me that, in spite of two-and-a-half years of wartime service, I was still very sensitive and had not been hardened by military discipline. He gave me as his major piece of advice to acquire military hardness as soon as possible without suspecting that my biggest worry all the time was how to stay untouched by it. And the latter objective I attained to my utmost satisfaction.

Since 21 December we have been in Ossegliano in our R & R zone. I have already met the doctor who was sent here to replace me. He's

Assistant Doctor Miele. This man, however, immediately reported as sick. He has a rather advanced form of tuberculosis of the lungs. I must therefore stay with the battalion until someone else comes, which cannot take very long as an immediate replacement was promised by army high command.

On the 22nd, 23rd and 24th I carried out a cholera vaccination for the whole battalion. We experienced very bad weather throughout.

On Christmas Eve we had a quite small, very modestly decorated Christmas tree and a gramophone served up instrumental music. Only a few records were at our disposal and so each piece was played over and over again. We all listened devoutly for this was an event for us.

Today the battalion has again taken up a position. I could not go with them as I have been suffering for the last few days from sciatica all down the left side of my body. Walking causes me great pain. I was therefore obliged to report myself as sick. The consequences of this really primitive, tiring way of life that is full of privations never go away. I naturally asked for a locum for the duration of my illness. Lance Corporal Assistant Doctor Stannoch, medical head of the 2nd Battalion was appointed, although until now he has been at the 'Primakueich' medical centre. There are enough doctors here in divisional headquarters. Why is it that none of these is appointed to such a post? They are kept out of it because, one way or another, they have succeeded in currying the favour of doctors on the General Staff.

So, I'm staying on in Ossegliano. The medical centre left here at 5 pm. With it went my ensign, Sadek Franz, a serious, intelligent, sensitive, sympathetic young man. He took his leave of me with tears in his eyes. He could not utter a single word because of his depression. He knew that, in all probability, I would very soon be out of here myself and he wouldn't see me again. I am sorry to see him go …

Chapter 4

From the Isonzo to the Piave

Introduction by Hew Strachan

On 24 October 1917 – too late in the year for an offensive in the judgement of many – the twelfth battle of the Isonzo opened. It did so not with the long preparatory bombardments typical of its predecessors but with a short and intense counter-battery fire targeting the enemy's artillery, which was obligingly placed forward, rather than his trenches and fortifications. These lacked depth and the initial infantry attack, which followed immediately, was quickly converted into a complete breakthrough. The attackers were not the Italians but the Central Powers, and the front on which they did so was much further north than any of the preceding eleven battles. It ran from Flitsch (today Bovec) in the north to Tolmein in the south. Here the front line followed the high ground in a nearly straight line, but the river ran south-west through Caporetto (to the Italians, for whom this was their local headquarters, but known as Karfreit to the Germans and Kobarid in today's Slovenia), before turning south-east back to Tolmein. The broad valley provided good ground for the opening stages of the offensive, even if there were successive mountain ranges behind Caporetto, and here the river itself was broad and fordable.

Alarmed by the state of the Austro-Hungarian army at the end of the eleventh Isonzo battle, the Germans had reinforced it with seven divisions, under the command of Otto von Below of the 14th Army. Its chief of staff, Krafft von Dellmensingen, a Bavarian expert on mountain warfare, planned the battle. Unlike Cadorna, who had sought to dominate the high ground before advancing, Krafft urged his units to maintain their momentum by following the valley bottoms. Against an army configured for its own advance but also wracked by mutinies and poor morale, the 14th Army gathered speed the further it penetrated.

The German divisions, including specialist mountain troops, formed the army's left and an Austro-Hungarian corps commanded by Alfred Krauss its right. Within four days, the 14th Army was out of the mountains and facing Cadorna's headquarters at Udine. The Italians fell back behind the line of the River Tagliamento. Krauss crossed the river further upstream in the mountains, so outflanking the Italians, who were dislodged and continued their retreat.

The Germans' intentions were more limited than the results they had achieved. They had wanted to relieve the pressure on their allies in the Carso, but their combined offensive had now unhinged the whole Italian position in the north-east. The breakthrough threatened the lines of communication between Italy and its armies on the lower Isonzo. The Italians had to fall back across their front. By mid-November, their losses totalled 700,000, of whom only 40,000 had been killed or wounded; 280,000 had been captured and about 350,000 had deserted. Italy's British and French allies rushed divisions to Italy to help plug the gaps. Vittorio Orlando formed a coalition government and, when Cadorna refused to resign, the king dismissed him and appointed Armando Diaz in his stead. The Austro-Hungarians too reconfigured their command arrangements. On 1 November an army group made up of the formations from south Tyrol, including the 10th and 11th Armies, was placed under Conrad von Hötzendorf. On his left Archduke Eugen led a front formed of two army groups, one led by von Below and containing the 14th German Army and its associated Austro-Hungarian formations, and the other in the south led by Boroević, whose 5th Army was reconfigured as the 1st and 2nd Isonzo armies.[1]

Barasch was recalled to active duty on 20 October 1917, four days before Caporetto. He joined the 55th Infantry Regiment as its regimental doctor at Laibach, and he remained with it for the remainder of his front-line service. Together with the 15th Infantry Regiment, it was in the 21st Brigade (commanded by Friedrich von Weisz), which served in the 10th Infantry Division, commanded by Emil von Gołogórski. The division was part of XXIII Corps, which

---

1. *Österreich-Ungarns letzter Krieg*, Vol. VI, Beilage 23.

had been formed in November 1916 and served continuously on the Italian front, now within the 1st Isonzo Army. By 29 October, Boroević's army group was on the move, approaching the lower Isonzo in conformity with the breakthrough to its north. The Italians destroyed the bridges as they retreated and the river rose, hindering 10th Division's crossing, but by 1 November it was over and already halfway to the Tagliamento.

Given that this was Barasch's first experience of mobile war and that his army was advancing – and doing so without encountering effective opposition, his diary might be expected to luxuriate in the flush of victory. It does not. His hopes of the war ending were vested not in what was occurring on his front, but in the Russian Revolution. Reports that the Bolsheviks wanted to negotiate reached him on 2 November 1917. He attributed the success against the Italians to the Germans, not to his own army, whose indiscipline as it advanced along the Adriatic coast appalled him because of its wastefulness. Soldiers were permitted to loot and plunder when the high command should have organised the riches of the Venetian plain in a more systematic manner. He is scathing about its staff work, noting on 11 November 1917 how Gołogórski's chief of staff, Karl Tarbuk von Sensenhorst, struggled with his map reading. His diary bears witness to an army which was spent a year before its final surrender: Barasch even praises the Italian army for the superior quality of its equipment, despite its defeat.

On 10 November, the Italians rallied behind the Piave. Conrad's army group, with Below's 14th Army on his left, attempted to get behind their left wing by pushing down from the mountains and the Asiago plateau but he was checked. As Barasch describes, Boroević's army group also made half-hearted and ill-planned frontal attempts to cross the Piave but, with the year closing and the Austro-Hungarians' own communications in disarray thanks to the rapidity and extent of their advance, the line stabilised. The Germans withdrew the 14th Army in January and relations between the two allies remained fraught: the Austro-Hungarians were constrained to commit two divisions they could ill afford to a front – France – in which they had no interest. Not until the following summer, on 15 June 1918, did the

Austro-Hungarian army mount a set-piece major offensive to cross the Piave. It failed and the Italians counter-attacked, forcing Boroević to retreat back across the river. By 23 June, the Italians were again on the river line and there they stayed – despite pressure from their allies – until October. Although Barasch had been recalled to service on 3 June, his health had collapsed by the 15th and on 12 September he died. On 3 October Germany requested an armistice, prompting Austria-Hungary to do so too, but unlike Germany it received no direct response. The Italians began their own offensive on 24 October, the first anniversary of Caporetto, launching a diversionary attack towards Asiago and establishing bridgeheads across the Piave on the 27th. The Austrians renewed their effort to seek an armistice on 29 October, when the Italians reached Vittorio Veneto, and agreed terms at Villa Giusti on 4 November. The Hungarians did so in Belgrade on 13 November. Two months after Barasch's death, the empire which he had served no longer existed.

28 April 1917
Since 6 January I have been in Fiume. To begin with in the Reserve Hospital, which is housed in the Naval Academy, under the command of Medical Staff Doctor, Colonel Richard Pfeffers. Since March 15 I have been allocated to the Red Cross Hospital.

Yesterday I was in the company of Professor Cori, his wife and the female Dr Bacie in Abbazzia. While here we visited the female painter [Leo Von] Littrow [1860–1925], a highly-strung, lively, well-educated, refined lady who is 60 years old and who showed us her many fine pictures and her very rich collection of various antiques. The pictures are, for the most part, seascapes and studies of islands, very atmospheric, and I spent a fine afternoon in this likeable company. Also in Abbazzia, I made the acquaintance of Miss Celebrim, the daughter of Councillor Celebrim, the medical expert retained by state dignitaries in Trieste for Istria.

On 1 May I am going on holiday to Vienna.

On 20 May I got back from holiday. From now on I will be serving the troops and the prisoners of war.

On 6 and 7 July I was on duty in the isle of Veglia (a workplace in Besca Vecchia) and San Gregorio. I had there to examine workers employed in the bauxite mines, bauxite being an aluminium-bearing ore.

On 12 August 1917 I had to report to Lieutenant General Istvanovic. Major Hoch, who commands a battalion in the 79th Infantry Regiment, took me to see him. And why? Because I am too assiduous with my morning visits, send too many people to hospital in Zagreb and declare too many illnesses. I'm too much of a doctor and not enough an army doctor. These are the reproaches constantly being levelled at me by lay people, by men who are not in the least bit qualified to diagnose a person's state of health. But yesterday I had to listen to the same thing from a doctor, Colonel Richard Pfeffers, who even went as far as to threaten me with possibility of losing my position here for this very reason. And today, I was placed on report and the same thing was relayed to me again.

26 August 1917
A trip in my capacity as a doctor to Besca Vecchia to the premises of Bauxite Limited (an imperial German company.)

Last night at half-past one in the morning we left on the commercial steamer that goes back and forth between Fiume and Ragusa. At seven in the morning we reached our destination, and soon after, I had to make my medical inspection of the workers since they were needed to load the ship with bauxite, which they did throughout the day. In all, fifty-one men are employed here, almost all weak, sick, undernourished, and overworked. Many have been doing this hard job, without a break, without having a single day off, for more than two years. For ten hours a day they work in the mines, with poor food and exposed to the enormous heat and breathe in the dust.

About 1 o'clock in the afternoon I went by sailboat and favourable winds to Ponte. I had a look round this old, rather big, and poor place. It has a population of approximately 4,000.

About 6.30 pm we started our journey back.

27 September 1917, Midnight
Directly after my arrival from the isle of Arbe, I had to inspect the Mondaneo bauxite mine and gather facts relating to the case of a soldier who had died suddenly two days earlier.

Yesterday at 2 o'clock in the morning we left Fiume aboard the small, old, dirty steamer *Dalmatia* belonging to the Hungary-Croatia Company. About seven in the morning we arrived today at our destination. Here I was kept busy until about 11 o'clock, whereupon I proceeded on foot to the main town on the island, also called Arbe. After a march of one-and-a-quarter hours in scorching heat along a steep, rocky path fallen into disrepair, I reached the town. I found a hotel where I had a modest repast after visiting this beautiful, remote old town on the Karst limestone plateau. The ancient, grey, mostly ruined city walls, the old gates, the slim, proud towers, the imposing wide cathedral, the inscriptions on the old houses well preserved only in a few places, the narrow streets, all these are eloquent witnesses of centuries long gone. In one of the churches I found a Rubens that has been well looked after by the present population. Croatian, but also a Habsburg possession, this island is already part of Dalmatia.

1 October 1917
Homecoming from a business trip to Besca Vecchia (a bauxite mine) on the isle of Veglia.

20 October 1917, 5 am
An agonising night without any sleep whatsoever. Last night in the mess Chief Medical Officer Pfeffers informed me that I had had a wire from army headquarters ordering me back to the front. I must go 'immediately' to the front to join the 55th Infantry Regiment. It struck me as a highly unpleasant and quite unexpected piece of news.

How abandoned and alone in the midst of all these strange, completely indifferent, cold, self-seeking people do I feel just now. The most they can do is force themselves to express superficial and conventional condolences and sympathy, which only hurts and offends me. The times can afford nothing more inward or deeper. If I only had a warm, sympathetic, pure soul next to me – I long for one so much – I should like to tell it so many things. I should like to pour out all my sorrow, keep it far from the dirt there is in life and love it so deeply, so profoundly with every fibre of my being and my soul. And where are you now, the one I'm looking for, the one I long for so much, the one I await so impatiently? A single, warm, loving glance from you could confer on me a reservoir of spiritual strength to help me hold out at this difficult time, could bring me hope and faith for the future. Perhaps this uncanny, dreadful war is responsible for us not being able to find each other?!

Today I must leave Fiume. I have spent many happy hours here at the seaside. Unfortunately, my sojourn here was a very short one.

Yesterday I visited an acquaintance to whose home I was invited, Mr Szögö Pali (Via Verneda 5). Here I came across a large group of people including Dr Aladar Rapoch, April C.F. Zgl. Jaksie, Sau. Lieutenant Grünbaum (Gabor), Levaggi, Assistant Doctor Neuschass. I was not able to stay there long. Most of them were playing cards. I took my leave of them quite quickly and went home to write various letters before my departure.

On 21 October 1917 at 6 o'clock in the morning I left Fiume. In the train I encountered OG A Dr Munk from Lemberg who was also going to the front to join the 73rd. In addition, there was OG A Dr Spit, who had been assigned to a column of a division.

During the journey I stopped off in Adelsberg and sought out the army medical chief, General Staff Officer Dr Weil Gustav. He is a most kind, extremely understanding man, but once an order is issued he is unable to change it. There was nothing else for it. I had to go to the front to join my regiment. From Adelsberg I proceeded that night to Laibach on a goods train. It was cold and rained heavily. I got to Laibach at 11 o'clock at night and found with great difficulty lodgings at the Hotel Elephant. Laibach is bursting at the seams with military personnel. I stayed here till 6 o'clock in the morning on 23/X. I went to visit the wife of the vet, Dr Lamprer, to say goodbye.

On 23 October 1917 at 6 o'clock in the morning I continued my journey. From there I went via Divacca to Opeina where I received further information at the local collection point for convalescents. I now need to go via Prosecco, Gabrovica and Bayta to Kresja. In the last place, I will make my way to Gullen in an ancient lorry which I will need to take so as to know the way back. On the same day I proceeded on to Trieste. I stayed here till the following day, i.e. early in the morning of the 24th and then went back to Opeina by tram. From Opeina I went to Prosecco where I had to wait for a second lorry to take me further. After a long time I found one and continued on to Kresja. From there I had to proceed on foot in very unpleasant and cold rainy weather by way of paths that were soaking wet through on to Samotorce, where my regiment was stationed.

There, on the very same day, I relieved Assistant Doctor Ludwig Landau of his duties. I am now Regimental Chief Doctor of the 55th Infantry Regiment [Barasch's headstone give his rank as *Oberazt*, suggesting that this was an acting rank only].

Already the following day, i.e. on the evening of 25 October, I had to go via Vicenik, Mavhinje and Cerovlje to take up my position. We are at the foot of the peak of Hermaola, the apple of the enemy's eye and hotly disputed. The first aid post is in the camp at Mideazza. The barracks there is small, rather badly built, damp, dull, and dark, and this is where we have to live and work. And, in addition, we must share this small space with another regiment. The first aid post of the

3rd Infantry Regiment is also housed here with OG A Dr Berl from Vienna and his medical orderly Herr Bauer (also from Vienna).

In order to build other first aid centres along these lines there is a shortage of helpful equipment. Drilling machines are needed for the construction of spacious and well-built barracks for command centres well away from the front line. The lives of commanders are so precious. Doctors and medical orderlies can be replaced easily. But commanders of divisions and their immediate subordinates like doctors on the general staff, who are currently vegetating in Ternica, well in the rear, are absolutely irreplaceable.

We must keep our mouths shut and make do with the little that there is on hand.

Before marching off to my position, I reported to the Divisional Doctor St. A. Dr Tintner. This hero from Turnovica received me in a most unfriendly manner, but I have completely stopped caring about such things.

The following doctors and medics are with the regiment: A.A. Dr Pejša (1st Battalion), Medical Orderly Lieutenant Sperling, A.A. Dr Havranek, New 2nd Battalion Medical Orderly Peter Janosz, Medical Orderly Lieutenant Schopper (4th Battalion along with Herr Redluh), Medical Orderly Rothfeld from Lemberg, who is with us at the first aid centre.

28 October 1917, 8 o'clock in the Morning

For almost two hours we have found ourselves in the medical centre in the so-called Third Reserve line that stretches from Iwege to Flondar. At 9 o'clock I must set off and march towards Pietra Rossa. We are in pursuit of the enemy who is retreating all along the line.

29 October 1917, 8 pm in St Canziano

After long and very strenuous forced marches in most unfavourable weather we arrived here yesterday. Our march itinerary took us via Selz, Roùche, Dobbia and so on till we reached the Isonzo. We could not cross this river as the enemy had left all the bridges behind him in flames. We had to call a halt and proceed to the construction of a bridge. We had to spend the whole night in the open out in the streets tired, frozen, hungry, and soaked to the skin in inclement weather. All the bridges along the Isonzo and in several places roundabout were merrily ablaze due to fires set by the Italians to cover their retreat. A huge pall of smoke and columns of fire rose up on all sides high in the sky. Truly it was a sight worthy of Nero.

We were told that weakened enemy patrols were still in the area. From time to time a dull bang could be heard from over there. The men on our side did not know what it meant. Our leadership, as always, had not been sufficiently careful on this occasion. Soon we felt the consequences. Towards midnight the level of the water near the left bank of the Isonzo rose, and we were all standing up to our navels in water. The whole area for miles around looked like one big lake. We were in danger of drowning. Enemy patrols had brought this about and our leaders, as usual, had not noticed it in time. Now we had to get a grip on a bad situation. Whole units of sappers with specially trained dogs were entrusted with this task.

30 October 1917, 12.30 pm
Since midday we have been ready to march. We have to cross the Isonzo in this inclement weather. An ice-cold, violent north-easterly is blowing without abating and it is raining heavily – all the streets are deep under water. We are wading through cold water up to above our knees. My shoes and clothes are wringing wet.

* * *

Sappers are working on building pontoon bridges. Tonight we are again standing on the bank of the Isonzo and waiting till we can get across.

Our march takes us directly through Papariano-Arvignone-St Giorgio di Nogara-Muzzama-Palazzolo to Latisana.

Towards half-past nine it is our turn to march across the quite narrow and rickety bridge constructed by us. In front of us there were some other regiments who had forded the river in this way.

1 November 1917, 8 o'clock in the Morning
We are already in St Giorgio di Nogara, a small Italian town that has been almost completely abandoned by its population and badly damaged by fleeing Italian soldiers. We arrived here yesterday towards 9 o'clock at night after a tiring ten-hour-long march.

The previous night we spent in Cervignano to which we came after crossing the Isonzo around midnight. This fine little town was ill served by retreating Italians and in large part plundered and destroyed. The work of looting and destruction was only ended when our own hordes of soldiers showed up. Unfortunately, out of deference to them just in case, further looting was not prevented. Whole units raged through the town where, throughout the length and breadth of its shops, they brought to light the best wines, chocolate, meat, fruit, and tinned stuff. Only a minimal civilian population had remained in the town. Most of them fled along with the enemy troops, even though Cervignano actually belongs to Austrian Friuli. Houses that were still inhabited were, by a stroke of good fortune, spared. Our hordes of soldiers went on the rampage only in abandoned houses and shops. This was a scandal and an unforgiveable mistake on the part of our ever short-sighted military high command who left the regiments to stay overnight in the town. Many fine things were destroyed needlessly which had been spared by the enemy in their haste to make themselves scarce.

I visited there a hospital in which I found about a hundred badly wounded Italians. With them was an Italian doctor, an army chaplain, and two medics. One of the medics there was a first-rate radiographer. He led me to the very big, well-managed, well-equipped, valuable x-ray department, which had, unfortunately, been totally wrecked by soldier vandals.

We left Cervignano at 11 o'clock in the morning in fine, bright weather. We marched through the fertile, far-flung plain. On the way, lying about everywhere on the paths, in ditches and bogs, dead horses, oxen, and cattle which had been shot by a retreating enemy as they could no longer be taken along. There were spiked big guns and broken-down lorries. Many houses, for the most part depots and stores, were in flames. A terrible spectacle. There were thousands of bottles of wine, tins, new and good shoes just lying about there. About half-past twelve in the afternoon, we crossed the border into Italy. Now we were marching through enemy territory. On the way we saw whole units consisting of prisoners of war in varying sizes from small to large being led to Cervignano.

1 November 1917, During the Night
I am living here in a small farmhouse with Lieutenant Tunis, a high-school colleague I met here by chance, after not having seen him for seven years. Lieutenant Mossoczy is also sleeping here. He reported to me yesterday as sick because of a pulled ligament in a knee joint and I excused him from duty for a few days. The latter in civilian life is an opera singer (bass) in Lemberg. About 1 o'clock in the morning my sleep was disturbed, and I could not fall asleep again. The regimental chaplain came by. This gentleman was well in the rear with a provisions convoy where he could feed his face accordingly and had comfortable living quarters at his disposal. While we are living outside in small, damp, dark, dull dumps in the Karst plateau region and having to endure hunger, and not only that, but having constantly to stand in the open air and be in danger of loss of life and limb. This mean, dirty parasite, this boring, grovelling, self-serving representative of a profession that cares for souls is really not bothered about the poor people who are suffering out there and who are having to die for the fatherland. For this 'reverend' the war is a godsend. This quite young, poor, lazy man is filling his pockets and for him this is the most important thing. Now, when we are temporarily out of danger, he comes here all amiable and laid-back so as once again, after such a long time, to say a Mass in the field and to encourage people to persevere in the war effort. The state pays him a captain's wages for this. These 'noble' and devout Christians have now completely forgotten about Christ's teaching of love thy neighbour, since they could now no longer maintain it, and preach, for high wages, hate, vengeance, murder, and the annihilation of that neighbour who does not pay them. And to think that men are blind enough to be pleased about this and to put up with it.

2 November 1917, 6 o'clock in the Morning

At 4 o'clock this morning I received the command to leave this location at 8 o'clock and march to Muzzama. We are getting closer and closer to the River Tagliamento where heavily armed enemy rearguard patrols are still putting up a lot of resistance. The enemy's main force is involved in a full and far-flung, orderly retreat, according to news from the 2nd Battalion of our regiment, which is functioning as a so-called pursuit battalion. In this pursuit some small skirmishes developed, in which, in any case, we sustained only inconsiderable losses. These included among others the battalion commander, Major Böhm, a brave, energetic, serious, self-sacrificing officer. The regiment suffered a very great loss from his going. The regiment could be proud of this man. Other than that, very few troops of great strategic worth are to be found here. The regimental commander himself, Colonel Ulvsiant, is a heavy drinker for whom the consequences of alcoholism are already apparent, and allowances have to be made for him. He is a figure of fun. Fortunately, he has a most energetic, intelligent, diligent adjutant in the shape of Captain Tandy, but he is being sent to hospital tomorrow because of illness. Most of the other officers are, for the large part, young, inexperienced gentlemen, active, of course, but seldom to be found.

Despite such circumstances, for the most part, an everyday occurrence, despite poor leadership and inadequate organisation, we still enjoy renewed military succes. And this while our enemy is far and away superior to us in terms of technical resources.

He is also better logistically. What is the secret of our success? Only the historian of the future will be able to account for this. Our soldiers have made themselves most comfortable in enemy territory. They were trapped for months on end in monotonous and difficult trench warfare. Now they have made their home in the terrible land of the enemy.

Everything is being taken away from the local population: cows, oxen, poultry, horses, various cereal crops, wine, anything one stumbles upon is requisitioned. If only one could proceed without extravagance. Our powers of organisation are too defective for that. A lot is destroyed and thrown away uselessly. And this is happening at a time when people are having to queue up for hours just for a piece of bread, a piece of meat, etc. and having to pay exorbitant prices for them into the bargain. And until our indolent leadership stirs its stumps, most of it gets wasted anyway. It always turns up too late with its rules and regulations. Oh! Poor Austria.

3 November 17
Yesterday towards 11 am we reached Muzzama where we will also spend time. Today about 2 am I received the news that at 9 am we are to continue our march to Casa Bianca. It was once again a fine, bright, and warm day. Yesterday the 11th and 12th Honved (i.e. Hungarian) divisions started their march. As soldiers they are both robust and totally ruthless. Our own soldiers despise the Hungarians a lot.

The broken bridges over the Tagliamento have now been repaired.

3 November 1917, 9 pm
We are located next to the Casa Bianca (= white house), approximately 6km from Latisana. We are drawn up in marching order. Tonight troops, who are still in front of us, will force a crossing of the Tagliamento. The regiment is stationed in the open air.

5 November 1917
Early this morning we finally managed to cross the river on pontoons. Now the bridge will be erected over which we will have to continue our march. A fine, bright, and cheerful autumn day. Everything is in readiness for the continuation of our march. There is hustle and bustle in the ranks. For the last three days an ever-growing menagerie of cows, calves, mules, donkeys, and pigs have been brought forth and assembled. Some were left behind by the fleeing population, some have been requisitioned from the remaining population. The requisitioning is ruthless. Animals are being slaughtered indiscriminately, more and more just so that they can be cooked. Many are indeed ill from having eaten too much. What they cannot eat is being thrown away, while, at the same time, behind the lines, people are constantly suffering. No commander worries about this, no one intervenes to organise all this. Good wheat, white flour is brutally trampled underfoot. It is difficult to watch this happening.

8 November 1917, 4 am, in Corbolone on the River Livenza
The bridges over the river have been blown up. Strong enemy patrols are offering firm resistance on the west bank and temporarily preventing a crossing. We had already reached Corbolone the day before yesterday, i.e. on the 6th about 8 pm after a tiring day's march and did battle immediately with the enemy patrols already in position on the other bank where enemy patrols still exist. To our left, the 15th Infantry Regiment managed at a short stretch near St Steno di Livenza, where the river describes a sharp bend, to cross it and to attack the enemy directly on the west bank. Enemy resistance has, however, not yet been broken. These enemy patrols have been given the task at each river to hold us up for a certain time and to cover in this way their retreat, so that they can withdraw in an orderly fashion.

The enemy was able to do this where the Tagliamento was concerned. Along the whole stretch from the Tagliamento to the Livenza we found no one to kill. The enemy had been able to cover their retreat completely. Perhaps they will also succeed in doing so between Livenza and Piave. What is going to happen now is anybody's guess. All the locals have assured us that the enemy intends to draw back beyond the Po and only then to mount a concerted resistance. Our way from Latisana onwards lay through S. Giorgio Arisopoli to Teglio Veneto where we spent the night of the 5th to the 6th. Out in the open, of course. On the 6th at 7 am we carried on marching by way of Boldana, Giai della Sega, Belfiore, Giai di Spadacenta, Loucou, and Corbolone. Under pressure from German and Austro-Hungarian troops from Carinthia and the Tyrol the enemy is <u>retreating as fast as he can</u>. We are already deep in Veneto.

9 November 1917, 2 am
Early yesterday the enemy rearguard finally withdrew. A bridge was built in haste and we crossed the river on a gloomy, rainy day. We marched in the direction of Cessalto towards the canal, the so-called Piavone, behind which the enemy rearguard has installed itself to oppose us. Heavy infantry machine-gun and artillery fire opened up very quickly. Our regiment went on the attack. We are not properly informed about the disposition of the enemy's forces. The regimental

commander, Lieutenant Colonel P., worries about everything but the fate and well-being of his regiment. He is for the most part intoxicated and is only on the look out for places where he can get good wine and good nosh. It is a really sad state of affairs. Every enlisted man and officer feels at a loss because of it. Fortunately, our regimental adjutant, Lieutenant Colonel Fischer, is a sensible, industrious man. But he is still too young. He is only 21 years old and already has to decide the fate of a whole regiment. Older, more experienced officers on active service are for the most part well to the rear in positions where they are not really needed. Now and again one of them trusts himself to go as far as the front to collect some prestigious decoration and then immediately after getting it disappears into the back country. Our lieutenant colonel too wants at all costs to be awarded the Order of Leopold and, with this in mind, constantly sends reports and sketches, given to him by his adjutant, which he then countersigns, to brigade headquarters.

And such a man is entrusted with a whole regiment.

We also sustained quite a few losses, both on our flanks and frontally respectively, as our vanguard was perpendicular to that of the foe and we therefore drew heavy fire onto our flanks. Our 4th Battalion had indeed to withdraw temporarily to a distance of about 1km. And even under such adverse circumstances and such inadequate leadership we won the victory over the Italians who are, in terms of their weaponry, technically so much more advanced than we are. How did this come about? On the one hand, your average Italian soldier is not patient enough to hold out for a long time either resisting or attacking. On the other hand, we have the collaboration of the Germans to thank for this present surprising victory, who are putting a great deal of pressure on the enemy.

9 November 1917, 9 pm
After a long, tiring march, we came today to St Donnà di Piave, a small town on the River Piave almost completely abandoned by its inhabitants. The enemy today withdrew early in the day from the Piavone Canal and we went after them in hot pursuit. Strong enemy patrols have dug themselves in on the west bank of the Piave after having blown up the bridges over the river.

11 November 1917, 7 am
From early yesterday we have been located in Calvecchio not far from St Donnà di Piave. The enemy still occupies the west bank of the river. We are waiting for him very soon to withdraw. These are only strong rearguard forces that are standing against us. In all probability we will continue our march tomorrow.

On the march to Calvecchio yesterday I met our division general, Vice Marshal Gołogórski, along with his chief of staff. Each of them was provided with various maps of this area and were incapable of orientating themselves in order to get to the railway station building at St Donnà di Piave. I had to give them precise instructions on which roads they should take to arrive at the railway track. I would not have expected this from an Austrian general and leader of men. To begin with, he would have to travel through this region, through which he would have to lead the troops entrusted to him and would have to know with total precision the narrowest of paths, all the ditches, canals, swamps, and hills in order to be able to give correct orders. And how does all of this look in reality?

* * *

Last night I was at the regimental command post for the evening meal. We sat there in a small, abandoned house in front of an open fire and warmed ourselves. It had been a cold and rainy day. In front of a merrily crackling and blazing fire we chatted until 10 o'clock at night, whereupon I took my leave and went to the medical centre. Here it was so cold that I could scarcely get warm.

12 November 1917, 10 o'clock at Night
The west bank of the Piave is still in enemy hands. Today too he kept us pinned down all day long under heavy artillery fire. The 2nd Battalion had many killed and wounded. The 2nd Battalion's medical centre suffered a direct hit which, fortunately, was not a particular problem for us. Only Medical Officer Eckert was injured by the blast. I went myself in person to investigate on the spot and gave orders for the medical centre to be transferred to another house.

Towards evening several shells and shrapnel exploded in the vicinity of my medical centre (at a distance of twenty to thirty paces). So, our enemy is very impatient and living on his nerves. There were constant attempts made on our part to get to the west bank. Until now we haven't entirely succeeded. Tomorrow at 6 o'clock in the morning an energetic, serious, well-prepared attack will be set in motion by us to attain this end. The 2nd Battalion will be shipped across so that, under their protection, the 4th can build a bridge there.

I have also given orders in this respect, namely in the disposition of the medical centres. I myself will move forward at 5 o'clock tomorrow morning with my prefabricated medical centre.

* * *

Tonight I sent to hospital Lieutenant Romuald von Mossoczy, a most sympathetic, intelligent gentleman, because he had suffered a bad stroke.

13 November 17, 3 o'clock in the Morning
A very difficult day is now behind me. Namely yesterday. The planned operation failed, and our regiment sustained considerable losses as a result. Five officers were wounded, and one killed (Lieutenant Colonel Dumkovsky) and going on for seventy men wounded and ten others fatally.

The operation started as planned at 6 am. I proceeded in time with my medical centre to the Italian barracks near St Donnà. There I have also had installed the medical centres for the 1st Battalion (under the aegis of Assistant Doctor Peyše) and the 4th (under the aegis of Medical Orderly Lieutenant Schopper). I have also taken all necessary precautions for the wounded to be quickly bandaged and taken to Divisional Medical Collection Centre 10. This succeeded even despite all the difficulties we encounter at every turn with our high command.

15 November 1917
Yesterday early I had to go via Ceggia to Cessalto to see Divisional Medical Officer Dr Fintner. He has transferred me quite unexpectedly

to another regiment according to a telephone call I got and given my post to a certain Dr Tevčan. I protested against this vehemently. And not without success. The order was cancelled, which the General Staff Doctor was most reluctant to do. My advocate, who was already at the present location of my regiment, had now to go back to Cessalto.

Just before 3 pm I came back to Calvecchia and proceeded directly to the cemetery of St Donnà di Piave where the funeral took place of those who fell in vain the day before yesterday.

These were new victims of our careless leadership, of the hollow ambition of our leaders, of the tedious chase after decorations and honours who were laid to rest in those graves. One of our leaders has the desire to obtain the Maria Theresa Order of Merit. Because of this he wanted to push for a crossing of the Piave in as short a time as possible regardless of casualties. He did not leave himself enough time to make the appropriate preparations – on the one hand, to bring up sufficient artillery and ammunition, on the other, to ascertain through aerial reconnaissance the strength and position of the enemy. We were of the opinion that we had little opposition to face from the enemy. Our poor regiment had to advance in the absence of a necessary bombardment beforehand by big guns to pave the way. The necessary preparations had scarcely been made on our side to ferry our troops over and the enemy commenced a heavy bombardment of us that lasted for more than two hours. Guns of the most varied calibres, mortars, machine guns, and infantry rifles opposed us without respite. And this took its toll on us. The attempted crossing had to be abandoned after we had suffered considerable losses. And our leader is very upset about it. Not because of the number of casualties and fatalities. There's another reason. In his dreams he had already come near to achieving his highest ambition – the Maria Theresa Order of Merit. And now how far he is from it.

16 November 1917, 6 o'clock in the Morning
I'm writing this after a sleepless night. I am as strung up as can be. I'm feeling really down. I've just experienced something very unpleasant. And this from a 'gallant gentleman' I have only known for two days. The gentleman in question wanted to have his revenge on me for having

endeavoured to stay with the regiment I've now settled down with and his being unable to take my place as a result. I only did that which I was fully entitled to do. And now I have Herr Tevčan to contend with. Yesterday afternoon he showed up again at regimental headquarters and then, after a short interview with Lieutenant Colonel Pollak, went back to Cessalto. To my horror l learned very quickly what all this was about: a mean trick, a base denunciation. Lieutenant Colonel Pollak told me briefly what it was about. The new senior doctor had told him that I had insulted him (Herr Tevčan) in front of the former and called him a drunken lout. An action worthy of a scoundrel. And what unpleasant consequences it had for me. I was also extremely upset by it. And this all the more as Lieutenant Colonel Pollak is a very nice and sympathetic good man.

I therefore had to react right away. I proceeded with all due haste to Cessalto and set out the facts of the case to two duty officers, Lieutenant Colonel Wodnansky and Captain Steinbach. They will lead an honourable investigation into this treatment …

A new bitter disappointment, a new experience. But none of this helps me unfortunately. I am always too gullible and open-hearted. And this always rebounds on me. And it's incorrigible.

17 November 1917
Yesterday afternoon I witnessed a terrible tragedy befall a family. Two little cute farm children were blown to pieces while playing with an unexploded Italian mortar bomb.

And their poor parents and siblings were deserving of pity in large measure. Their grief was boundless. They shouted, wailed, threw themselves on the ground, crumpled up, tore their hair out from their head, cried, covered the corpses with their own bodies and kissed them, cried some more. A picture of the highest degree of human misery.

* * *

We are still in Calvecchia. The enemy, despite all expectations of our high command, is still in possession of the west bank of the Piave and fire on us continuously day and night. It's true that they will soon have to withdraw under pressure from the north (Tyrol).

18 November 1917, 11 pm
Still in Calvecchia. The enemy fire is heavy here. The fine little town of St Donnà has been in large measure destroyed. We are now waiting for those troops of ours to cross the river in the north and south who are now gathering on the west bank to enable them to attack the enemy. He will then be compelled to retreat.

Today a report about the progress of the war was made. Dr Oplatka, an editor of the *New Free Press* [*Neue Freie Presse*, one of the best-known Viennese newspapers. Theodor Herzl, founder of the Jewish state, was a correspondent], came to do it and will stay with us for a few days.

Today I am unable to get to sleep. I have been especially on edge for a few days now. I have various family problems to think about ...

21 November 1917, 1 o'clock in the Morning
Since yesterday at midday we are in Grassaga as a so-called divisional reserve. We were relieved by the 21st Bohemian Infantry Regiment and marched at 8 am out of St Donnà di Piave or rather Calvecchia in very fine clear weather. On the way the new regimental commander, Lieutenant Colonel Szatanek, who came to us on the 19th, inspected the regiment. He is too strict a soldier and too much a stickler for discipline who makes disproportionate demands on already war-weary men. He has apparently forgotten that we are already in the fortieth month of the war and that men just as much as officers have had more than enough of this wicked war.

At the front a great many shots are being traded by both sides. The enemy is still holding on tight to the west bank of the Piave. On our side, a plan to encircle the enemy is being made in order to force him to retreat even more.

* * *

I have been billeted in a small house with a poor Italian farming family. Two other refugee families are being housed there so that the space I have at my disposal is very small. Unfortunately, the three families who together live here have lots of children. This is par for the course in the Veneto. Families here with eight to ten children are an everyday occurrence.

24 November 1917, Grassaga
This morning I was with Assistant Doctor Havranek in Cessalto with the division's doctor, Medical Officer of Health Dr Tintner. At half-past two in the afternoon I was obliged, on the orders of the new regimental commander, to give a lecture to all the regiment's officers. I explained for more than an hour the fundamental principles of hygiene in the field. A quite thankless task in which I acquitted myself rather well. Everyone was well satisfied and thanked me for the trouble I had taken.

25 November 1917, Grassaga, 10.30 pm
A misty, dark, cold, rainy day. At midday we had a high-ranking guest, Major General Weiss, our brigadier, a highly sympathetic, intelligent, and energetic gentleman.

Appropriate preparations were made, and we had an excellent substantial dinner consisting of several courses. Toasts were drunk and the best Italian wines and liqueurs and French champagne put on the table.

During this excellent banquet we heard the truly unpleasant news that we would, on the 28th, be brought up out of the army reserve in order to force a new crossing of the Piave. A difficult and dangerous task awaits us. Who knows which of us fate will overtake?

27 November 1917
Since yesterday Grassaga and the surrounding villages are being evacuated on the orders of the army high command. The whole civilian population must get out of there to occupy places that have already been agreed upon. Young and old must leave their homes and be nomads. Men, for the most part, old and sick (the younger and healthier among them had to follow the fleeing Italians). Women and children are dragging themselves in large hordes through the streets

with piled-up wagons and carts. All of them with complaining and questioning eyes on the great uncertain future. A picture of misery and misfortune. A heart-wrenching sight.

28 November 1917, Grassaga
Tonight we will leave this place and march forward. Our regiment is tasked, on the 29th, at 5 am, with forcing a crossing of the Piave again between Code and Testa Dura. A very dangerous and difficult task which, when it was tried on the 13th of this month, failed. The regimental high command and probably the regimental medical centre will be permanently based in Calvecchia. Many here will be hauled in by death. Many will be badly wounded. This is very important to bear in mind. Our new regimental commander does not have the Order of Leopold yet. He must obtain this decoration whatever the cost. This silly chasing after orders is our greatest misfortune. Our regiment, which has accomplished so much, has been due some rest and recreation for a long time now. After all the great losses sustained up till now its companies are small in numbers. But there's no other way. The Order of Leopold must come to adorn the heroic breast of the new colonel.

This order is the great dream of nearly all our staff officers and it usually costs the blood of a lot of men. The bloodier and the more losses involved in an operation or a skirmish, irrespective of the eventual result, the better and more certain the award of the order. The poor anonymous infantryman, who has been forced to and trained for so-called heroic deeds, is the true order-martyr, the victim of the empty, base ambition of colonels. On him will, if he escapes with his life from this common battle, very seldom and exceptionally, be hung some decoration or other. His duty is to suffer for the good of colonels, to sacrifice himself and be exposed to the hardest privations. He has to. Woe to him who doesn't do it. The bare, usually quite idle hand of the colonel is raised up against him and punishes him mercilessly. Otherwise, a colonel in such a battle sits well to the rear and awaits its outcome … For forty months we have lived under such wretched conditions. And all this in the twentieth century. And the so-called man of culture puts up with this. How ignominious, what a disgrace.

29 November 1917
A pleasant surprise for the regiment today. Our old commander, Colonel Fleischer, came back to the regiment today and took over command of it. Because of this change the planned operation was postponed.

30 November 1917, In Grassaga
Today again a bright warm day. Only the nights are cold, frosty, which I feel in my small, cold, windowless room. The noonday sun, on the other hand, is really quite strong. Today, after the midday meal, I sunbathed.

2 December 1917
Conditions in the regiment have at present turned out unpleasantly and unfavourably for me. First of all, there is the stupid anti-Semitism that one gets to feel all the time here at the front as well. And besides, the new commander is a relative of that Dr Tevčan with whom I had the unpleasant set-to not so long ago. This affair is far from having been cleared up and is still in the hands of the tribunal. Difficulties are being made for me at this time with the regiment, which is something that I find most disagreeable.

Today, according to the military grapevine, our representatives are supposed to have started peace negotiations with Russia. Perhaps we are close to the end of the war now. Perhaps I will be able soon to attain my own personal freedom again. Perhaps it will soon be made possible for me to quit this narrow, empty, superfluous, hard life as a soldier. If only I could once again become a civilian!! But I'm a pessimist. I have been disappointed all too often in the things I hoped for during this war and can therefore no longer believe so easily. I only wish for it now. I long so much for the untroubled spirit of peace. And how much longer will I have to wait for it?

We are still in Grassaga. Other regiments are continually trying to cross the Piave but come up against the enemy's dogged resistance. Until now all attempts to do so have proved futile. The 21st Bohemian Infantry Regiment suffered very great losses in so doing. New attempts are being made notwithstanding. Our high commands are convinced that this plan must succeed. Perhaps they will be right for once in their predictions!

A lot depends on the progress made by the Tyrolean unit of Franz Conrad von Hötzendorf [now commanding an army group which bore his name and contained the 10th and 11th Armies]. And this is going forward very slowly. The enemy is offering steely resolve and resistance. French and English divisions are to play a part soon. In accordance with this, our army units will be strengthened there too by German troops recently brought up for the purpose. Perhaps the planned advance in the north will succeed. Only then will crossing the Piave and further progress be possible.

12 December 1917
For three days now we have been encamped in the area between Corbolone and Belfiore, east of the Livenza. I am living in the Casa Loucou with my medical centre. My state of health is getting worse and worse. I am constantly very depressed and always in a bad mood. I feel so alone and abandoned. My occupation here can bring me no satisfaction whatsoever, no emotion whatsoever and is not the least bit reassuring. It is a wretched form of vegetating which oppresses and hurts me very much. My nervousness grows more and more intense under all these miserable circumstances. Sleeplessness tortures me night after night. Such a state, in the long run, is quite unbearable.

At 9 o'clock in the morning I will go today to Corbolone to a meeting of doctors which is due to take place at the home of Medical Officer of Health Dr Tintner. I will also take this opportunity to visit a sick Italian man called Professor Calzavara, a most intelligent and sympathetic gentleman. I have already been to see him twice. He has rheumatoid paresis in his legs and has been bedbound for two years because of this illness. He lies there deprived of appropriate help and care. His wife and daughter are in Milan and he is quite alone in this poor state of health. I have done for him everything I could.

Last night four cases of measles in the civilian population were reported by Medical Lieutenant Schopper in the area covered by Battalion 4. I had to proceed here immediately in order to check this. I had to cover on foot a rather long distance as one cannot travel along that bad path that lies through fields and made soft by the rain. It was a dark and rainy night. After a lot of hunting about I finally found the house, 'Casa Speranza' ('Hope House'), in which were the four cases reported.

I found them living under very strained circumstances. The biggest part of this very roomy house is occupied by Machine Gun Company 4. Only a small, dirty, stinking stable and a part of the roof space is for the civilians and refugees ... About eighty refugees live there in these tiny spaces in the unhealthiest of conditions. Children, old people, women, men, the sick, all of them packed together. The children sick with measles are housed in the stable together with healthy children and oxen. I attended to their most pressing needs. I had the sick children placed in isolation. I also made a report on overall conditions to high command. Today I will bother about the rest. I will start with having the children taken to hospital.

14 December 1917
This morning I was in Belfiore where I must erect for the regiment a bathhouse and delousing station with the most primitive of means. Our command headquarters themselves bother about nothing. They only issue written orders which is, of course, easy to do. The way in which these orders are then carried out is of precious little interest to them. All this looks very good on paper. The reality is quite different. Everywhere one encounters the greatest difficulties, regardless of form-filling, requisitions, and priorities. The massive indolence of bureaucrats is, of course, to blame for this. Nothing can appear by magic. Provision has to be made for it.

I got the command from division to build the bathhouse and delousing station but have not been given the necessary materials for it from the technical division. For two days now we have been having damp, murky, unpleasant weather. Daily in the morning I had to go to Belfiore because the building of the bathhouse and delousing station is already past the planning stage. I have already overcome the major difficulties with it. I already have, due of course to unremitting effort on my part, enough workers and material. In four to five days everything will be ready. The poor men who slipped away at the beginning of August and had no chance to have a bath could have had a bath and been deloused already. This would have been a number one priority. People here in point of fact are dirty and full of lice. Scabies is widespread among them. They also suffer from skin mites, which are very painful and prevent them from sleeping. Then I received the unlooked for and unpleasant news that we must leave this area and move into more backward-lying places.

All my efforts up until now have therefore been quite fruitless. We must wander off again to new billets after having made ourselves somewhat more comfortable here. Now we will have to start work afresh until we can sort out all the new billets. I will have to start all over again with the setting up of a bathhouse and a delousing station for the regiment. Also, with the organisation of a house for the regiment. And so these poor people are not allowed their well-earned rest. And who is to blame for that? Only our comfortably off general staff officers. They should have foreseen that we would not be able to stay long in the region of Loucou-Bogdano-Bova-Belfiore and sent us right away to a more rearguard position. This was not important to these short-sighted, elegant, well-nourished, demanding, and comfortably off gentlemen and nor was making provision for the somewhat more distant future and thinking about it in advance. This is a cancer for us, the root cause of all our shortfalls, problems, and failures.

What our army has achieved here on this south-west front is in no way attributable to our leaders, but wholly and solely on the one hand to the participation of the German army and, on the other, to the weakness of the enemy. The Italian soldier lacks iron perseverance and long-lasting stamina, both of which he could do with. It was for this reason that the Italian army had to retreat so much, even though organisationally, technically, administratively it is far superior to ours. Everywhere we went during our march forward we were able to convince ourselves of this. We were also able to realise, from the huge amount of booty valued at billions of liras that fell into our hands, just how far behind them we are in this respect. And yet we were successful. And we ourselves were not responsible for our success, only the enemy himself was. He was disorientated, quite unexpectedly attacked in the north by the German [14th] Army under [Otto von] Below, demoralised, impatient. And so we have this great procession of cultural artefacts during which the enemy has lost more than his military equipment. The enemy only has himself to blame that we have now occupied so great a part of the rich, fertile, and handsomely endowed Venetian plain. The enemy has it on his conscience that the country's population in its own rich home territory has had to suffer hunger now for six to seven weeks and is going to the dogs. When the Italian high command learns of this after the war, it will have nightmares over it. This will be a blemish on their reputation that they will not be able to erase so quickly.

* * *

Yesterday afternoon I was once again with Professor Calzavara in Corbolone. It was a farewell sick visit. The sick gentleman was very upset when he learnt that I would no longer be able to visit him again soon. He asked me for my address and promised to write to me often. The army has now got hard times to get through. His wife and daughter are in Milan and he is lying here all by himself in a small, cold room and cannot leave his bed because of his paralysis. He is a most sympathetic, intelligent, and sensible gentleman. I shall miss him a lot.

25 December 1917
Since the evening of the 19th we have been in Teglio Veneto and surrounding area (Cintello, Zuzzolino). We are resting ... A small, nice place with some fine old houses belonging to gentry, short but rather broad and straight streets and a wide square in the centre, in which the small old church with its high, proud campanile is situated. Many among the populace, especially all the wealthy people, have fled with the enemy troops. Poor people had to stay behind, despite their great fear of us. Now they are truly to be pitied. They have certainly not, as they feared, been killed and raped. But there has been a fair amount of robbing and looting even so. These poor people have lost all their worldly goods and now they have to starve in their so rich

and blessed homeland. Now, after our troops have helped themselves, so that everything is, for the most part, squandered and reduced to nothing, orders come to us forbidding looting under pain of death. As always with our high command, too late, of course. Nearly always they are far too slow and longwinded to have an immediate effect.

The priest and the doctor left with the refugees. The former did not forget to take his own cook with him. He surely did it out of Christian love of his neighbour. Oh! What a comedy. What a lie. What deception everywhere we go. And human society is too short-sighted to see this and will pick up the tab for it at the end of the day.

The doctor in question was an elderly gentleman of Bohemian extraction called Dr Dobrowolny who had to go because of his sick wife.

The regimental general staff has stayed in the fine, big town hall. Unfortunately, the rooms there are all almost empty. The high command of sixteen Corps, which was housed there before us, has taken nearly all the furniture with it: beds, tables, armchairs, sofas, Venetian mirrors, expensive carpets, all the many pictures, etc., etc. They took these away in carts and cars. They are allowed quite openly to plunder treasures while ordinary soldiers and officers who have done so much at the front are under sentence of death for it. These are the double standards of our high command, their twisted logic, and against these things we can do nothing. We put up with all this because we are far too cowardly, because we do not have the courage to stand in the way of it.

The owner of this villa is a Hungarian Jew who owns a lot of property here and whose son is a serving captain in the Italian army.

We found in this villa a most elegant, already fitted bathroom and are making use of it to our heart's content. I was finally able, after three months, to have a bath. Our command centres care very little about poor soldiers. A bathhouse could have been set up for both officers and men a long time ago behind the front. Besides we would only queue to have baths, even well to the rear, only if we were to appear on a parade ground. Why were they not made a priority? A far too difficult task for the soft grey matter of our general staff.

I found too in Zuzzolino, in the garrison town of the 1st Battalion, an impeccably erected bathhouse for men. It's a good thing that the Italians prepared this for us in advance as otherwise our men would have had to wait a long time before a bathhouse of our own could have been erected under such miserable conditions. And yet the men must still wait to have a bath. There is no soap and there are no clean clothes to be had. We must be patient and wait. An appeal has been made.

1 January 1918, 3 am
Until now we've been celebrating New Year's Eve in the Villa Reiss in Teglio. The gentlemen of the 1st and 4th battalions were also invited to command HQ. Altogether there were approximately fifty of us. A lot of wine was drunk, singing, games, and speeches. And yet, there was an indefinable something belying our good humour. The wine soon had its effect on some and, although these were bright sparks, laid back even, most of us were in a downbeat mood. I should have liked to leave early but that wouldn't have been right. I felt an obligation to stay.

5 January 1918, 3.30 pm
I have been travelling since 6 o'clock in the morning yesterday. I've been given a seven-day leave of absence. Travelling now, of course, is very complicated, tiring, strenuous, and disagreeable. Train compartments are full to overflowing. Due to coal shortages they are unheated, and I am forced to shiver with the cold all the time. Even the windows are missing in some of the compartments and naturally, owing to our usual slipshod approach to things, are not replaced. Everywhere, thick clouds of smoke, dust, and dirt. At all the stations along our route to beyond Cervignano the train halted for a very long time. At Cervignano, for instance, the train stopped for one-and-a-half hours.

On the 6 January 1918 I was ordered to Vienna to attend a course on the effects of gas. I left my regiment in Teglio Veneto and travelled to Vienna via Portogruaro and Cervignano.

On 27 January 1918 I suddenly fell ill with a high fever (39.2º) and was taken into the Garrison Hospital. Lieutenant Colonel Professor Steyskal and Dr Boudy.

On 18 February I was transferred to Cobenzl to the sanatorium.

On 3 June 1918 I received a cable recalling me to service in the field. General Medical Officer of Health A. Thoman leaves no doctor in peace. This noble knight already has the health of many doctors on his conscience. He is ruthless in the true sense of the word.

On 5 June 1918 I arrived in Udine in Field Hospital 1313. Here I was examined by the neurologist Regimental Doctor Richter (Vienna). As luck would have it, an understanding, nice man. Regimental Doctor Franke, a doctor from Prague, is the veritable right-hand man of Dr Thoman.

Here I came across several sick doctors, none of whom Thoman is willing to allow to pull back, although they are all really ill and need treatment. Among others here I met Dr Baar (Senior Doctor) and Dr Frommer (Assistant Doctor). The latter in particular was a most sympathetic person.

I don't know yet what is going to happen to me.

On my journey back to the front line I made a detour on the 3rd and 4th to Nagy Kamzsa. Here I visited Dr Aladar Rapoch and the family of L. Zeikovitz. I spent two pleasant evenings in their company.

9 June 1918
Still in hospital in Udine. Yesterday I had to speak to no fewer than five army doctors. They don't want to leave me in peace. These were just pathetic, strolling actors each with a pitiful role to play. One observes, another supervises, a third inspects and so on. These faithful companions and helper's helpers of that feared tyrant, that ruthless despot, who sits up there in his office and commands, to whom no human victim is one too many in order to go up the ladder another rung and to be able to acquire a new decoration. And who are these poor victims? Hundreds of doctors who have no privileged connections with high-ups or attractive young women or are far too proud to make use of such connections and seek the way of truth and justice. What a base system of cliques, what a demeaning mess of you-scratch-my-back-I'll-scratch-yours. And such a system can still exist after four hard, bloody years of war. No one can manage to bring it down.

I am curious to know when they will take their dirty paws off me. I have already delivered enough victims to the god of war. My whole nervous system has been undermined and shaken to the core.

They have to admit that too despite all their bad will. Of course, they will hold various consultations and discussions. None of this helps them much. They'll have to send me back and I need treatment.

There are still several sick doctors in this hospital who need thoroughgoing treatment away from the front line. However, only a few of them manage to get it. Most are simply not believed. They are forced to assume some kind of duty irrespective of their legitimate grievances. There is an assistant doctor here, a Hungarian, a short, weak, thin, pitiful, but still presentable little man who suffers from attacks of hysterical weeping and a constant deep sense of unease. He will soon be leaving here. He will be allocated duties in some hospital or other. A second doctor, a senior doctor with a stomach ulcer, will remain here and be treated. Whether any kind of treatment here could lead to a successful outcome beggars belief. Another doctor, also a senior doctor, a Bohemian, has arthrosclerosis and a high degree of deafness. He too will soon have to take up duties in some hospital or other.

A senior doctor, Dr Baar, who suffers from asthma attacks, also will not be left here long and will soon be assigned to medical duties elsewhere, and so on and so on.

But Assistant Doctor Klinger will soon be sent as a patient to a clinic in Budapest. He will be spared examinations by all these army doctors. His father in Budapest is Archduchess Amalie's dentist.

And Senior Doctor Fischer (from Nagy-Bečskerek) will also in the next few days be able to go home as some great bigwig has had a word with Thoman about it. This is how things look with us as far as justice is concerned.

11 June 1918, 3 o'clock in the Afternoon
I left Udine in a Maltese Cross train. Our way lay through Cormos, Gorizia, St Lucia and Auzza terminating in Laibach. Here we detrained. The sick were taken into care in various hospitals. I was sent to Reserve Hospital 1 (an army barracks). I must wait here to be sent even further away from the action …

... I must be very careful now. I could quite easily have run away and then the hospital would have had to carry the can for it. This is the eternal fear of serving officers confronted by good manners that sometimes makes them commit glaring blunders. The most important thing for them is only that they always stay in the good books of higher authority, that they are recognised as diligent in the performance of their duties. Their deeds are not governed by the iron laws of sound reason but directed solely by the mostly useless rules of bureaucratic regulations according to the orders given them. They only want to save their necks and keep their jobs. They have no higher aims and objectives. And to gentlemen like these, a decisive role falls, militarily speaking. If, purely by chance, someone is employed in this post who thinks more freely about things, he will never amount to much in the army. Most people here are cowardly, have closed minds and tell lies. I asked the head doctor here yesterday, for instance, for my clothes to be returned to me as going around without clothes in front of all these people would be dreadfully demoralising for me. I asked permission besides to be allowed to go into the blocked-off garden. This narrow-minded, duplicitous gentleman said to me with a smile that the only person I could approach in this matter was Colonel Regimental Doctor Welider. This gentleman, who had spoken to me with such friendliness, later outside told the Regimental Doctor not to let me have my clothes back and not to let me into the garden. I have just learnt this today from the Regimental Doctor himself who wanted to justify his behaviour toward me after the event. These gentlemen show goodwill of this kind to the poor victims entrusted to their care. And against this kind of thing one can do nothing. One is quite powerless against them. Forward in the realm of fire, these serving officers are nowhere to be seen, but here, behind the lines, they are great heroes and seek to build a career on their ruthlessness.

Yesterday at 5 o'clock in the afternoon I had a visitor. The vet, Dr Lamprer, and his wife sought me out and stayed with me for nearly two hours. This visit gave me a lot of pleasure.

While here I got to know a young, sympathetic, intelligent law student by the name of Arthur Zanini from Istria (20km from Parenzo).

15 June 1918
I have been since last night in a narrow, dirty, single cell on the psychiatric ward of Laibach Hospital.

16 June 1918
I have now spent three nights in this single cell. Throughout the day I walk around the corridors, under the constant, watchful, unpleasant gaze, of course, of attendants and orderlies. I have asked several times to be allowed out into the garden so that I can at least breathe in some fresh air for a while. In the corridors there is an unbearable stench emanating from the cells of the seriously ill, the disorientated, the stark raving. Apart from that, I find myself in the corridors in very unpleasant, peculiar, depressing company. The less sick patients walk about in large numbers. One of them pulls various faces quite arbitrarily, another laughs, whistles and constantly jumps about, yet another shouts and swears while another voices out loud an incomprehensible, disconnected monologue. And yet another patient shrieks and makes idiosyncratic motions in the air. And I had to live through three days in this kind of company, because Regimental Doctor Rubida saw fit to let me. He wants revenge on me for the quarrel I had with him and which he himself started. This man is a cocaine addict, a man the soundness of whose mind is at times quite questionable and yet his word carries weight with the military because he has three stars on his tunic, because he is a regimental doctor. On such people depends the fate of so many. His word is law. He can make or break like no one else. Yesterday even Senior Medical Officer of Health Dr Lussenberger came to see me. He was very friendly, apologised to me and explained that this regimental doctor had been compelled to arrange my internment. In the army you have to do these things. With him I have occasion now and again to speak. He is under observation here because of epileptic fits. Apart from with him I am friendly here with a military cadet by the name of Kynce from Prague, whose state of mind is being observed here as a consequence of legal proceedings against him. The poor man has been here for nearly three months.

18 June 1918

I am still in the cell on the psychiatric ward. Today Dr Lamprer's wife came to see me and stayed with me for approximately two hours. She has set the wheels in motion to ensure that my stay in this narrow, awful prison will be as short as possible. She has already seen General Medical Officer Geduldiger three times on my behalf and met with Dr Lussenberger this afternoon. Meanwhile telegrams with pleas to grant admission have come from hospitals in Vienna. I have already cabled various heads of department – Dr Ernst, Mr Fug Lazanes, Dr Schmerer, Kenedis. Probably I will be able to leave this cell tomorrow afternoon and travel to Vienna.

The regimental doctor has in the meantime realised just what a big mistake he has made in this case and this evening allowed me to enter the locked-up garden. How lucky for me.

23 June 1918

Since the afternoon of the day before yesterday I have been in Vienna in Garrison Hospital 1 accompanied by a letter of introduction from Regimental Doctor Rubida of the Department of Pyschiatry. After a long, tiring journey of over forty hours in a special train for sick people I arrived in Vienna on the 21st of the month about 2 o'clock in the afternoon. Here in the hospital I am under observation. A truly unpleasant, painful existence here too as I am under constant strict supervision and am treated almost like a criminal. And the only crime I have committed was to have stayed too long under fire on the front line and to have everywhere done my duty in a spirit of the greatest self-sacrifice and selflessness and not to have looked around, like many others, for connections and protection.

For the first and second day I was together with an Italian prisoner of war, Senior Doctor Pietro di Laura from Piacenza, a most likeable, sympathetic man who would soon be sent off to the Steinhof Psychiatric Institution. A state of depression, due to be treated at the Steinhof, had manifested itself in him following his monastic existence in captivity and the strong yearning that he had to be reunited with his wife and children. Certainly no doctor could ever hope to cure him. Only going back to his family would heal his innermost soul.

The acting duty doctor, Senior Doctor Kohle, proprietor of the Rekawinkel Sanatorium, told me today that I would very soon get away from here. He is going to send me to the convalescent home at Cobenzl.

Afterword

A Belated Wreath from Your Translator by Michael Wooff

In Ernest Hemingway's 1948 introduction to *A Farewell to Arms*, a novel set against the backdrop of the Italian front in the First World War, he writes that 'wars are fought by the finest people that there are …'. The author of these diaries definitely falls into that category: he was, first and foremost, a fine human being.

He had already, prior to his arrival in Komen on the Carso, or limestone plateau, in what is now Slovenia, gone through his baptism of fire in the aftermath of the particularly bloody Battle of Doberdò, which had taken place in August 1915, and in which the number of lives lost, on both sides, was enormous.

There are many deaths recorded in these diaries and also many burials, but, on the part of Dr Barasch, there is always compassion. The nameless lieutenant he treats for syphilis prompts him to deplore the moral laxity that war has given rise to: 'The woman has caught it … She infects with it … Along with her … wished and longed for love she imparts this fierce poison'. He is sorry to say goodbye to a medical orderly who has served him well and we have every reason to believe that the orderly will miss him just as much. He always does, to the best of his ability, what he is called on to do, whether that be giving a lecture on hygiene to an audience of officers during his time in Grassaga or reacting to four cases of measles in civilian children. Sometimes he is forced to witness what he cannot hope to remedy: the body in no-man's-land of a dead Italian, the deaths of children: 'Two little cute farm children were blown to pieces while playing with an unexploded Italian mine.' Their family and siblings are devastated by the incident. What can he do? It is for him a picture of 'the highest degree of human misery'.

He regards it as a misfortune for humanity at large that 'men like Grey, Kitchener, Poincaré, Salandra and their cronies' cannot experience the bloodshed directly for themselves and think differently. Through it all, however, amid the most eloquent expressions on his part of righteous indignation at superiors who take a back seat and all those who profit and enrich themselves at the expense of others, thinking only of their pockets and their stomachs, he retains the utmost respect for what is genuine, especially art. He enjoys meeting the then famous female Impressionist painter Leo von Littrow in Abbazia, now Opatija in Croatia. He writes a letter to Karl Scholz, a Viennese painter, and expresses the hope that they might one day meet up in Vienna. He talks of a painting by Rubens in a church on the island of Arbe off the coast of Dalmatia. He mentions a Lieutenant Mossoczy who, before the war, had been an opera singer in Lemberg (Lviv) not far from his own place of birth. Such things obviously matter to him.

To echo the words at the end of the first stanza of the poem composed by George Peele for Queen Elizabeth I in 1590, the title of which finally furnished the title for the Hemingway novel I allude to above:

> Beauty, strength, youth are flowers but fading seen.
> Duty, faith, love are roots and ever green.

Dr Barasch's relatively short life – he died aged 33 – was deeply rooted in exactly those three things. *Ruhe sanft nach schwerem Lebenskampf!* Rest easy after life's hard struggle! You will always be missed and so will your humanity.

Index

IB is used to denote Isaak Barasch
Page numbers in bold refer to plate illustrations

Abbazzia 181, 214
Adelsberg 184
Adriatic Sea 3, 11, 12, 24, 59, 179
air balloons, observation 163
Albania 12, 16
Alla Baita gorge 166
Alps, the 3, 36, 106, 137
Ampezzo valley 115
Anatolia 17
anti-Semitism 2, 3, 8, 25, 26, 27, 200
Arbe, island and town 182, 214
Arz zu Straussenburg, Arthur 23, 24
Asiago plateau 107, 108, 138, 179, 180
Austria 2, 4, 20, 26, 106, 190
Austria-Hungary 1, 2, 3, 4, 6, 7, 10, 13, 15, 16, 18, 48, 105, 106, 182
    collapse of 4, 25, 35
    cultural diversity 3
    formation of dual monarchy 1
    religion and freedom of worship 3
    support of Jews 8, 25
Austro-Hungarian army 19–25
    III Corps 61, 106
    VII Corps 22–3, 61
    1st Alpine Detachment 127
    1st Honved Infantry Regiment 71
    2nd Alpine Detachment 145
    4th Mountain Brigade 139, 173
    5th Army 61, 64, 108, 138, 139, 174, 178
    5th Battalion (37th Army Infantry Regiment) 75
    7th Corps 101
    15th Infantry Regiment 178, 191
    21st Bohemian Infantry Regiment 197, 200
    21st Mountain Brigade 107, 109, 117
    23rd Third Reserve Infantry Regiment 171
    32nd Landsturm Infantry Regiment 61
    37th Landsturm Infantry Regiment 61
    43rd Hungarian Regiment 72
    43rd Schützen Division 139
    55th Infantry Regiment 178, 183, 184
    75th Landsturm Battalion 139, 172
    85th Infantry Regiment 139
    102nd Bohemian Regiment 100
    106th Austrian Landsturm Infantry Division 61
    110th Landsturm Brigade 61
    187th Landsturm Brigade 61
    background 19–20
    construction of trenches 123
    ethnic make-up 22
    Jewish officers and soldiers 26–7
    lack of supplies and equipment 153, 185
    logistics 77–8, 91
    medical services 28–37
        disease 35–6
        hygiene 35, 78–9, 198, 202–3, 205–6
        organisation and structure 30–1
        shortages of medicines and supplies 34, 70, 124
        sick doctors 207, 208
        treatment of casualties 32–4, 107–8, 112, 124, 134, 143–4, 145
    military collapse 24–5
    numbers of sick, injured, missing and dead 37, 60, 139, 141
    officers 21
    requisitioning 189–90, 190
    senior commanders 23
    structure and size 20–3
    treatment of Jewish soldiers 28
    treatment of prisoners 133

Baar, Dr 207, 208
Bainsizza plateau 140, 141

Balkan Mountains 3
Balkan wars 5, 6, 7, 10, 11, 13, 15, 29
Balkans 5–6, 7, 9, 11, 14, 15, 17, 24
Baltic states 17, 105
Barasch, Cecilia (Tzilla; sister of IB) 48, 49, 54
Barasch, Isaak Arthur (IB) **1–8**
   VII Corps 22, 23
   4th Mountain Brigade 139, 173
   21st Mountain Brigade 107, 109, 117
   32nd Landsturm Infantry Regiment 62
   37th Landsturm Infantry Regiment 61
   55th Infantry Regiment 178, 183, 184
   75th Landsturm Battalion 139, 172
   85th Infantry Regiment 139
   appreciation of the arts 119–20, 181, 182, 188
   appreciation of natural world and landscape 76, 109, 111, 113, 114, 115, 116–17, 162
   army medical career 31, 121
   attitude to the church 80–2, 115, 188, 205
   attitude to Italy 18
   attitude to medical role 86–7, 87–8, 131, 147–8
   background 4, 49–50
   birth 48–9
   criticism of superiors 21, 31, 64, 66, 68, 69, 81–2, 85, 92–4, 101–2, 132, 142–3, 145, 151–2, 154–5, 159, 161–2, 165–6, 173–4, 175, 181, 185, 192, 195, 199, 202, 203, 210
   criticism of system 34–5, 70, 124, 131–2, 142, 150, 152, 153–4, 154–5, 155, 164–5, 207–8
   death 38, 48, 180
   description of effect of war on the land 162
   description of field hospital 144
   description of wartime conditions 63–4, 70, 82, 83, 92–3, 132, 147, 150–1, 161, 164
   disciplinary record 65–6, 181, 195–6, 200
   disillusionment with war 39, 67, 68, 69, 81–2, 98, 102, 117–18, 130–1, 132–3, 156–7, 169, 197, 200
   distress at burial of dead 80
   education 8, 27, 51
   establishing medical facilities 131, 142–3, 159–60, 163, 202
   family 49, 51–4
   gives lecture on hygiene 198
   lack of rations 147, 148, 161, 163, 164, 165, 173
   languages 51
   leisure and pastimes 52, 63, 114–15, 122, 124, 129, 176, 206
   medical duties 76, 86, 95, 134, 145–6, 153–4, 175
   mental health 37, 63, 69, 83–4, 94, 95, 103, 110, 114, 117–18, 119, 121, 155, 161, 168–9, 183, 195–6, 197, 201, 211
     admitted to Garrison Hospital 1 211
     admitted to Laibach hospital 37, 210
   military honours 47, 128
   physical health 155, 159, 161, 176
     admitted to Garrison Hospital 206–7
     criticism of care 209, 210, 211
   traumatic events 79–80, 96–7, 152–3, 156, 196
   working conditions 78–9, 79, 87, 87–8, 95, 131, 139
Barasch, Leon (Leib; brother of IB) 49, 50, 53–4, **2, 8**
Barasch, Yanka (Yenta; sister of IB) 48, 49, 50, 53, 54
Barasch/Jung, Klara (Donia/Kaila; sister of IB) 48, 49, **2**
Barasch Mehlsak, Lea (mother of IB) 49, **1**
Bardach, Bernhard 27
Barth, Lieutenant Colonel von 112, 114
bauxite, mining of 181, 182, 183
Belfiore 191, 201, 202, 203
Below, Otto von 177, 178, 204
Belzec 53, 54
Berchtold, Leopold 6
Berlin 6, 53
Besca Vecchia 181, 182, 183
Bethmann Hollweg, Theobald von 7
Bismarck, Otto von 2, 9
Bohemia 4, 8, 9, 25
Bonetti 82, 88, 96, 157, 160, 166
Boroević, Svetozar 60, 61, 62, 64, 138, 140, 141, 174, 178, 179, 180
Bosnia-Herzegovina 1, 4, 6, 20
Bozen 107, 109, 110
Brenner, A.G. 76, 95, 101, 102
Brunech 107, 110, 111, 113, 124, 132, 137, 142, 146

Brusilov, Aleksey Alekseyevich 108
  Brusilov offensive 8, 137
Budapest 1, 15, 25, 26, 32, 122, 208
Bukovina 8
Bulgaria 2–3, 6, 10, 14, 17, 29, 105
Bülow, Bernhard von 14, 16

Cadorna, Luigi 13, 18, 60, 107, 108, 137, 138, 140, 141, 177, 178
Calvecchia 195, 196, 197, 199
Calzavara, Professor 201, 204
Caporetto 24, 129, 177, 178, 180
Carpathian Mountains 3
Cattaro 16
Central Powers 13, 14, 15, 17, 24, 68, 105, 137, 140, 177
Cervignano 187, 188, 206
Cessalto 191, 194, 195, 196, 198
Chantilly/plan 137
civilian population, effect of war on 73
Cobenzl (sanatorium) 207, 212
Col Becchei di Sopra 126, 128
Col de Bois 129, 133
Col Rosa 116, 123, 126, 127, 130
Conrad von Hötzendorf, Franz 2, 6, 7, 19, 105, 178, 201
Corbolone 191, 201, 204
Cresta Bianca 116, 134
Croatia 12, 102, 214
Croda d'Anconca 118, 121, 125
Cruihrib 74, 88, 90, 97, 98
Czechoslovakia 4

Dalmatia 12, 16, 17, 101, 182, 214
depression, brought on by war 211
Devetak 88, 92
Diaz, Armando 178
Doberdò 63, 72, 74, 75, 76, 77, 79, 80, 83, 88, 90, 91, 92, 94, 98, 99, 100, 103, 106, 128
  battle 54, 213
  lake 41, 74, 82, 96, 97
  plateau 62, 74, 75, 101, 103
Dodecanese Islands 17
Dolomites 54, 106, 107
  fortifications, admiration for 134–5, 147
  landscape, appreciation of 111, 115, 116, 146–7
Dual Alliance 9
Dunant, Henri 28, *see also* Red Cross

Entente Cordiale 68
Entente powers 11, 13, 16, 17, 18, 19, 24, 61, 105, 137, 138, 140
entertainment 65, 99
Erlsbacher, Lieutenant Colonel 130, 147
Etsch, River 106, 109, 110
Eugen, Archduke 23, 106, 108, 178

Faiti Hrib 170, 173
Falkenhayn, Erich von 105, 106, 108, 138
Fanes/Fanestal 116, 118, 121, 122, 123, 125, 126, 127, 133, 143, 145
  Gross Fanes 121, 127, 130, 133, 134
  Little Fanes 113, 121
Fiammes 116, 135
Fingerhut, Irene (niece of IB) vi, 52
Firenzesattel 126, 128
Fiume 12, 175, 181, 182, 183
Flick, Lieutenant Colonel 127, 129
Fodara Vedla 112, 113
Forcella della fontana negra 128, 130
France 9, 10, 14
  French Revolution 2
Franz Ferdinand, Archduke 3, 6, 12
  assassination 1, 6, 51
  politics 1–2, 19
Franz Josef, Emperor 1, 2, 9, 11, 19, 23
  accession 2
  death 23, 52, 172
  held in high regard by Barasch family 52
  politics 3, 6, 15
  support for Jews 52
Freiherr von Kirchbach auf Lauterbach, Karl 106
French army 28, 61, 178, 201
Freud, Sigmund 3, 50
Friedrich, Archduke 23, 174
Furcia Rossa 128, 130, 147

Galicia 4, 7, 8, 13, 15, 17, 22, 25, 27, 32, 48, 49, 52, 61, 105, 106, 108, 138, 139
Garda, Lake 12, 106
gas attack, threat of 73
Geneva Convention 29, 32
Germany 2, 5, 6, 9, 10, 11, 12, 14, 15, 16, 17, 18, 21, 23, 24, 25, 53, 105, 108, 140, 180
Giolitti, Giovanni 16, 17
Gliniany 50, 52
Gołogórski, Emil von 179, 193

Gorizia (Görz) 16, 18, 59, 60, 61, 104, 106, 208
  battle of 137–76
Gorlice-Tarnow 17
Grassaga 197, 198, 199, 200, 213
Greece 3, 10, 14
Grey, Sir Edward 5, 11, 18, 69, 81, 214

Habsburg empire *see* Austria-Hungary
Havranek, Dr 185, 198
Hill 70 100
Hill 171 166, 167, 170, 171, 173
Hoitas, Dr 82, 83
Holy Roman Empire/Emperor 2, 50
Horn of Africa 10, 17
Hudilog 87
Hungary 1, 6, 8, 20, 22, 25, 26

Iamiano 73, 74
Il Fallè 116, 121, 123, 126
Il Zurlong 134
influenza 37–8, *see also* Spanish flu
Innsbruck 107, 127, 129, 147
Isonzo front 18, 22, 24, 34, 59–104, 106, 137–41, 169, 177–9
Isonzo River 12, 35, 41, 59, 60–1, 96, 138, 162, 185–7
Istria 171, 181, 209
Istvanovic von Ivanska, Nikolaus 44, 181
Italian army 11–12, 14, 17, 24, 59, 173, 205
  2nd Army 60
  3rd Army 60
  7th Alpini Regiment 133
  arrives on the Isonzo front 59
  IB's opinion of 179, 203
  war dead 60, 61, 138, 141, 178
Italian front 22, 23, 24, 53, 129, 179, 213
  geography 18
Italy 9, 24, 51, 129, 178, 188
  colonial expansion 9–10, 12
  Entente 17, 18, 68
  Risorgimento 9, 12, 17
  Treaty of London 16–17
  Triple Alliance 9–10, 10–11, 12, 13, 14, 15, 16–17
  at war with Austria-Hungary 8–18

Jews 8, 205
  in Austria-Hungary 25–8, 50
  in Austro-Hungarian army 26–7, 28
  discrimination 8, 26

farming 50
marriage tax 49
populations 8
support of Franz Josef, Emperor 52
Josef, Archduke 64, 65, 101
Jugendstil 3, 55
Julian Alps 12, 59, 76
Jung, Dr (Head Doctor) 45, 83, 156
Jung, Dr Schilem (cousin and brother-in-law of IB) 51, 53, **2**

Karl, Emperor/Kaiser 23, 24, 69, 141, 172
Karlik, Captain 76, 87, 175
Karst (Carso) plateau 35, 36, 59, 60, 62, 63, 64, 106, 138, 140, 153, 156, 178, 182, 188
  geography 96, 103
Kitchener, H.H. 18, 69, 214
Kletter, Ernst 61, 94, 101
Komen 61, 63, 64, 65, 67, 69, 167, 170, 213
Konrad, Captain 118, 122
Korer, Dr 63, 69
Kostanjevica 69, 75, 77, 80, 83, 84, 85, 86, 88, 90, 91, 95, 96, 99, 103, 169, 170
Kövess von Kövesshaza, Hermann 106, 109
Krafft von Dellmensingen, Konrad 113, 177
Kraina Vas 103
Krauss, Alfred 23, 106, 178
Kresja 184

Lagaco, valley 127
Laibach 37, 60, 103, 104, 106, 139, 178, 184, 208, 210
Lamprer, Dr (and wife) 184, 209, 211
Lana-Burgstall 109
Latisana 186, 190, 191
Lavinores 112, 116
Lazarevič, Ensign Jovan 148
League of the Three Emperors 9
Lechner, Dr 114, 115
Lemberg 8, 27, 48, 49, 51, 53, 54, 183, 185, 188, 214
Limojoch 123, 126
Littrow, Leo von 181, 214
Livenza, River 191, 201
Lloyd George, David 140
Lokvica 95, 148, 169
Lombardy 2
looting 179, 187, 204–5, 205

Loucou 191, 201, 203
Lueger, Karl 3
Lussenberger, Dr 210, 1211

Magyars 1, 15, 20, 21, 26
'Makuči' medical help centre 174
'Ma Mokrim' medical centre (Cronberg) 142, 147, 148, 149, 151, 161, 164, 166, 167
Mandolfo, Lieutenant Colonel 121, 122, 133, 175
Marcella, Dr 78, 83
Marcotirei 71
Marmolata 118, 126, 127
Mehlman, Helen (Hinda; sister of IB) vi, 52, 53
Mehlman, Dr Yoel Chaim (brother-in-law of IB) 52, **8**
Mehlsak, Moses (father of IB) 49–51, **2**
Metternich, Klemens von 2, 5, 11
Mikoli 73, 74, 75, 82, 83, 85, 88, 91, 92, 95, 96, 99
Milan 133, 201, 204
military awards, and IB's attitude towards 144–5, 192, 195, 199
Moltke, Helmuth von 7, 12, 13
Monfalcone 41, 59, 60, 90, 96, 138
Montal 111, 117
Monte dei sei Busi 61, 74, 75, 89, 90, 98, 100
Monte Cadini 112, 115, 116
Monte Cristallo 112, 116
Monte Pezzovica 116
Monte Sabotino 139, 158, 173
Monte San Daniele 142
Monte San Gabriele 141, 142
Monte San Marco 170, 171, 172, 173
Monte San Michele 59, 60, 62, 69, 75, 88, 90, 92, 94, 138
Monte Santo 117, 141
Monte Sella Hotel 55, 111, 112, 120
Monte Vallon Bianco 123, 125, 126, 128, 130, 144, 146, 147
Monte Viano 110
Montenegro 3
morality, effect of war on 84
Moravia 8, 25
Mossoczy, Romuald von 188, 194, 214
Mount Rombon 59
Mrazek, Ensign 114, 115
Muzzama 186, 189, 190

New York City vi, 52, 53, 54
Nice 9, 18
Niedersdorf 110, 111
Nova Vas 75, 97

Olang 110
Opeina 184
Oppacchiasella 92
Orlando, Vittorio 178
Oslavija 60, 104, 137, 150
Ossegliano 171, 173, 174, 175, 176
Ossek 148, 154, 159, 166, 171
Ottoman empire 3, 4, 5, 9, 10, 14, 17

Panowitzer Forest 167, 168
Pedern 112, 113, 121, 124, 125, 131, 134, 143, 144, 146
Peutelstein 116, 118
Pfeffers, Dr Richard 45, 181, 183
Piave, River 24, 25, 36, 179, 180, 191, 192, 193, 195, 196, 197, 198, 200, 201
Piavone 191, 192
Piedmont 2, 9
Pietro di Laura, Dr 211
Plaschke, Siegfried 27
Podgora 137, 150
Poincaré, Raymond 10, 18, 69, 91, 214
Pola 12, 16
Poland vi, 15–16, 17, 25, 48, 53, 54, 105
Pollak, Lieutenant Colonel 196
Pollio, Albert 12, 13
Prosecco 184
Prussia 1, 2, 4, 7, 9
Przemysl, fortress/siege 16
Puster, valley (Pustertal) 107, 110, 111, 113, 117, 125, 142
   railway 127

Radomcić, Petar 103, 109, 114, 157
Ragusa 114, 172, 184
Rapoch, Dr Aladar 183, 207
Red Cross 28, 65, 84, 153, 181
   Austrian Red Cross 29
   establishment 28–9
   Geneva Convention 29
rest and recovery 171, 174, 175
Rienz, River 110, 111, 113, 117
Ritter von Eiss, General Alexander vii
Romania 3, 6, 14, 15, 19, 24, 54, 129, 138
Rosental, valley 139, 166, 167, 168, 170
Rubida, Dr 210, 211

Russia 3, 4, 6, 7, 8, 9, 11, 12, 15, 16, 17, 18, 24, 25, 26, 28, 53, 105, 108, 138, 200
Russian Revolution 179

Sadek, Medical Orderly 176, **4**
St Caterina sector 150, 152, 157, 173
St Donnà di Piave 192, 193, 194, 195, 197
St Giorgio di Nogara 186, 187
St Vigil in Enneberg 40, 54–5, 111, 112, 113, 116, 117, 120, 121
Salandra, Antonio 16, 17, 18, 69, 81, 214
Salata, valley 113, 116
San Martino, mountain 75, 88, 90, 92
San Pauses 116, 126
Sarajevo 1, 51
Savoy 9, 18
Schmidl, Erwin 47
Scholz, Karl 119–20, 214
Schopper, Medical Orderly Lieutenant 185, 194, 201
Segetti 69, 71, 99
Seiwerth, Major 67, 71
Selz 99, 100, 185
Serbia 3, 5, 6, 7, 10, 11, 13, 15, 16, 17, 18, 24, 105
Seton-Watson, Robert 4, 5
Slavs 1, 4, 12, 15, 20, 22
Slovenia 24, 59, 63, 173, 177, 213
Soča, River 59
Somme offensive 137, 138
Sommer, Lieutenant Colonel of Artillery 126
Sonnino, Sidney 16, 17, 81
Sowabensky, Lieutenant 112, 113
Spalato 101, 171
Spanish flu vi, 38, 54
Standschutzen troops, attitude to 122
Stannoch, Dr 174–5, 176
Stehlik, Dr 102
Strafexpedition (punishment expedition) 106, 108
Stuva 113, 116, 117, 118, 129, 135

Tagliamento, River 178, 179, 189, 190, 191
Teglio Veneto 191, 204, 206
Tel Aviv 52, 54
Temner, Lieutenant Colonel 117, 118
Temnica 69
Temo, Ensign 121, 122
Tevčan, Dr 195, 196, 200
Theumer, Lieutenant Colonel 109

Thoman, Dr 207, 208
Tintner, Dr 185, 198, 201
Toblach 110
Tofana Massif 116, 125–8
Tolmein 104, 138, 177
Transylvania 6
Travenanz/Travenanzestal (valley/ravine) 125, 127, 128, 129, 131, 133, 134, 145
Treaty of London 5, 16–17
Trentino 15, 16, 17, 108
Trient 106
Trieste 12, 16, 17, 23, 60, 63, 65, 66, 67, 68, 84, 86, 104, 181, 184
Triple Alliance 9, 10–11, 12, 13, 14, 16, 17
Triple Entente 11
Tyrol 12, 105ff., 137, 138, 139, 178, 191, 197

Udine 60, 133, 178, 208
Field Hospital 1313 207–8

Valkišcie 73, 75, 79, 82, 92
Valone valley 73, 86, 88, 95, 96, 98
Veglia, island 181, 183
venereal disease, effects of 84
Venetian Alps 12
Venetian/Veneto plain 12, 24, 107, 179, 204
Verdun 65, 105, 108
Vienna 1, 3, 4, 5, 6, 7, 8, 11, 13, 15, 16, 19, 25, 26, 27, 29, 37, 38, 46, 48, 50, 51, 52, 68, 70, 86, 105, 120, 181, 185, 206, 207, 211, 214
flourishing of culture 50
Villa Giusti 180
Villach 104
Vilpian 109, 119, 120
Vippacco, River 138, 139, 141, 142, 167, 173
Vittorio Veneto 25, 180

Wahesina 65
weapons 73, 89, 127, 149, 153
Wiener Zentralfriedhof (Vienna) 53, **8**
Wilhelm II, Emperor 6
Wilson, Woodrow 5, 25
'Fourteen Points' 5

Zanini, Arthur 209
Zillertaler Alps 127
Zloczow 48, 51, 52
Zuzzolino 204, 206